The
VOCABULARY
GUIDE
to
BIBLICAL
HEBREW
and
ARAMAIC

Other Resources by Miles V. Van Pelt and Gary. D Pratico

Basics of Biblical Hebrew Grammar

Basics of Biblical Hebrew Workbook

Charts of Biblical Hebrew

Graded Reader of Biblical Hebrew

Old Testament Hebrew Vocabulary Cards

Biblical Hebrew Vocabulary in Context

Biblical Hebrew Laminated Sheet

Other Resources by Miles V. Van Pelt

English Grammar to Ace Biblical Hebrew

Biblical Hebrew: A Compact Guide

Basics of Biblical Hebrew Video Lectures

Basics of Biblical Hebrew Vocabulary Audio

Basics of Biblical Aramaic: Complete Grammar, Lexicon, and Annotated Text

Basics of Biblical Aramaic Video Lectures

SECOND EDITION

The — VOCABULARY GUIDE *to* BIBLICAL

HEBREW *and* ARAMAIC

MILES V. VAN PELT
GARY D. PRATICO

ZONDERVAN

The Vocabulary Guide to Biblical Hebrew and Aramaic
Copyright © 2003, 2019 by Gary D. Pratico and Miles V. Van Pelt

ISBN 978-0-310-53282-8 (softcover)

ISBN 978-0-310-53283-5 (ebook)

Requests for information should be addressed to:
Zondervan, *3900 Sparks Dr. SE, Grand Rapids, Michigan 49546*

Cover design: LUCAS Art & Design
Typesetting: Miles V. Van Pelt

Printed in the United States of America

19 20 21 22 23 24 25 26 27 28 29 /LSC/ 15 14 13 12 11 10 9 8 7 6 5 4 3 2 1

To Laurie

רַבּוֹת בָּנוֹת עָשׂוּ חָיִל וְאַתְּ עָלִית עַל־כֻּלָּנָה

Proverbs 31:29

To Mary

וּשְׂמַח מֵאֵשֶׁת נְעוּרֶךָ

"I do"

Proverbs 5:18b

בְּאַהֲבָתָהּ תִּשְׁגֶּה תָמִיד

"I am"

Proverbs 5:19b

To Madeline Pearl and Melissa Grace,
with our love and devotion

וְאָהַבְתָּ אֵת יְהוָה אֱלֹהֶיךָ
בְּכָל־לְבָבְךָ וּבְכָל־נַפְשְׁךָ וּבְכָל־מְאֹדֶךָ

Deuteronomy 6:5

To Aaron, Martha, and Jon,
with our love

יְבָרֶכְךָ יְהוָה וְיִשְׁמְרֶךָ׃
יָאֵר יְהוָה פָּנָיו אֵלֶיךָ וִיחֻנֶּךָּ׃
יִשָּׂא יְהוָה פָּנָיו אֵלֶיךָ וְיָשֵׂם לְךָ שָׁלוֹם׃

Numbers 6:24-26

כּוֹשֵׁל יְקִימוּן מִלֶּיךָ

Job 4:4a

Table of Contents

Preface viii

Introduction x

Bibliography of Works Consulted xiv

Abbreviations and Symbols xv

Hebrew Word Lists

Hebrew Words Arranged by Frequency 1

Hebrew Words Arranged by Common Root 85

Aramaic Word List

Aramaic Words Arranged by Frequency 131

Appendices

Hebrew Homonyms 159

Hebrew Nominals

    a. Nouns with Common Gender 167

    b. Endingless Feminine Singular Nouns 170

    c. Segholate Nouns 173

    d. Adjectives 182

    e. Prepositions 188

Hebrew Verbs

    a. All Verbs 191

    b. I-נ 224

    c. I-י 229

    d. I-Guttural 232

    e. I-Guttural and III-ה 239

    f. II-Guttural 242

    g. III-ה 251

    h. III-ח/ע 257

    i. III-א 261

    j. Biconsonantal 264

    k. Geminate 269

Indices

Index of Hebrew Words 273

Index of Aramaic Words 296

Preface
First Edition

One of the essential tasks in learning any language is the memorization of vocabulary. Regardless of the language, vocabulary memorization is required of the beginning, intermediate, and advanced student. Ideally, the study of vocabulary should focus on high frequency words but, in the setting of most language courses, it is not always possible for a student to learn only frequency vocabulary. Nevertheless, the gradual mastery of the most common words in Hebrew is an essential part in becoming proficient with this biblical language. *The Vocabulary Guide to Biblical Hebrew* was written for this purpose. This volume presents, in a number of different ways, all of the Hebrew vocabulary of the Old Testament that occurs ten or more times.

In the preparation of this volume, we utilized a number of excellent resources. For the creation of initial lists and the calculation of frequency statistics, we used the computer software *Accordance* with the *GRAMCORD Hebrew MT* (Groves-Wheeler Westminster Hebrew Morphology) database. It was distributed by Oaktree Software, Inc. At this point, it will be appropriate to note that minor discrepancies in frequency numbers are observable throughout the various lexical sources. Except for occasional and minor adjustments for the sake of consistency, we have followed those frequency numbers derived from *Accordance*—which is, in our opinion, the best resource of its kind. In addition to *Accordance*, the lexical resources commonly referred to as BDB, *HALOT* (or KB), and *NIDOTTE* were used in our shaping and presentation of a Hebrew word's range of meaning. Full bibliographic information for these lexical resources is provided at the end of this section, following the introduction.

We are indebted to a number of individuals and institutions. We would like to thank Zondervan for their support in the preparation of this volume—especially Verlyn Verbrugge and Jack Kragt. We also recognize Bob Buller and Lee Fields for their editorial work and Paul Sumner for his preparation of the index. Special thanks are due to Jonathan Kline for his expert work in numerous aspects of the preparation of this volume for print. Finally, we are indebted to our families, and especially our wives, whose encouragement, support, and love have sustained us in our work.

Miles V. Van Pelt
Gary D. Pratico
April, 2003

Preface
Second Edition

In this second edition, we have added a frequency list including all of the Aramaic words that appear in the Old Testament. We have also removed the list with proper nouns and slightly rearranged the content of the *Vocabulary Guide*. The list with Hebrew words arranged by frequency is followed by the list of Hebrew words arranged by common root. After these first two lists, we have positioned the list of Aramaic words arranged by frequency. Supplementary lists now appear in the appendices with Hebrew Homonyms (formerly, "Identical Words with Different Meanings") as the first appendix. Most importantly, we have carefully unified the contents of the *Vocabulary Guide* with the vocabulary lists in *Basics of Biblical Hebrew Grammar*, 3rd ed. (Grand Rapids: Zondervan, 2018) and the *Old Testament Hebrew Vocabulary Cards*, 2nd ed. (Grand Rapids: Zondervan, 2018).

We are grateful for the opportunity to revise and update these important Hebrew language resources. It is always a pleasure to partner with our friends at Zondervan, especially Nancy Erickson who has shepherded numerous updated and revised editions of our work over the last couple of years. Special thanks are also due to CL Pearce for his expert work in numerous aspects of the preparation of this volume for print.

Miles V. Van Pelt
Gary D. Pratico
October, 2018

Introduction

We all recognize that vocabulary memorization can be one of the most painful aspects of language acquisition. Most students who complete their first year of Hebrew language instruction resonate with the words of Job 19:2, "How long will you torment me and crush me with *words*?" Nevertheless, few things will hinder a student's proficiency and enjoyment of a language more than an inadequate stock of basic vocabulary. In fact, those who would minimize the issue of vocabulary memorization will almost certainly struggle with proficiency in the language and find it difficult to fully realize the benefits of studying and reading Hebrew. Stated plainly, vocabulary memorization is vitally important.

Let the student be encouraged, however. A little vocabulary can go a long way in providing a good measure of competence with reading Hebrew. By memorizing only the first fifty words in the frequency vocabulary list, students will be equipped to recognize almost 55 percent of the total words that occur in the Hebrew Old Testament (419,687). Students who master the 641 words that occur fifty or more times will be able to recognize over 80 percent of all words. Finally, those who are brave enough to master all 1,903 words in the frequency vocabulary list will be equipped to recognize almost 90 percent of all words that occur in the Hebrew Old Testament. In other words, memorization of only 22 percent of the total stock of Hebrew vocabulary (1,903 out of 8,679 total lexical items) will enable a student to recognize 90 percent of all words appearing in the Hebrew Bible. The remaining 6,776 lexical items occur only 49,914 total times, a figure significantly less than the number of occurrences of the Hebrew conjunction ן (and).

A glance at the table of contents will reveal that this volume is composed of a number of different vocabulary lists. The first list is the most important. Entitled *Hebrew Words Arranged by Frequency*, this list contains all of the Hebrew words that occur ten or more times in the Old Testament (excluding proper nouns). This list is arranged by frequency, beginning with the most frequent Hebrew words and progressing to those that occur only ten times. The entries in this list are sequentially numbered from 1–1903. These numbers are a helpful point of reference and provide a convenient system for breaking the words into discrete groups for memorization. Please note that this is the only list in the book that contains all of the Hebrew words (excluding proper nouns) that occur ten or more times. All subsequent lists contain only parts of this list, arranged in various ways in order to provide a number of venues for memorization, review, and reference.

Entry Format

The format of each entry in the vocabulary lists is arranged as follows. The Hebrew word appears in the left column. In the larger, right-hand column, lexical and other related information is provided. There is sometimes an abbreviation that appears in parentheses, identifying the part of speech or another point of grammatical information, such as gender and/or number. Note that not all entries have been identified by part of speech. Verbs will be easy to recognize because each verbal entry begins with an abbreviation that identifies the verbal stem, such as Q (Qal) or Ni (Niphal). Following any initial abbreviations, the student will find a brief selection of translation values that will provide a sense of the word's "semantic range" or "semantic field." The selection of translation values is based largely on frequency of occurrence. With verbal entries, it is especially important to observe that we have not included definitions for derived stems that occur fewer than ten times with a particular verbal root. It is also worthy of note that a Qal stem definition may be provided as a point of reference even if the Qal stem is not attested more than ten times with the verbal root.

Following the selection of translation values, we have oftentimes provided the spelling of various inflected forms or grammatical constructions. In each case, these forms have been provided because of the frequency with which a particular form or construction appears in the Hebrew Old Testament. We have been careful to provide the spellings of irregular plural (see entries #22 and #23) and irregular construct (see entry #25) forms. Additionally, nouns, prepositions, and others words are sometimes shown with pronominal suffixes (see entry #16). We have also included, in selected instances, defective spellings (see entry #97), full or *plene* spellings (see entry #12), and occasionally, special or significant uses of a particular word (see entries #107 and #132). At times we will also designate the frequency of alternative spelling(s) (see entries #54 and #72) in order to provide the student with a sense of the distribution and significance of that particular spelling. Finally, entries conclude with a number in parentheses that identifies how many times a word occurs in the Old Testament. Occasionally, other information may follow, such as a reference to a related or cognate form (see entries #50, #51 and #52).

Distinguishing Between Identical Roots

While verbal entries are quite straightforward in the format of their presentation, the reader must be alerted to how we have handled the numerous instances of verbal roots that are spelled the same. Traditionally, standard lexicons and vocabulary guides have designated verbal roots having identical spelling with Roman numerals such as I שָׁבַר (to smash, shatter) and II שָׁבַר (to buy grain). In this volume, we have opted not to designate identical roots in this way. The rationale for departure from this widely practiced system of designation was based, in large measure, on the frequent inconsistencies between and within standard lexicons with respect to the assignment of Roman numerals. Additionally, most Hebrew students, and even a few instructors, give little attention to the memorization of the Roman numeral designations that are assigned to identical roots. With a view to simplicity of presentation, notably for the beginning student, identical verbal roots and other words that appear in the "frequency" list have been cross-referenced (see entries #280 and #1238). Additionally, we have provided a catalogue of all "identical" Hebrew words that occur more than ten times (see Hebrew Homonyms beginning on page 159).

Understanding and Using the Different Lists

In any number of configurations, students can utilize the first major list of frequency vocabulary to complement their Hebrew language studies. For the beginning student, an appropriate level of vocabulary mastery for a single academic year would be those words that occur fifty times or more. The 642 words that fall into this category could be spread throughout an academic year. In an academic year with ten weeks in each of the two semesters, a mere 32 words per week would equip a student with this level of vocabulary. In those institutions with a greater number of weeks in each semester, fewer words per week would be required to reach this modest goal. Some will prefer a less rigorous course of study and others will want to be more aggressive. Either way, a simple calculation of the number of words to memorize in the time allotted for memorization will accommodate any academic schedule or personal aspiration.

The second major list in this volume is an alphabetical listing of words that share a common root. This type of list is sometimes called a "cognate" list. In language study, the term "cognate" refers to words that are related by derivation. For example, the verb מָלַךְ means "to reign" or "to be(come) king." Understanding the idea of a verbal root as a grammatical abstraction, we can say that there are a number of forms that derive from the root מלך, such as מֶלֶךְ (king), מַלְכָּה (queen) and מַלְכוּת (kingdom). The essential nuances of "being king," "reigning," or "exercising royal authority" are inherent in the meanings of each of these derived or cognate forms. They are etymologically related to one another and to the triconsonantal root מלך. Recognizing and understanding these types of relationships are of great benefit for building vocabulary. Please note that this list, together with all of the following lists, do not contain all of the Hebrew words that occur more than ten times. Only the "frequency" list has all 1,903 words that fall into this category. All other lists (except the list of proper nouns) contain only portions of the frequency list, organized and presented in various ways.

In the third major list of this second edition, we have now included a list all Aramaic words, including proper nouns, that occur in the Aramaic portions of the Old Testament. Words are arranged by frequency, from the most to the least frequent. There are 705 words. In this list, for the sake of convenience and reference, each word is numbered sequentially. By way of convention, verbal roots are listed without vowels.

Following the first three major word lists, we have included three appendices: Hebrew Homonyms, Hebrew Nominals, and Hebrew Verbs. These lists provide students with an opportunity to focus on specific word categories to facilitate review, reference, and testing.

Bibliography
of works consulted

Andersen, F. I., and A. D. Forbes. *The Vocabulary of the Old Testament*. Rome: Pontifical Biblical Institute, 1992.

_____ . *Spelling in the Hebrew Bible*. Rome: Pontifical Biblical Institute, 1986.

Brown, F., S. R. Driver, and C. A. Briggs. *The New Brown-Driver-Briggs-Gesenius Hebrew and English Lexicon*. Peabody: Hendrickson, 1979.

Holladay, W. L. *A Concise Hebrew and Aramaic Lexicon of the Old Testament*. Grand Rapids: Eerdmans, 1988.

Köhler, L., W. Baumgartner, and J. Stamm. *The Hebrew and Aramaic Lexicon of the Old Testament*. Study Edition. 2 vols. Translated and edited by M. E. J. Richardson. Leiden: E. J. Brill, 2001.

Landes, G. M. *Building Your Hebrew Vocabulary: Learning Words by Frequency and Cognate*. Atlanta: Society of Biblical Literature, 2001.

Mitchel, L. A. *A Student's Vocabulary for Biblical Hebrew and Aramaic*. Grand Rapids: Zondervan, 1984.

VanGemeren, W. A., ed. *The New International Dictionary of Old Testament Theology and Exegesis*. Grand Rapids: Zondervan, 1997.

Accordance Bible Software with the *GRAMCORD Hebrew MT* (Groves-Wheeler Westminster Hebrew Morphology) database. Distributed by Oaktree Software, Inc. (www.accordancebible.com).

Abbreviations and Symbols

Adjective	adj		Masculine	m
Adverb	adv		Negative	neg
Collective	coll		Niphal	Ni
Common	c		Noun	n
Compare with	cf		Participle	ptc
Conjunction	conj		Passive	pass
Construct	cstr		Personal	pers
Demonstrative	dmstr		Piel	Pi
Dual	d		Plural	p
Feminine	f		Prefix	pref
Hiphil	Hi		Preposition	prep
Hithpael	Hith		Pronoun	pron
Hophal	Hoph		Pual	Pu
Idiomatically	idiom		Qal	Q
Interrogative	interrog		Relative	rel
Infinitive	inf		Singular	s
Literally	lit		Suffix	suff

\#   preceding a number (#718), identifies an entry in the frequency list

x   following a number (816x), indicates the number of times a particular form occurs

ˈ   located over a Hebrew letter (אֶ֫רֶץ), identifies Hebrew words with penultimate stress (next-to-last syllable)

Hebrew Words
Arranged by Frequency

The following list contains all Hebrew words, except proper nouns, that occur ten times or more in the Hebrew Old Testament. Words are arranged by frequency—from the most to the least frequent. There are 1,903 words. In this list, for the sake of convenience and reference, each word is numbered sequentially.

1   וְ   (conj) and, but, also, even, then (50,524)

2   · הַ   (definite article) the (24,058)

3   לְ   (prep) to, toward, for (20,321)

4   בְּ   (prep) in, at, with, by, against (15,559)

5   אֵת   (definite direct object marker) not translated; also spelled אֶת־ with loss of accent or (with 3ms suff) אֹתוֹ (10,978); cf אֵת (#50)

6   מִן   (prep) from, out of; also spelled · מִ (Nun assimilates as Daghesh Forte) when prefixed to another word (7,592)

7   עַל   (prep) on, upon, on account of, according to (5,777)

8   אֶל־   (prep) to, toward, into; (with 3ms suff) אֵלָיו (5,518)

9   אֲשֶׁר   (rel pron) who, that, which (5,503); cf שֶׁ (#287)

10   כֹּל   all, each, every; (cstr) כָּל־ (5,415)

11   אָמַר   (Q) to say; (Ni) be said, called; (Hi) declare, proclaim (5,316)

12   לֹא   (neg particle) no, not; also spelled לוֹא (5,189)

13   בֵּן   son; (ms cstr) בֶּן־; (mp) בָּנִים; (mp cstr) בְּנֵי (4,941)

14   כִּי   that, because; (adversative) but, except; (emphatic) indeed, truly (4,487); כִּי־אִם but, except; cf אִם (#42)

15   הָיָה   (Q) to be, become, happen, occur; (Ni) be done, brought about, come to pass, occur (3,576)

16   כְּ   (prep) as, like, according to; (with 2ms suff) כָּמוֹךְ (3,053)

17   עָשָׂה   (Q) to do, make; (Ni) be done, made (2,632)

18   אֱלֹהִים   God, gods (2,602)

19   בּוֹא   (Q) to go in, enter, come to, come upon; (Hi) bring (in), come (in); (Hoph) be brought (2,592)

20   מֶלֶךְ   king, ruler (2,530)

21   אֶרֶץ   (fs) land, earth, ground (2,505)

22   יוֹם   day; (mp) יָמִים (2,301)

23	אִישׁ	man, husband; (mp) אֲנָשִׁים (2,188)
24	פָּנִים	(cp) face, front; לִפְנֵי (prep לְ prefixed to cstr) before, in front of (2,126)
25	בַּיִת	(ms) house, household, (metaphorically) dynasty; (1497x ms cstr) בֵּית; (mp) בָּתִּים (2,047)
26	נָתַן	(Q) to give, put, place, set; (Ni) be given (2,014)
27	עַם	people; (mp) עַמִּים (1,869)
28	יָד	(fs) hand; (metaphorically) power (1,627)
29	הָלַךְ	(Q) to go, walk, (metaphorically) behave; (Pi) go, walk; (Hith) walk about, move to and fro (1,554)
30	דָּבָר	word, matter, thing (1,454)
31	הוּא	(3ms pers pron) he, it; (ms dmstr pron and adj) that (1,398)
32	רָאָה	(Q) to see, perceive, understand; (Ni) appear; (Pu) be seen; (Hi) let or cause someone to see (something) (1,311)
33	עַד	(prep) until, as far as (1,263); cf עֵד (#678)
34	אָב	father, ancestor; (ms cstr) אֲבִי; (mp) אָבוֹת (1,210)
35	זֶה	(ms dmstr pron and adj) this (1,178)
36	שָׁמַע	(Q) to hear, listen to, understand, obey; (Ni) be heard; (Hi) proclaim (1,165)
37	דָּבַר	(Q) to speak (rare in Q); (Pi) speak (1,136)
38	יָשַׁב	(Q) to sit (down), dwell, inhabit; (Hi) cause to sit or dwell, settle (a city) (1,088)
39	עִיר	(fs) city, town; (fp) עָרִים (1,088)
40	יָצָא	(Q) to go or come out; (Hi) cause to go or come out, lead out, bring out (1,076)
41	שׁוּב	(Q) to turn back, turn, return; (Hi) cause to return, bring back, restore; (Polel) bring back, restore (1,075)
42	אִם	if (1,070); כִּי־אִם but, except, only; cf כִּי (#14)
43	הִנֵּה	behold, look; (with 1cs suff) הִנְנִי (1,061)

44	עִם	(prep) with, together with; (with 3ms suff) עִמּוֹ (1,048)
45	אֶחָד	one; (fs) אַחַת (976)
46	לָקַח	(Q) to take, grasp, capture, seize; (Ni) be captured, taken away (967)
47	יָדַע	(Q) to know, know sexually (have intercourse with); (Ni) be(come) known, reveal oneself; (Hi) make known, inform (956)
48	עַיִן	(cs) eye, spring (900)
49	עָלָה	(Q) to go up, ascend; (Ni) be taken up; (Hi) bring or lead up or out, offer up (sacrifice) (894)
50	אֵת	(prep) with, beside; also spelled אֶת־ with loss of accent or (with 3ms suff) אִתּוֹ (890); cf אֵת (#5)
51	שָׁנָה	year; (fp) שָׁנִים (878); cf שֵׁנָה (#1534)
52	אֲנִי	(1cs pers pron) I (874); cf אָנֹכִי (#136)
53	שֵׁם	name, reputation (864)
54	לֵב	heart, mind, will; (mp) לְבּוֹת; also spelled לֵבָב (854)
55	שָׁלַח	(Q) to send, stretch out; (Pi) send, stretch out, send away, expel; (Pu) be sent away (off) (847)
56	מוּת	(Q) to die; (Hi) kill, put to death; (Hoph) be killed (845)
57	שָׁם	there, then, at that time (835)
58	אָכַל	(Q) to eat, consume; (Ni) be eaten, consumed; (Hi) feed (820)
59	עֶבֶד	slave, servant (803)
60	אַיִן	(particle of nonexistence) is not, are not, nothing; most often spelled אֵין (790); cf אַיִן (#1361)
61	אִשָּׁה	woman, wife; (fs cstr) אֵשֶׁת; (fp) נָשִׁים (781)
62	אָדוֹן	lord, master; (of God 439x) אֲדֹנָי Lord (774)
63	גַּם	also, even (769)
64	שְׁנַיִם	(md) two; (fd) שְׁתַּיִם (769)

4

65	נֶפֶשׁ	(fs) soul, life, person, neck, throat (757)
66	כֹּהֵן	priest; (mp) כֹּהֲנִים (750); cf כָּהַן (#1147)
67	אַתָּה	(2ms pers pron) you (749)
68	אֵלֶּה	(cp dmstr pron and adj) these (744)
69	כֵּן	so, thus (741); cf כֵּן (#1122, #1783)
70	קָרָא	(Q) to call, summon, proclaim, read aloud, give a name to; (Ni) be called, summoned, proclaimed (739); cf קָרָא (#301)
71	אַל	(neg particle) no, not (729)
72	אַחֲרֵי	(prep) after, behind; also spelled אַחַר (718)
73	דֶּרֶךְ	(cs) way, road, journey (712)
74	הֲ	(interrog particle) prefixed to the first word of a question (664)
75	נָשָׂא	(Q) to lift, carry, raise, bear (load or burden), take (away); (Ni) be carried, lifted up, exalted; (Pi) lift up, exalt; (Hith) lift oneself up, exalt oneself (659)
76	אָח	brother; (ms cstr) אֲחִי; (mp) אַחִים (629)
77	קוּם	(Q) to rise, arise, get up, stand (up); (Hi) set up, put up, cause to arise, establish (627)
78	שָׁלֹשׁ	(ms) three; (fs) שְׁלֹשָׁה; (mp) שְׁלֹשִׁים thirty (606)
79	זֹאת	(fs dmstr pron and adj) this (605)
80	רֹאשׁ	head, top, chief; (mp) רָאשִׁים (600); cf רֹאשׁ (#1735)
81	שִׂים	(Q) to set (up), put, place, set in place, establish; also spelled שׂוּם (588)
82	בַּת	daughter; (fp) בָּנוֹת (587); cf בַּת (#1616)
83	מַיִם	water; (md cstr) מֵי (585)
84	מֵאָה	hundred; (fp) מֵאוֹת; (fd) מָאתַיִם two hundred (583)
85	כֹּה	thus, here (577)
86	מָה	(interrog pron) what? also spelled מַה and מֶה (571)
87	גּוֹי	nation, people; (mp) גּוֹיִם (567)

88   הֵם   (3mp pers pron) they; (mp dmstr) those; also spelled
               הֵמָּה (565)

89   הַר   mountain, hill, hill country; (mp) הָרִים (558)

90   עָבַר   (Q) to pass over, pass through, pass by, cross; (Hi)
               cause to pass over, bring over, cause or allow to pass
               (through), cause to pass through fire, sacrifice (553)

91   אָדָם   man, mankind, humankind (546)

92   טוֹב   (adj) good, pleasant (530); cf טוֹב (#714)

93   גָּדוֹל   (adj) great, big, large (527)

94   עָמַד   (Q) to stand (up), take one's stand, stand still; (Hi)
               station, set up, appoint, designate (524)

95   תַּחַת   (prep) under, below, instead of (510)

96   חָמֵשׁ   five; (fs) חֲמִשָּׁה; (mp) חֲמִשִּׁים fifty (508)

97   קוֹל   voice, sound, noise; also spelled קֹל (505)

98   נָכָה   (Hi) to strike, smite, beat, strike dead, destroy;
               (Hoph) be struck down dead, beaten (501)

99   יָלַד   (Q) to bear (children), give birth, bring forth, beget;
               (Ni) be born; (Pi) help at birth, serve as midwife; (Pu)
               be born; (Hi) become the father of, beget (499)

100   פֶּה   (ms) mouth, opening; (ms cstr) פִּי (498)

101   אֶלֶף   thousand; (md) אַלְפַּיִם two thousand (496); cf אֶלֶף
               (#1749)

102   צָוָה   (Pi) to command, give an order, charge; (Pu) be
               ordered, be told, receive a command (496)

103   עֶשֶׂר   ten; (fs) עֲשָׂרָה; (mp) עֶשְׂרִים twenty, twentieth (492)

104   הִיא   (3fs pers pron) she, it; (fs dmstr pron and adj) that;
               also spelled הוּא in the Pentateuch (491)

105   עוֹד   again, still, as long as (491)

106   שֶׁבַע   (ms) seven; (fs) שִׁבְעָה; (mp) שִׁבְעִים seventy (490)

107   צָבָא   (cs) host, army, war, service; (cp) צְבָאוֹת (487); יְהוָה
               צְבָאוֹת "Yahweh of Hosts;" cf צָבָא (#1589)

6

108	קֹדֶשׁ	holiness, something that is holy (470)
109	שָׁמַר	(Q) to watch (over), guard, keep, observe, preserve, protect, take care of; (Ni) to be kept, protected, on one's guard (469)
110	מָצָא	(Q) to find (out), reach, obtain, achieve; (Ni) be found (457)
111	אַרְבַּע	four; (fs) אַרְבָּעָה; (mp) אַרְבָּעִים forty (455)
112	עוֹלָם	forever, everlasting, ancient; also spelled עֹלָם (439)
113	נָפַל	(Q) to fall, fall upon; (Hi) cause to fall, bring to ruin (435)
114	עַתָּה	now, after all, at last, then (435)
115	מִשְׁפָּט	judgment, decision, ordinance, law, custom (425)
116	מִי	(interrog pron) who? (424)
117	שַׂר	ruler, prince (421)
118	שָׁמַיִם	heaven, sky (421)
119	רַב	(adj) great, many; (mp) רַבִּים (419); cf רֹב (#974)
120	חֶרֶב	(fs) sword (413)
121	בֵּין	(prep) between (409)
122	נָא	(emphatic particle) please, now, surely (405)
123	כֶּסֶף	silver, money (403)
124	מִזְבֵּחַ	altar; (mp) מִזְבְּחוֹת (403)
125	מָקוֹם	place, location; (mp) מְקֹמוֹת (401)
126	יָם	sea; (mp) יַמִּים (396)
127	זָהָב	gold (392)
128	יָרַד	(Q) to go down, descend; (Hi) bring down, lead down (382)
129	רוּחַ	(cs) spirit, wind, breath; (cp) רוּחוֹת (378)
130	בָּנָה	(Q) to build (up), rebuild, build (establish) a family; (Ni) be built, have a child (by or from) (377)
131	אֵשׁ	(cs) fire (376)

132	נְאֻם	utterance, announcement, revelation (376); נְאֻם־יְהוָה "says (declares) Yahweh"
133	שַׁעַר	gate (373)
134	נָגַד	(Hi) to tell, announce, report, declare, inform; (Hoph) be told, announced, reported (371)
135	דָּם	blood; bloodshed (361)
136	אָנֹכִי	(1cs pers pron) I (359); cf אֲנִי (#52)
137	רָעָה	evil, wickedness, calamity, disaster (354); cf רַע (#153), רָעָה (#255), and רֹעַ (#1310)
138	מָלַךְ	(Q) to be(come) king or queen, reign, rule; (Hi) make someone king or queen, install someone as king or queen (350)
139	אֹהֶל	tent (348)
140	לֶחֶם	bread, food (340)
141	סָבִיב	around, about; (substantive) surroundings (338)
142	עֶשֶׂר	ten; (fs) עֲשָׂרָה; used in constructions to express numerals eleven to nineteen (337)
143	עֵץ	tree, wood (330)
144	שָׂדֶה	(ms) field, pastureland (329)
145	בָּרַךְ	(Q Pass ptc) blessed, praised, adored; (Pi) bless, praise (327)
146	כְּלִי	vessel, implement, weapon; (mp) כֵּלִים; (mp cstr) כְּלֵי (325)
147	אוֹ	(conj) or (321)
148	בְּתוֹךְ	(prep) in the midst (middle) of, inside (319); combination of (prep) בְּ and (n) תָּוֶךְ (middle, center); also מִתּוֹךְ (68x) and אֶל־תּוֹךְ (22x)
149	מִלְחָמָה	war, battle, struggle (319)
150	יָרֵא	(Q) to fear, be afraid, in awe of, reverence; (Ni) be feared, held in honor (317); cf יָרֵא (#539)
151	נָבִיא	prophet (317)

152	עָנָה	(Q) to answer, respond, reply, testify; (Ni) be answered (316); cf עָנָה (#449, #1467)
153	רַע	(adj) bad, evil, wicked, worthless; also spelled רָע (312); cf רָעָה (#137)
154	מִשְׁפָּחָה	family, clan (304)
155	פָּקַד	(Q) to attend (to), pay attention to, take care of, miss (someone), number, appoint; (Ni) be missed, visited, appointed; (Hi) appoint, entrust (304)
156	מְאֹד	very, exceedingly (300)
157	חַטָּאת	sin, sin offering; (fs cstr) חַטַּאת; (fp cstr) חַטֹּאות and חַטֹּאת (298)
158	סוּר	(Q) to turn (aside), turn off, leave (off), desist; (Hi) remove, take away, get rid of (298)
159	עֵת	(cs) time, point of time; (cp) עִתִּים and עִתּוֹת (296)
160	חָזַק	(Q) to be(come) strong, have courage; (Pi) make strong, strengthen; (Hi) strengthen, seize, grasp, take hold of; (Hith) strengthen oneself, show oneself as strong or courageous (290)
161	כָּרַת	(Q) to cut, cut off, cut down; (idiom) to make a covenant (with בְּרִית); (Ni) be cut off (down); (Hi) cut off, destroy, exterminate (289)
162	עָבַד	(Q) to work, serve, toil (289)
163	בְּרִית	covenant (287)
164	עֹלָה	whole burnt offering (sacrifice that is completely burned) (286)
165	אֹיֵב	enemy (285)
166	אַתֶּם	(2mp pers pron) you (283)
167	חֹדֶשׁ	month, new moon (283)
168	חָיָה	(Q) to live, be alive, revive, restore to life; (Pi) preserve alive, let live, give life; (Hi) preserve, keep alive, revive, restore to life (283)
169	קָרַב	(Q) to approach, draw near, come near; (Hi) bring (near), present, offer a sacrifice or offering (280)

170	אַף	nostril, nose; (metaphorically) anger; (md) אַפַּיִם (277); cf אַף (#309)
171	אֶבֶן	(fs) stone; (fp) אֲבָנִים (276)
172	צֹאן	(cs) flock(s), flock of sheep and goats (274)
173	שֵׁשׁ	six; (fs) שִׁשָּׁה; (fs cstr) שֵׁשֶׁת; (mp) שִׁשִּׁים sixty (274); cf שֵׁשׁ (#800)
174	לְמַעַן	(prep) on account of, for the sake of (272)
175	בָּשָׂר	flesh, meat, skin (270)
176	מִדְבָּר	wilderness, desert, pasture (269)
177	רָשָׁע	(adj) wicked, guilty (264)
178	חַי	(adj) living, alive; (mp) חַיִּים (254)
179	מַטֶּה	(ms) staff, rod, tribe; (mp) מַטּוֹת (252)
180	מָלֵא	(Q) to be full, fill (up); (Ni) be filled (with); (Pi) fill, perform, carry out, consecrate as priest (252); cf מָלֵא (#554)
181	גְּבוּל	border, boundary, territory (251)
182	רֶגֶל	(fs) foot (251)
183	אַמָּה	cubit (distance between elbow and tip of middle finger), forearm (249)
184	חֶסֶד	loyalty, faithfulness, steadfast love, lovingkindness (249)
185	חַיִל	strength, wealth, army (246)
186	חָטָא	(Q) to miss (a goal or mark), sin, commit a sin; (Pi) make a sin offering; (Hi) cause to sin (240)
187	נַעַר	boy, youth, servant (240)
188	אֵל	God, god (237)
189	שָׁלוֹם	peace, welfare, wholeness (237)
190	זָכַר	(Q) to remember; (Ni) be remembered, thought of; (Hi) remind (235)
191	מַעֲשֶׂה	(ms) work, deed, act (235)

192   לַיְלָה   (ms) night; (mp) לֵילוֹת (234)

193   עָוֹן   transgression, iniquity, guilt, punishment (of sin); (mp) עֲוֹנוֹת (233)

194   יָרַשׁ   (Q) to inherit, take possession of, dispossess, impoverish; (Hi) cause to possess or inherit, dispossess (232)

195   זֶרַע   seed, offspring, descendants (229)

196   רָבָה   (Q) to be(come) numerous, great, increase; (Hi) make many, make great, multiply, increase (229)

197   קֶרֶב   inner part(s), organ(s), body; (prep) בְּקֶרֶב (155x) in the middle of, among (227)

198   בָּקַשׁ   (Pi) to seek, search for, look for, discover, demand, require; (Pu) be sought (225)

199   כָּתַב   (Q) to write (upon), register, record; (Ni) be written (225)

200   מוֹעֵד   appointed time (of feast), meeting place, assembly (223)

201   תּוֹרָה   law, instruction, teaching (223)

202   אֲדָמָה   ground, land, earth (222)

203   נַחֲלָה   inheritance, property, possession (222)

204   אֵם   (fs) mother; (with 3ms suff) אִמּוֹ (220)

205   כּוּן   (Ni) to be established, steadfast, ready, arranged, stand firm; (Hi) establish, set up, prepare, make ready, make firm; (Polel) set up, establish (219)

206   אָהַב   (Q) to love (of human and divine love); (Pi ptc) lover (217)

207   שָׁתָה   (Q) to drink (217)

208   בֶּגֶד   clothes, garment, covering (216)

209   נָטָה   (Q) to spread out, stretch out, extend, pitch (a tent), turn, bend; (Hi) turn, incline, stretch out, spread out (216)

210   מַחֲנֶה   (cs) camp, army; (cp) מַחֲנוֹת and מַחֲנִים (215)

211	עָזַב	(Q) to leave, leave behind, forsake, abandon, set free (214)
212	בֹּקֶר	morning (213)
213	יָסַף	(Q) to add, continue (to do something again); (Hi) add, increase, do again and again (213)
214	מַלְאָךְ	messenger, angel (213)
215	נָצַל	(Ni) to be rescued, delivered, saved; (Hi) tear from, take away, deliver from (213)
216	שָׁכַב	(Q) to lie down, have sexual intercourse (with) (213)
217	מִנְחָה	gift, offering, tribute (211)
218	כָּלָה	(Q) to be complete, finished, at an end, accomplished, spent, exhausted, come to an end; (Pi) complete, finish, bring to an end (207); cf כַּלָּה (#1184)
219	צַדִּיק	(adj) righteous, just, innocent (206)
220	יָשַׁע	(Ni) to be delivered, victorious, receive help; (Hi) help, save, deliver, rescue, come to the aid of (205)
221	שָׁפַט	(Q) to judge, make a judgment, decide (between), settle (a dispute or controversy); (Ni) go to court, plead, dispute (204)
222	אֲרוֹן	(cs) ark, chest, coffin (202); אֲרוֹן הַבְּרִית "the ark of the covenant"
223	אָסַף	(Q) to gather (in), take in, take away, destroy; (Ni) be gathered, taken away, assemble (200)
224	כָּבוֹד	glory, splendor, honor, abundance (200); כְּבוֹד יְהוָה "the glory of Yahweh"
225	רוּם	(Q) to be high, exalted, rise, arise; (Hi) raise, lift up, exalt, take away; (Hoph) be exalted; (Polel) exalt, bring up, extol, raise (children) (197)
226	כַּף	(fs) hand, palm, sole of the foot (195)
227	יָכֹל	(Q) to be able, capable of, endure, prevail (193)
228	שֶׁמֶן	oil, fat (193)

12

229	חָצֵר	(cs) courtyard, village, settlement; (cp) חֲצֵרִים and חֲצֵרוֹת (192)
230	סֵפֶר	book, scroll, document (191); סֵפֶר הַתּוֹרָה "the book of the law"
231	בְּהֵמָה	animal(s), beast(s), cattle (190)
232	שֵׁבֶט	rod, staff, scepter, tribe (190); שִׁבְטֵי יִשְׂרָאֵל "the tribes of Israel"
233	אֹזֶן	(fs) ear; (fd cstr) אָזְנֵי (188)
234	רֵעַ	friend, companion, neighbor (188)
235	גָּלָה	(Q) to uncover, reveal, disclose; (Ni) uncover, reveal oneself, be revealed, exposed; (Pi) uncover, reveal, disclose; (Hi) take (carry away) into exile (187)
236	שָׁבַע	(Ni) to swear (take) an oath; (Hi) cause to take an oath, plead with someone (186)
237	אָבַד	(Q) to perish, vanish, be(come) lost, go astray; (Pi) cause to perish, destroy; (Hi) exterminate (185)
238	מִצְוָה	commandment; (fp) מִצְוֹת (184); מִצְוֹת יְהוָה "the commandments of Yahweh"
239	בָּקָר	cattle, herd (183)
240	רִאשׁוֹן	(adj) first, former; (fs) רִאשֹׁנָה; (mp) רִאשֹׁנִים (182)
241	זָקֵן	(adj) old; (n) elder, old man (180); cf זָקֵן (#1055)
242	לָמָּה	why? also spelled לָמָה (178)
243	שָׂפָה	lip, language, edge, shore (178)
244	שָׁאַל	(Q) to ask (of), inquire (of), request, demand (176)
245	חָוָה	(Hishtaphel) to bow down, worship (173)
246	בָּחַר	(Q) to choose, test, examine (172)
247	אַיִל	ram, ruler; (adj) mighty (171); cf אַיִל (#1173)
248	בִּין	(Q) to understand, perceive, consider, give heed to; (Ni) be discerning, have understanding; (Hi) understand, teach; (Hith) show oneself perceptive (171)

249	לָחַם	(Q, Ni) to fight, do battle with (rare in Q) (171)
250	עֵדָה	congregation, assembly (171)
251	קָדַשׁ	(Q) to be holy, set apart or consecrated; (Ni) be honored or treated as holy; (Pi) set apart, consecrate or dedicate as holy; (Hi) consecrate, dedicate or declare as holy; (Hith) show or keep oneself holy (171)
252	דּוֹר	generation; also spelled דֹּר; (mp) דֹּרוֹת and דֹּרֹת (167)
253	הָרַג	(Q) to kill, slay (167)
254	מְלָאכָה	work, occupation, service (167)
255	רָעָה	(Q) to pasture, tend (flocks), graze, shepherd, feed (167); cf רָעָה (#137)
256	אַחֵר	(adj) other, another; (fs) אַחֶרֶת (166)
257	דָּרַשׁ	(Q) to seek, inquire (of or about), investigate, require, demand (165)
258	חוּץ	outside, street; (mp) חוּצוֹת; (prefixed with prep מִן) מִחוּץ from outside, outside (164)
259	פֶּתַח	opening, entrance, doorway (164)
260	סָבַב	(Q) to turn (about), go around, surround; (Ni) turn; (Hi) cause to go around, lead around; (Polel) encompass with protection (163)
261	זֶבַח	sacrifice (162)
262	טָמֵא	(Q) to be(come) unclean; (Ni) defile oneself; (Pi) defile, pronounce or declare unclean; (Hith) defile oneself, become unclean (162); cf טָמֵא (#417)
263	אַךְ	only, surely, nevertheless (161)
264	בַּעַל	owner, master, husband, (divine title) Baal (161)
265	לְבַד	alone, by oneself; (with 3ms suff) לְבַדּוֹ (161)
266	גִּבּוֹר	(adj) mighty, valiant, heroic; (n) hero (160)
267	נוּס	(Q) to flee, escape (160)
268	צְדָקָה	righteousness, righteous act, justice (159)

269	שָׂמַח	(Q) to rejoice, be joyful, glad; (Pi) cause to rejoice, gladden, make someone happy (156)
270	שֵׁנִי	(adj) second; (fs) שֵׁנִית (156)
271	חָכְמָה	wisdom, skill (153)
272	כָּסָה	(Q) to cover, conceal, hide; (Pi) cover (up), conceal, clothe (153)
273	מָוֶת	death, dying; (ms cstr) מוֹת (153)
274	צָפוֹן	(fs) north, northern (153)
275	שָׁחַת	(Pi, Hi) to ruin, destroy, spoil, annihilate (152)
276	נֶגֶד	(prep) opposite, in front of (151)
277	נָגַע	(Q) to touch, strike, reach; (Hi) touch, reach, throw, arrive (150)
278	רֹב	multitude, abundance, greatness (150)
279	שָׂנֵא	(Q) to hate; (Pi ptc) enemy (148)
280	שָׁבַר	(Q) to break (up), break in pieces, smash, shatter; (Ni) be smashed, broken, shattered or destroyed; (Pi) shatter, smash, break (148); cf שֶׁבֶר (#1238)
281	שְׁמֹנֶה	eight; (fs) שְׁמֹנָה; (mp) שְׁמֹנִים eighty (147)
282	הָלַל	(Pi) to praise, sing hallelujah; (Pu) be praised, praiseworthy; (Hith) boast (146); cf הָלַל (#1501)
283	נָסַע	(Q) to pull (out or up), set out, start out, depart, journey (146)
284	עֲבֹדָה	work, labor, service, worship (145)
285	רָדַף	(Q) to pursue, follow after, chase, persecute (144)
286	חָנָה	(Q) to decline, camp, encamp, pitch camp, lay siege to (143)
287	שֶׁ	(prefixed rel pron) who, which, that (143); cf אֲשֶׁר (#9)
288	אָז	then, since, before (141)
289	יַיִן	wine; (ms cstr) יֵין (141)
290	יָמִין	(fs) right hand, south (141)

291	חַיִּים	life, lifetime (140)
292	מֵעַל	above, upward, on top of (140); cf מַעַל (#992)
293	נוּחַ	(Q) to rest, settle down, repose; (Hi) cause to rest, secure rest, set, leave (behind or untouched) (140)
294	מִשְׁכָּן	dwelling place, tabernacle; (mp) מִשְׁכָּנוֹת (139)
295	נְחֹשֶׁת	copper, bronze (139)
296	חָכָם	(adj) wise, skillful, experienced (138)
297	יֵשׁ	(particle of existence) there is, there are (138)
298	סוּס	horse (138)
299	נַחַל	stream, brook, wadi (137)
300	פָּתַח	(Q) to open (up); (Ni) be opened, loosened, set free; (Pi) let loose, loosen (136)
301	קָרָא	(Q) to meet, encounter, happen; inf cstr with prep לְ (לִקְרַאת) toward, against, opposite (136); cf קָרָא (#70) and קָרָה (#1198)
302	חָלַל	(Ni) to be defiled, profaned, defile oneself; (Pi) profane, pollute, defile; (Hi) let something be profaned (135)
303	כִּסֵּא	seat, chair, throne (135)
304	זָבַח	(Q) to slaughter (for sacrifice), sacrifice; (Pi) offer sacrifice, sacrifice (134)
305	מִסְפָּר	number (134)
306	עֶרֶב	evening, sunset (134)
307	פָּנָה	(Q) to turn (toward, from, to the side, away) (134)
308	שֶׁמֶשׁ	(cs) sun (134)
309	אַף	(conj) also, indeed, even (133); cf אַף (#170)
310	חוֹמָה	wall (133)
311	פֶּן־	lest, otherwise (133)
312	פַּר	bull, ox, steer (133)
313	קָבַר	(Q) to bury; (Ni) be buried (133)

314	שָׁאַר	(Ni) to remain, be left over, survive; (Hi) leave (someone or something) remaining (133)
315	חֹק	statute, appointed time, portion; (mp) חֻקִּים (131); cf חֻקָּה (#373)
316	נָשִׂיא	chief, leader, prince (130)
317	שָׁכַן	(Q) to settle (down), abide, reside, dwell, inhabit; (Pi) abide, dwell (130)
318	אֱמֶת	truth, fidelity; (with 2ms suff) אֲמִתֶּךָ (127)
319	קָבַץ	(Q) to collect, gather, assemble; (Ni) be gathered, assembled; (Pi) gather together, assemble (127)
320	כֹּחַ	strength, power (126)
321	עֶצֶם	(fs) bone, skeleton (126)
322	בּוֹשׁ	(Q) to be ashamed; (Hi) put to shame (125)
323	חֵמָה	wrath, heat, poison (125)
324	חֲצִי	half, middle (125)
325	נָגַשׁ	(Q) to draw near, approach; (Ni) draw near; (Hi) bring (near), offer (a sacrifice) (125)
326	שָׁלַךְ	(Hi) to send, throw, cast; (Hoph) be thrown, cast (125)
327	חָשַׁב	(Q) to think, consider, devise, plan, value, reckon; (Ni) be reckoned, accounted, considered (as); (Pi) think, consider, devise, plan (124)
328	צֶדֶק	righteousness, equity (123)
329	קָהָל	assembly, community, crowd (123)
330	אֲנַחְנוּ	(1cp pers pron) we (121)
331	לָכַד	(Q) to take, capture, catch, seize; (Ni) be caught, captured (121)
332	אוֹר	(cs) light, daylight, sunshine (120); cf אוֹר (#707)
333	בְּכוֹר	firstborn, oldest offspring (120)
334	רֶכֶב	chariot, (coll) chariots or chariot riders (120)
335	אָחוֹת	sister, relative, loved one (119)

336	יָשָׁר	(adj) upright, just (119)
337	נָהָר	river, stream; (mp) נְהָרוֹת and נְהָרִים (119)
338	פְּרִי	fruit, offspring (119)
339	בָּטַח	(Q) to trust, rely upon (118)
340	פַּעַם	(fs) foot, pace, time; (fp) פְּעָמִים (118)
341	תּוֹעֵבָה	abomination, abhorrence, offensive thing (118)
342	גָּדַל	(Q) to grow up, be(come) great, strong, wealthy, important; (Pi) bring up (children), make great, extol; (Hi) make great, magnify, do great things (117)
343	יָטַב	(Q) to be well with, go well with, be pleasing (to); (Hi) make things go well for, do good to, deal well with, treat kindly (117); cf טוֹב (#714)
344	לָשׁוֹן	(cs) tongue, language (117)
345	מַמְלָכָה	kingdom, dominion, reign (117)
346	קָדוֹשׁ	(adj) holy, set apart (117)
347	שָׂרַף	(Q) to burn (completely), destroy; (Ni) be burned (117)
348	שָׁפַךְ	(Q) to pour (out), spill, shed (blood) (117)
349	שָׁלֵם	(Q) to be complete, finished; (Pi) complete, finish, make whole, restore, reward; (Hi) bring to completion, consummate (116); cf שָׁלֵם (#1024)
350	נָבָא	(Ni) to prophesy, be in a state of prophetic ecstasy; (Hith) speak or behave as a prophet (115)
351	קָטַר	(Pi) to make a sacrifice go up in smoke, offer (a sacrifice) by burning; (Hi) cause a sacrifice to go up in smoke (115)
352	בָּכָה	(Q) to weep (in grief or joy), weep (for) (114)
353	כָּבֵד	(Q) to be heavy, weighty, honored; (Ni) be honored; (Pi) honor; (Hi) make heavy, dull or insensitive, harden (heart) (114); cf כָּבֵד (#773, #1563)
354	מִגְרָשׁ	open land, pasture (114)
355	שֶׁקֶר	lie, deception, falsehood (113)

356	בִּלְתִּי	(negates inf cstr) not, except; also spelled לְבִלְתִּי (86x) with prep לְ (112)
357	לָבַשׁ	(Q) to put on a garment, clothe, be clothed; (Hi) clothe (112)
358	עַמּוּד	pillar, column, tent pole (112)
359	יָדָה	(Hi) to thank, praise, confess; (Hith) confess (111)
360	כָּנָף	(fs) wing, edge, extremity (111)
361	שַׁבָּת	(cs) Sabbath, day or period of rest; (cp) שַׁבָּתוֹת (111)
362	עָפָר	dust, dry earth (110)
363	רַק	only, still, but, however (109)
364	נָחַם	(Ni) to be sorry, regret, have compassion (on or for); (Pi) comfort, console (108)
365	שְׁלִישִׁי	(adj) third; (fs) שְׁלִישִׁית and שְׁלִישִׁיָּה (108)
366	הֵן	behold, if (107)
367	כֶּבֶשׂ	lamb, sheep (107)
368	סָפַר	(Q) to count; (Pi) count, recount, make known, proclaim, report, tell (107)
369	בָּמָה	(cultic) high place, sacred hill; (fp) בָּמוֹת (106)
370	יָתַר	(Ni) to be left over, remain; (Hi) have (something) left over or remaining (106)
371	בְּעַד	(prep) behind, through (104)
372	גָּאַל	(Q) to redeem, act as kinsman (perform the responsibilities of the next-of-kin), avenge (104); cf גָּאַל (#1756)
373	חֻקָּה	statute, ordinance (104); cf חֹק (#315)
374	רוּץ	(Q) to run (104)
375	תָּמִיד	continually (104)
376	מַרְאֶה	vision, sight, appearance (103)
377	כָּפַר	(Pi) to cover (over), atone (for), make atonement (102)

378	שָׁכַח	(Q) to forget; (Ni) be forgotten (102)
379	מְעַט	(adj) little, few (101)
380	רֹחַב	width, breadth, expanse (101)
381	רָעָב	famine, hunger (101)
382	יַעַן	on account of, because; 33x with אֲשֶׁר (#9) as יַעַן אֲשֶׁר (100)
383	עוֹר	skin, hide, leather (99)
384	רָעַע	(Q) to be bad, evil or displeasing; (Hi) do evil, do wickedly, do injury, harm, treat badly (98)
385	שְׁבִיעִי	(adj) seventh; (fs) שְׁבִיעִית (98)
386	שָׁרַת	(Pi) to minister, serve (98)
387	אָמַן	(Ni) to be reliable, faithful or trustworthy; (Hi) believe (in), trust, have trust in, put trust in (97)
388	יֶתֶר	rest, remainder, excess (97)
389	שָׂבַע	(Q) to be satisfied, have one's fill (of), eat or drink one's fill; (Hi) satisfy (97)
390	חַיָּה	animal, beast, living thing (96); cf חַיָּה (#1768)
391	חֲמוֹר	donkey (96)
392	טָהוֹר	(adj) clean, pure (96)
393	יַחְדָּו	together, at the same time (96)
394	אֹרֶךְ	length (95)
395	הָפַךְ	(Q) to turn, overturn, overthrow, destroy; (Ni) be destroyed, turned into, changed (95)
396	חָלָל	(adj) pierced, slain, defiled (94)
397	טָהֵר	(Q) to be clean (ceremonially), pure (morally); (Pi) cleanse, purify, pronounce clean; (Hith) purify or cleanse oneself (94)
398	כֶּרֶם	vineyard (94)
399	מָלַט	(Ni) to escape, flee to safety, slip away; (Pi) let someone escape, save someone, leave undisturbed (94)

400	שִׂמְחָה	joy, gladness (94)
401	חָרָה	(Q) to be(come) hot, burn with anger, become angry (93)
402	פֶּשַׁע	transgression, rebellion (93)
403	גֵּר	stranger, sojourner, alien (92)
404	חֵלֶב	fat; (metaphorically) best, choice part (92)
405	עֵבֶר	beyond, other side, edge, bank (92)
406	קָצֶה	(ms) end, border, outskirts (92)
407	שָׁמֵם	(Q) to be deserted, uninhabited; (Ni) be made uninhabited, desolate, deserted; (Hi) make deserted or desolated (92)
408	זְרוֹעַ	(fs) arm, forearm; (metaphorically) strength or power; (fp) זְרֹעוֹת (91)
409	כְּרוּב	cherub; (mp) כְּרוּבִים cherubim (91)
410	מַלְכוּת	kingdom, dominion, royal power (91)
411	סָגַר	(Q) to shut (in), close; (Hi) deliver (up), hand over, surrender, give up (91)
412	תָּמִים	(adj) blameless, perfect, honest, devout (91)
413	שָׁמַד	(Ni) to be exterminated, destroyed, or annihilated; (Hi) exterminate, annihilate, destroy (90)
414	יֶלֶד	child, boy, youth (89)
415	דֶּלֶת	door (88)
416	דַּעַת	knowledge, understanding, ability (88)
417	טָמֵא	(adj) unclean (88); cf טָמֵא (#262)
418	שִׁיר	(Q) to sing (of); (Q and Polel ptc) singer (88); cf שִׁיר (#455) and שִׁירָה (#1675)
419	שֶׁקֶל	shekel, measurement of weight (88)
420	לָמַד	(Q) to learn; (Pi) teach (87)
421	עָנָן	(coll) clouds (87)
422	עֵצָה	counsel, plan, advice (87)

21

423	שֶׁלֶם	peace offering (87)
424	פֵּאָה	corner, side, edge (86)
425	שִׁית	(Q) to set, put, place, set one's mind to (86)
426	הָמוֹן	multitude, crowd, sound, roar (85)
427	קָנָה	(Q) to get, acquire, buy (85)
428	פָּלַל	(Hith) to pray, make intercession (84)
429	רָחוֹק	(adj) distant, remote, far away (84)
430	גּוּר	(Q) to sojourn, dwell (stay) as a foreigner or alien (82); cf גּוּר (#1839)
431	זָכָר	male, man (82)
432	סָתַר	(Ni) to be hidden, hide oneself; (Hi) hide (82)
433	עָזַר	(Q) to help, assist, come to the aid of (82)
434	פֹּה	here, at this place; also spelled פוֹ (82)
435	קָלַל	(Q) to be small, insignificant, of little account, swift; (Ni, Pi) declare cursed; (Hi) treat with contempt (82)
436	אָוֶן	iniquity, wickedness, evildoer (81)
437	מָהַר	(Pi) to hasten, hurry, go or come quickly (81)
438	מָשַׁל	(Q) to rule, reign, govern, have dominion (81); cf מָשַׁל (#1389)
439	שָׁחַט	(Q) to slaughter (animals for sacrifice) (81)
440	הֵיכָל	temple, palace (80)
441	חֹשֶׁךְ	darkness (80)
442	יָעַץ	(Q) to advise, counsel, plan, decide; (Ni) consult or take counsel together (80)
443	מָכַר	(Q) to sell, hand over; (Ni) be sold, sell oneself (into slavery) (80)
444	עוּר	(Q) to be awake, stir up; (Hi) arouse, rouse, wake up, stir up; (Polel) arouse, disturb, awaken (80)
445	עָנִי	(adj) poor, humble, afflicted (80); cf עָנִי (#853)
446	קָרְבָּן	gift, offering (80)

447	אוֹצָר	treasure, treasury, storehouse (79)
448	אוֹת	(cs) sign, mark, pledge; (cp) אֹתוֹת (79)
449	עָנָה	(Q) to be afflicted, humbled; (Pi) afflict, oppress, humiliate, violate (79); cf עָנָה (#152, #1467)
450	שׁוֹר	ox, bull, cow (79)
451	יְשׁוּעָה	salvation, help, deliverance (78)
452	מִשְׁמֶרֶת	watch, guard, responsibility (78)
453	נֶגַע	plague, affliction (78)
454	רָכַב	(Q) to ride, mount and ride; (Hi) cause or make to ride (78)
455	שִׁיר	song (78); cf שִׁיר (#418) and שִׁירָה (#1675)
456	תֵּשַׁע	nine; (fs) תִּשְׁעָה; (mp) תִּשְׁעִים ninety (78)
457	גּוֹרָל	lot, portion, allotment (77)
458	חָנַן	(Q) to be gracious to, show favor to, favor; (Hith) plead for grace, favor or compassion (77)
459	תְּפִלָּה	prayer (77)
460	בַּרְזֶל	iron (76)
461	מִקְנֶה	cattle, livestock, property (76)
462	נַעֲרָה	young girl, newly married woman, maidservant (76)
463	עֹז	strength, power, might; (with 3ms suff) עֻזּוֹ (76); cf עֹז (#1399)
464	קֶרֶן	(fs) horn (76)
465	קֶשֶׁת	bow, weapon (76)
466	תְּרוּמָה	offering, contribution, tribute (76)
467	חָלָה	(Q) to be(come) weak, tired, sick; (Ni) be exhausted; (Pi) appease, flatter (75)
468	מִקְדָּשׁ	sanctuary (75); 31x in Ezek
469	עָרַךְ	(Q) to set in order, lay out, set in rows, arrange, stack (wood), draw up a battle formation (75)
470	קָרוֹב	(adj) near, close (75)

471	חָפֵץ	(Q) to delight in, take pleasure in, desire, be willing (74); cf חֵפֶץ (#1632)
472	מָאַס	(Q) to refuse, reject, despise (74)
473	מִזְרָח	east, sunrise (74)
474	נָצַב	(Ni) to stand (firm), take one's stand, station oneself, be positioned; (Hi) station, set (up), place, establish (74)
475	סֶלָה	technical poetic notation of undetermined meaning; in Pss and 3x in Hab (74)
476	עֵז	(fs) goat, goat's hair; (fp) עִזִּים (74)
477	קָטֹן	(adj) small, young, insignificant; (fs) קְטַנָּה (74); cf קָטָן (#1048)
478	שָׁלָל	plunder, spoil (74)
479	אָסַר	(Q) to tie, bind, fetter, imprison (73)
480	אֶרֶז	cedar (73)
481	בַּל	(poetic) no, never (73); 69x in Isa, Pss, Prov
482	הֶבֶל	vanity, futility, breath (73); 38x in Eccl
483	זָעַק	(Q) to cry (out), call for help, summon (73)
484	חֶרְפָּה	reproach, disgrace, shame (73)
485	צוּר	rock, boulder (73); cf צוּר (#956)
486	קִיר	wall; (mp) קִירוֹת (73)
487	בֶּטֶן	(fs) belly, stomach, womb (72)
488	גִּבְעָה	hill (72)
489	מַדּוּעַ	why? (72)
490	צַר	adversary, enemy (72); cf צַר (#1047)
491	רָחַץ	(Q) to wash (with water), wash (off or away), bathe, bathe oneself (72)
492	רִיב	(Q) to strive, contend, quarrel, dispute, conduct a legal case (72); cf רִיב (#547)
493	שׁוֹפָר	trumpet, ram's horn; (mp) שׁוֹפָרוֹת (72)

494	בְּרָכָה	blessing, gift (71)
495	לִין	(Q) to remain overnight, spend the night (71)
496	עוֹף	(coll) flying creatures, birds, insects (71)
497	פָּלָא	(Ni) to be extraordinary, wonderful; (Hi) do something wonderful (71)
498	שָׁבַת	(Q) to stop, cease, rest; (Hi) put an end to, remove, put away (71)
499	שֻׁלְחָן	table; (mp) שֻׁלְחָנוֹת (71)
500	זָר	(adj) foreign, strange (70)
501	כְּסִיל	fool, shameless person (70)
502	מָשַׁח	(Q) to smear (with a liquid, oil, or dye), anoint (with oil) (70)
503	נָבַט	(Hi) to look (at or out), gaze, behold (70)
504	עֵמֶק	valley, plain (70)
505	צָרָה	distress, anxiety, trouble (70)
506	תָּקַע	(Q) to drive or thrust (weapon into a person), pitch (tent), blow (trumpet), clap one's hands (70)
507	חֵן	favor, grace, charm (69)
508	עֵד	witness (69)
509	קָדִים	east, eastern, east wind (69); cf קֶדֶם (#556)
510	רָפָא	(Q) to heal; (Ni) be healed, become whole; (Pi) heal, make healthy (69)
511	כִּכָּר	(fs) something round, talent (weight), valley; (fp) כִּכָּרִים (68)
512	אַתְּ	(2fs pers pron) you (67)
513	בּוֹר	pit, cistern, well (67)
514	כָּתֵף	(fs) side, shoulder (67)
515	פָּרַשׂ	(Q) to spread out (as with hands in prayer), stretch (out or over) (67)
516	קֶבֶר	grave, burial site; (mp) קְבָרִים and קְבָרוֹת (67)

25

517	קֵץ	end, border, limit (67)
518	אֲחֻזָּה	property, possession (66)
519	גֶּבֶר	strong man, young man, hero (66)
520	חֵלֶק	portion, share (66)
521	שְׁאֵרִית	remnant, remainder (66); 37x in Isa, Jer, Ezek; cf שְׁאָר (#1077)
522	אִשֶּׁה	(ms) offering by fire (65)
523	חֲלוֹם	dream (65)
524	כָּשַׁל	(Q) to stumble, totter, stagger; (Ni) be caused to stumble, stumble (65)
525	נָצַח	(Pi) to supervise, oversee or inspect works and activities related to the temple; מְנַצֵּחַ (ptc) used as title (superscription) in 55 psalms (65)
526	פּוּץ	(Q) to be spread, dispersed, scattered, overflow; (Ni) be scattered, dispersed; (Hi) scatter, disperse (65)
527	צָלַח	(Q) to succeed, prosper, be successful; (Hi) be successful, succeed, cause to succeed or prosper (65)
528	שְׁאוֹל	(cs) underworld, Sheol (65)
529	שָׁכַם	(Hi) to get up early, rise early, do (something) early (65)
530	תָּפַשׂ	(Q) to take hold of, seize, capture, grasp; (Ni) be seized, caught, captured, conquered (65)
531	גַּיְא	(cs) valley; also spelled גֵּיא (64)
532	יְאֹר	stream, river, Nile (64)
533	תָּמַם	(Q) to be(come) complete or finished, come to an end, cease, be consumed, burned out (64)
534	אָחַז	(Q) to seize, grasp, take hold (of), hold fast (63)
535	אָרַר	(Q) to curse (63)
536	בָּרַח	(Q) to run away, flee, go or pass through (63)

537	דָּרַךְ	(Q) to tread (often in the sense of pressing for wine or oil), march, draw a bow; (Hi) cause to tread, march or walk (63)
538	יָצַר	(Q) to form, fashion, shape, create (63)
539	יָרֵא	(adj) fearful (63); cf יָרֵא (#150)
540	נָצַר	(Q) to keep watch, watch over, guard, protect, preserve (63)
541	קָרַע	(Q) to tear, rend, cut up, tear away (63)
542	שִׁפְחָה	female slave or servant, maidservant (63); cf אָמָה (#587)
543	אֵצֶל	(prep) beside, near (62)
544	גְּבוּרָה	power, strength; (fp) גְּבוּרוֹת mighty deeds (62)
545	חַג	feast, festival, procession; also spelled חָג; (mp) חַגִּים (62)
546	קָנֶה	(ms) reed (62)
547	רִיב	dispute, quarrel, lawsuit (62); cf רִיב (#492)
548	שָׁקָה	(Hi) to give drink (to), irrigate (62)
549	אֶבְיוֹן	(adj) poor, needy (61)
550	אַחֲרִית	end, extremity, last (61)
551	אֵיךְ	how? (61)
552	אוּלָם	porch; also spelled אֵילָם (61); cf אוּלָם (#1273)
553	דּוֹד	beloved, uncle (61); 39x in Song
554	מָלֵא	(adj) full, filled (61); cf מָלֵא (#180)
555	עֵדוּת	witness, testimony; (fp) עֵדוֹת (61)
556	קֶדֶם	east, ancient times (61); cf קָדִים (#509)
557	אַלּוּף	tribal chief, leader (60)
558	בָּעַר	(Q) to burn (up), consume; (Pi) kindle, burn (60); cf בָּעַר (#1030)
559	זָנָה	(Q) to commit fornication, be a harlot (prostitute), be unfaithful (60)

560	חָמָס	violence, wrong (60)
561	מָגֵן	(cs) shield; (cp) מָגִנִּים (60)
562	נֶדֶר	vow; also spelled נֵדֶר (60)
563	נֶסֶךְ	drink offering; also spelled נֵסֶךְ (60)
564	עֲרָבָה	desert plain, Arabah (60)
565	פָּדָה	(Q) to ransom, redeem, buy out (60)
566	קְטֹרֶת	incense, smoke (60)
567	שָׂכַל	(Hi) to understand, comprehend, have insight, make wise, have success (60)
568	אֹרַח	(cs) road, path, way (59)
569	בְּלִי	without, nothing (59)
570	הֵנָּה	here (59); cf הֵנָּה (#982)
571	יָבֵשׁ	(Q) to dry up, be(come) dry, wither; (Hi) make dry (up), make wither (59)
572	יָכַח	(Hi) to reprove, rebuke, reproach, chasten, punish, decide, mediate, arbitrate (59)
573	נָחַל	(Q) to take (as a) possession, obtain (receive) property, give as an inheritance; (Hi) give as an inheritance (59)
574	נָטַע	(Q) to plant (59)
575	סֶלַע	rock, stone, cliff (59)
576	רָחַק	(Q) to be(come) far or distant, keep far from; (Hi) remove, put (keep) far away, keep at a distance (59)
577	שָׁדַד	(Q) to devastate, ruin, deal violently with, violently destroy; (Pu) be devastated (59)
578	אֱלוֹהַּ	God, god (58)
579	פָּעַל	(Q) to do, make, perform (58)
580	רֵיחַ	smell, odor, scent (58)
581	תְּהִלָּה	praise, song of praise (58)
582	אֶדֶן	base, pedestal (57)

583	חָזָק	(adj) strong, mighty, hard (57)
584	יַעַר	forest, woods, thicket (57)
585	מִזְמוֹר	psalm, song (57); all in Pss
586	פָּרָשׁ	horseman, horse (57)
587	אָמָה	female slave or servant, maidservant (56); cf שִׁפְחָה (#542)
588	זָרַע	(Q) to sow, scatter seed (56)
589	טֶרֶם	before, not yet; also spelled בְּטֶרֶם with prep בְּ (56)
590	מַחֲשָׁבָה	thought, plan, scheme (56)
591	רָצוֹן	pleasure, acceptance, favor (56)
592	שְׁמָמָה	desolation, waste, ruin (56)
593	אַלְמָנָה	widow (55)
594	גֶּפֶן	(cs) vine, grapevine (55)
595	דָּבַק	(Q) to cling, cleave to, stick to; (Hi) cause to cling, cleave or stick to, pursue closely (55)
596	חָדַל	(Q) to cease, end, stop, refrain (from) (55)
597	חָזָה	(Q) to see, behold, perceive (55)
598	חָלַק	(Q) to divide, share (with or in), apportion, distribute; (Pi) divide (in pieces), apportion, scatter (55)
599	חֵץ	arrow; (mp) חִצִּים (55)
600	חָתַת	(Q) to be shattered, dismayed, filled with terror (55)
601	כָּעַס	(Q) to be angry, vexed; (Hi) vex, provoke, provoke (God) to anger (55)
602	מִדָּה	measure, measurement (55)
603	צָעַק	(Q) to shout, cry (out), call for help; (Ni) be called together, summoned (55)
604	רְבִיעִי	(adj) fourth; (fs) רְבִיעִית (55)
605	שֵׁן	(cs) tooth, ivory (55)

606	אָבָה	(Q) to be willing, consent, yield to, want something (54)
607	גָּמָל	camel; (mp) גְּמַלִּים (54); 44x in Exod
608	דְּבַשׁ	honey (54)
609	יְרִיעָה	tent curtain (54)
610	מָרוֹם	height, elevation, pride (54)
611	סֹפֵר	scribe, secretary (54)
612	עָמָל	trouble, labor, toil (54)
613	עֶרְוָה	nakedness (54)
614	שְׂמֹאל	left, left side, north; also spelled שְׂמֹאול (54)
615	שָׁוְא	worthlessness, vanity, emptiness (54)
616	חָדָשׁ	(adj) new, fresh (53)
617	יוֹמָם	by day, daily, in the daytime (53)
618	יָצַק	(Q) to pour, pour out (liquid), cast (metal), flow (into); (Hoph) be cast, poured out, emptied out (53)
619	מְדִינָה	province, district (53)
620	מַצָּה	unleavened bread (53)
621	סֹלֶת	flour (53)
622	עֶלְיוֹן	(adj) upper; (divine title) Most High (53)
623	צֵל	shadow, shade, protection (53)
624	רָנַן	(Q) to call or cry aloud, shout with joy; (Pi) cry out (with joy), exult (53)
625	אַיֵּה	where? (52)
626	מָדַד	(Q) to measure, measure off (distance or expanse), measure out (grain) (52)
627	מָחָר	tomorrow (52); cf מָחֳרָת (#927)
628	שָׂעִיר	male goat (52)
629	אַחֲרוֹן	(adj) last, behind, west (51)

630	בָּקַע	(Q) to cleave, split, breach, break open; (Ni) be cleft, split (open); (Pi) split, rip open (51)
631	הוֹי	woe! oh! ha! (51)
632	כָּבַס	(Pi) to clean, cleanse, wash away guilt (51)
633	נָדַח	(Ni) to be scattered, banished, driven away, thrust out; (Hi) scatter, drive away, disperse, thrust out (51)
634	קֶרֶשׁ	board, plank (51); 48x in Exod
635	רֵאשִׁית	beginning, first (51)
636	תָּעָה	(Q) to err, wander (about), stagger, go astray (animal); (Hi) lead astray, cause to err (51)
637	בְּתוּלָה	virgin (50)
638	חָרַם	(Hi) to devote to the ban, dedicate to destruction, exterminate (50)
639	טַבַּעַת	ring, signet ring; (fp) טַבָּעֹת (50)
640	מוּסָר	discipline, correction, instruction (50)
641	נָכַר	(Hi) to recognize, know, investigate, be acquainted with, acknowledge (50)
642	נָשַׂג	(Hi) to reach, overtake (50)
643	אֱמוּנָה	faithfulness, reliability (49)
644	אֵפֹד	ephod, priestly garment (49)
645	בָּגַד	(Q) to act or deal treacherously, faithlessly or deceitfully with (49)
646	בַּעֲבוּר	on account of, in order that (49)
647	גָּאוֹן	majesty, exaltation, pride (49)
648	מַעֲלָה	ascent, step, stairs (49); cf מַעֲלֶה (#1188)
649	מִשְׁקָל	weight (49)
650	נָגַף	(Q) to smite, strike, injure; (Ni) be smitten, struck (with) (49)
651	פַּחַד	trembling, terror, dread (49)
652	פֶּסַח	Passover (49)

31

653	קָצִיר	harvest (49)
654	תְּכֵלֶת	blue or purple material (49)
655	תִּפְאֶרֶת	beauty, glory, splendor (49)
656	אֹמֶר	word, saying, speech (48)
657	בָּרָא	(Q) to create (only with God as subject); (Ni) be created (48)
658	גִּלּוּלִים	idols (48)
659	דַּל	(adj) poor, weak, needy (48)
660	חֶבֶל	rope, cord, field, region (48)
661	חִיל	(Q) to writhe, travail, be in labor, tremble; also spelled חוּל (48); cf חוּל (#1845)
662	חֲנִית	spear (48)
663	יָצַב	(Hith) to take one's stand, stand firm, station oneself, present oneself before (48)
664	לִשְׁכָּה	room, chamber, hall (48)
665	מַכָּה	wound, injury, defeat (48)
666	נְבֵלָה	carcass, corpse (48)
667	סָמַךְ	(Q) to support, uphold, sustain, help, lean or lay (hand upon); (Ni) lean (on or against), support oneself (48)
668	רָצָה	(Q) to be pleased with, favorable toward, well disposed toward, accept (with pleasure), become friends with (48)
669	שַׂק	sack, sackcloth (48)
670	שְׁבִי	captivity, captives (48)
671	שַׁדַּי	(divine title) Almighty, Shaddai (48); אֵל־שַׁדַּי "God Almighty" (of uncertain etymology)
672	אַרְיֵה	(ms) lion (47); cf אֲרִי (#861)
673	גִּיל	(Q) to shout with joy, rejoice (47)
674	חָרַשׁ	(Q) to be silent, deaf; (Hi) be(come) silent, deaf, keep still (47); cf חָרַשׁ (#1032)

32

675	יָרָה	(Hi) to instruct, teach (47); cf יָרָה (#1008)
676	מָתְנַיִם	(md) hips, waist, loins (47)
677	סָלַח	(Q) to pardon, forgive; (Ni) be forgiven (47)
678	עַד	forever, eternal; spelled וְעַד with conjunction וְ (47); cf עַד (#33)
679	פָּרַר	(Hi) to break (out), destroy, put an end to, make ineffectual (47)
680	צָפָה	(Pi) to overlay, plate (with gold) (47); cf צָפָה (#834)
681	צָרַר	(Q) to wrap (up), tie up, bind (transitive); be cramped, restricted, depressed (intransitive); (Hi) oppress, harass, afflict (47); cf צָרַר (#1070)
682	קָוָה	(Pi) to wait (for), wait with eagerness, hope (47)
683	רָחַם	(Pi) to show love for, have compassion (for), take pity on (47)
684	רָצַח	(Q) to kill, murder, slay (47)
685	שֶׂה	(ms) sheep, lamb (47)
686	שָׁבָה	(Q) to take captive, deport (47)
687	אָשָׁם	guilt, guilt offering (46); 27x in Lev
688	דֶּבֶר	plague, pestilence (46)
689	יַחַד	together, along with (46)
690	מִשְׁכָּב	bed, couch (46)
691	מִשְׁתֶּה	(ms) feast, banquet (46); 20x in Esth
692	נָכְרִי	(adj) foreign, strange; (fs) נָכְרִיָּה (46)
693	נְעוּרִים	youth (46)
694	עָצַר	(Q) to hold back, restrain, hinder, imprison; (Ni) be restrained, shut up, detained (46)
695	פָּגַע	(Q) to meet, encounter, fall upon, attack, assail, reach (46)
696	פָּרַץ	(Q) to break through (out or into), make a breach, burst open, spread out (46)

697	קוֹמָה	height (46)
698	קָשַׁב	(Hi) to give (pay) attention, listen carefully or attentively (46)
699	רָפָה	(Q) to sink, drop, relax, grow slack; (Hi) abandon, forsake, desert, leave (someone) alone (46)
700	אוּלַי	perhaps, maybe (45)
701	גָּרַשׁ	(Q) to drive out, banish; (Pi) drive out (away) (45)
702	זָמַר	(Pi) to sing, praise, make music, play an instrument (45)
703	חֲמִישִׁי	(adj) fifth; (fs) חֲמִישִׁית (45)
704	מִגְדָּל	tower; (mp) מִגְדָּלִים and מִגְדָּלוֹת (45)
705	סָרִיס	official, eunuch (45)
706	עִמָּד	(prep) with (45)
707	אוֹר	(Hi) to give light, shine, illuminate, light up (44); cf אוֹר (#332)
708	אַשְׁרֵי	blessed, happy (44); 26x in Pss
709	בָּחוּר	young man; (mp) בַּחוּרִים (44)
710	בָּלַל	(Q) to mix (up), confuse or confound (languages), mingle (44)
711	חָגַר	(Q) to gird, gird (oneself or someone), get ready (44)
712	חָלָב	milk (44)
713	חָלַץ	(Q) to draw out, take off, withdraw, be girded (ready for battle); (Pi) rescue, deliver (44)
714	טוֹב	(Q) to be good, pleasing, pleasant, joyful, well with (44); cf טוֹב (#92) and יָטַב (#343)
715	יִרְאָה	fear; (fs cstr) יִרְאַת (44); יִרְאַת יְהוָה "the fear of Yahweh"
716	מוֹשָׁב	dwelling, settlement, seat; (mp) מוֹשָׁבוֹת (44)
717	מָרָה	(Q) to be rebellious, obstinate or contentious; (Hi) behave rebelliously or obstinately (44)
718	מֶרְכָּבָה	chariot (44)

719	מַשָּׂא	load, burden (44); cf מַשָּׂא (#1254)
720	נָגִיד	leader, ruler (44); 21x in 1 and 2 Chron
721	נָקָה	(Ni) to be free (of), without guilt, innocent, exempt from (punishment); (Pi) leave unpunished, regard as innocent (44)
722	נֵר	lamp, light; (mp) נֵרוֹת (44)
723	קָשַׁר	(Q) to bind, be in league together, conspire (against) (44)
724	רוּעַ	(Hi) to shout, cry (out), shout a war cry (alarm of battle), sound a signal for war, cheer, shout in triumph (44)
725	שָׁבַר	break, fracture, collapse (44)
726	אֶפֶס	end, nothing (43)
727	בָּזַז	(Q) to plunder, spoil (43)
728	הָרָה	(Q) to conceive, be(come) pregnant (43); cf הָרֶה (#1502)
729	הָרַס	(Q) to tear down, demolish, destroy, throw down, overthrow, break through; (Ni) be ruined (43)
730	לוּחַ	tablet, board, plank (43)
731	מָתַי	when? (43)
732	נִיחֹחַ	soothing or pleasing scent; also spelled נִיחוֹחַ (43); 35x in Lev, Num
733	נֵצַח	forever, everlasting (43)
734	נָקִי	(adj) blameless, innocent (43)
735	פָּשַׁט	(Q) to take off (clothes), strip off, rush out, make a raid; (Hi) take off (clothes or armor), strip off (skin), flay (43)
736	קִנְאָה	jealousy, zeal (43)
737	רְחוֹב	(fs) public square, street (43)
738	תְּבוּאָה	produce, harvest (43)
739	אָנָה	where? עַד־אָנָה how long? also spelled אָן (42)

740	אֱנוֹשׁ	man, humankind (42); 31x in Pss, Job
741	בָּדַל	(Ni) to separate oneself, withdraw; (Hi) divide, separate, set apart, make a distinction (between), single out (42)
742	בָּזָה	(Q) to despise, regard with contempt (42)
743	בֶּטַח	security, safety (42)
744	בָּלַע	(Q, Pi) to swallow (up), engulf (42)
745	גּוֹלָה	captivity, exiles (42)
746	זוּב	(Q) to flow (away), suffer a discharge (42)
747	חָרְבָּה	desolation, ruin; (fp) חֳרָבוֹת (42)
748	יָחַל	(Pi, Hi) to wait (for), hope for (42)
749	יָפֶה	(adj) beautiful; (fs) יָפָה (42)
750	יָתוֹם	orphan (42)
751	כִּנּוֹר	lyre, harp; (mp) כִּנֹּרוֹת (42)
752	מַחֲלֹקֶת	division, portion (42)
753	מְנוֹרָה	lampstand (42); 20x in Exod
754	מַעֲלָל	deed, act (42); 18x in Jer
755	נוּעַ	(Q) to tremble, shake, totter, wave (of trees); (Hi) make unstable or unsteady, shake (up), disturb (42)
756	נָתַץ	(Q) to tear down, pull down, break down, demolish (42)
757	שָׁנִי	scarlet, crimson (42); 26x in Exod
758	שָׁקַט	(Q) to be quiet, peaceful, at peace, at rest; (Hi) give (keep) peace (42)
759	תְּבוּנָה	understanding, skill (42); 19x in Prov
760	אָזַן	(Hi) to give ear to, listen (to), hear, heed (41)
761	אָחוֹר	back, behind (41)
762	אָמֵץ	(Q) to be strong, be bold; (Pi) make firm, strengthen, harden someone's heart (41)
763	אָרַב	(Q) to ambush, lie in ambush, lie in wait (41)

764	בְּרִיחַ	bar (41)
765	בֹּשֶׁת	shame, disgrace (41)
766	גָּבֹהַּ	(adj) high, exalted; (fs) גְּבֹהָה (41)
767	גַּן	(cs) garden; (cp) גַּנִּים (41)
768	חָמַל	(Q) to have compassion (for), have pity (for), spare (41)
769	חָרוֹן	anger, fury, burning (41)
770	טַף	children (41)
771	יָסַד	(Q) to found, establish, appoint, destine, allocate; (Pi) found, appoint, establish (41)
772	יָסַר	(Pi) to teach, discipline, correct, chastise, rebuke (41)
773	כָּבֵד	(adj) heavy, severe, important (41); cf כָּבֵד (#353, #1563)
774	מָאֵן	(Pi) to refuse (41)
775	מְעָרָה	cave (41)
776	פָּשַׁע	(Q) to revolt, rebel (against), transgress, break with, break away from, behave as a criminal (41)
777	צָדֵק	(Q) to be in the right, have a just cause, be just (justified), be righteous; (Hi) justify, declare righteous, just or innocent (41)
778	צַוָּאר	neck (41)
779	רָגַז	(Q) to shake, quake, tremble, be agitated, perturbed, excited, upset (41)
780	אֵיפָה	a dry measurement of corn or wheat, ephah (40)
781	אֲשֵׁרָה	Asherah (pagan goddess), cultic pole; (fp) אֲשֵׁרִים and אֲשֵׁרוֹת (40)
782	בַּד	carrying pole, gate bar (40); cf בַּד (#1136)
783	גָּנַב	(Q) to steal, deceive (40)
784	דָּגָן	grain, corn (40)
785	מָשָׁל	proverb, wisdom saying (40)

786	נָטַשׁ	(Q) to leave, forsake, abandon, give up (something); (Ni) be forsaken (40)
787	עוּד	(Hi) to warn, admonish, witness, be a witness, testify (40)
788	עֹל	yoke; (with 3ms suff) עֻלוֹ (40)
789	צֵלָע	(fs) rib, side (40)
790	צִפּוֹר	(cs) bird; (cp) צִפֳּרִים (40)
791	רַחֲמִים	compassion, mercy (40)
792	בָּהַל	(Ni) to be terrified, horrified, dismayed, disturbed, hasty, make haste; (Pi) terrify, make haste, act hastily (39)
793	דַּי	what is required or necessary; (ms cstr) דֵּי (39)
794	חָרַד	(Q) to tremble, do something with trembling, shudder, quake; (Hi) startle (39)
795	מוֹט	(Q) to totter, shake, sway, stagger; (Ni) be made to stagger, stumble or totter (39)
796	מִרְמָה	deceit, deception (39)
797	נָחָה	(Q) to lead; (Hi) lead, guide, conduct (39)
798	קָהַל	(Ni) to assemble, meet together (intransitive); (Hi) assemble (transitive), summon (39)
799	שַׁמָּה	desolation, horror (39)
800	שֵׁשׁ	linen (39); 33x in Exod; cf שֵׁשׁ (#173)
801	תְּאֵנָה	fig tree, fig; (fp) תְּאֵנִים (39)
802	תּוֹלְדוֹת	(fp) generations, descendants; (fp cstr) תּוֹלְדֹת and תֹּלְדוֹת (39)
803	תּוֹלָעַת	worm (39); 27x in Exod
804	אֹכֶל	food (38)
805	אַרְגָּמָן	purple (38); 26x in Exod
806	בִּינָה	understanding, insight (38)
807	זַיִת	olive tree, olive; (mp) זֵיתִים (38)

808	זָרָה	(Q) to scatter; (Pi) scatter, disperse, spread (38)
809	חֶדֶר	room, chamber (38)
810	חֵיק	bosom, lap (38)
811	חֵפֶץ	delight, desire, pleasure, joy (38)
812	חָרַף	(Q) to taunt, reproach; (Pi) taunt, reproach, revile (38)
813	כּוּל	(Q) to comprehend; (Pilpel) contain, sustain, provide, support; (Hi) contain, hold (in), sustain, endure (38)
814	כָּלַם	(Ni) to be hurt, humiliated, ashamed, disgraced; (Hi) put to shame, humiliate, disgrace (38)
815	מָטָר	rain (38)
816	מְלֹא	fullness, abundance (38)
817	מִלָּה	word, speech (38); 34x in Job
818	מַר	(adj) bitter; (n) bitterness (38)
819	מָשִׁיחַ	(adj) anointed; (n) anointed one, Messiah (38)
820	עֵדֶר	flock, herd (38)
821	תִּירוֹשׁ	new wine (38)
822	בְּאֵר	(fs) well, pit, cistern (37)
823	גָּמַל	(Q) to complete, finish, wean, ripen, render; recompense, requite (37)
824	גֹּרֶן	(fs) threshing floor (37)
825	חָסָה	(Q) to seek or take refuge (37)
826	כּוֹכָב	star (37)
827	כָּכָה	thus, so (37)
828	לָקַט	(Q) to gather (together), glean; (Pi) gather (up), collect (37)
829	מִבְצָר	fortress, stronghold (37)
830	מָעוֹז	refuge, stronghold; (mp) מָעֻזִּים (37)
831	עָשַׁק	(Q) to oppress, exploit, wrong (someone) (37)
832	עֹשֶׁר	wealth, riches (37)

833	פִּילֶגֶשׁ	(fs) concubine; (fp) פִּילַגְשִׁים (37)
834	צָפָה	(Q) to keep watch, watch attentively, spy (37); cf צָפָה (#680)
835	שָׂחַק	(Q) to laugh, play; (Pi) play, entertain, dance, amuse (37)
836	שׁוֹעֵר	gatekeeper (37)
837	אָבַל	(Q) to mourn, lament; (Hith) observe mourning rites (36)
838	אִי	coastland, island; (mp) אִיִּים (36); 30x in Isa, Jer, Ezek
839	אִמְרָה	word, saying (36)
840	חָרֵב	(Q) to dry up (intransitive), lie in ruins; (Hi) cause to dry up, lay waste, make desolate (36); cf חָרֵב (#1850)
841	חָרָשׁ	craftsman (36)
842	טֻמְאָה	uncleanness, impurity (36)
843	יָקָר	(adj) precious, valuable (36)
844	יֵשַׁע	salvation, deliverance, help; (with 1cs suff) יִשְׁעִי (36)
845	כָּנַע	(Ni) to be subdued, humbled, humble oneself; (Hi) humble or subdue someone (36)
846	כָּרַע	(Q) to bow (down), kneel (down), fall to one's knees (36)
847	מוּל	(prep) in front of, opposite (36); cf מוּל (#925)
848	מוֹפֵת	wonder, sign, miracle (36)
849	מָעַל	(Q) to be unfaithful, act unfaithfully or treacherously (36)
850	מָשַׁךְ	(Q) to draw (out), pull, drag, prolong, stretch (36)
851	נֵכָר	foreigner, stranger (36)
852	נָסָה	(Pi) to test, put someone to the test, tempt (36)
853	עֳנִי	poverty, affliction, misery (36); cf עָנִי (#445)
854	פֹּעַל	work, deed (36)
855	קָצַר	(Q) to gather in, reap, harvest (36); cf קָצַר (#1598)

856	קָשֶׁה	(adj) difficult, hard, severe; (fs) קָשָׁה (36)
857	תֵּבֵל	(fs) world (36)
858	תְּהוֹם	(cs) primeval ocean, deep, depth (36)
859	תְּרוּעָה	shout, alarm, signal (36)
860	אוֹפַן	wheel (35)
861	אֲרִי	lion; (mp) אֲרָיוֹת (35); cf אַרְיֵה (#672)
862	אָשֵׁם	(Q) to be(come) guilty, commit an offense (35)
863	גֶּשֶׁם	rain, showers (35)
864	חָזוֹן	vision, revelation (35)
865	מַלְכָּה	queen (35)
866	מִשְׁנֶה	(ms) double, second (35)
867	נָקַם	(Q) to avenge, take vengeance (on), take revenge; (Ni) avenge oneself, take revenge (35)
868	סֵֽתֶר	hiding place, secret place, shelter (35)
869	עֵגֶל	calf, young bull (35)
870	עָרֵל	(adj) uncircumcised (35)
871	צָרַֽעַת	leprosy, skin disease (35)
872	קָצֶה	end, edge, tip, boundary (35)
873	רָשַׁע	(Hi) to condemn, declare or pronounce guilty (35)
874	אָלָה	oath, curse (34)
875	אָרַךְ	(Hi) to make long, lengthen, extend (34)
876	אָתוֹן	(fs) female donkey (34)
877	גָּבַהּ	(Q) to be high, tall, lofty, exalted or haughty; (Hi) make high, exalt (34)
878	הָמָה	(Q) to make (a) noise, make a sound, roar, growl, moan, groan, be boisterous (34)
879	זוֹנָה	prostitute, harlot (34)
880	זָרַק	(Q) to toss, throw, scatter, sprinkle (34)

41

881	חָבָא	(Ni) to hide (oneself), be hidden; (Hith) keep oneself hidden (34)
882	חֵטְא	sin (34)
883	חָסִיד	(adj) godly, faithful, pious (34)
884	יָרֵךְ	(fs) thigh, loin, side (34)
885	כַּלָּה	daughter-in-law, bride (34)
886	מָחָה	(Q) to wipe (out), destroy, annihilate (34)
887	נוּף	(Hi) to move back and forth, wave, brandish, wield (34)
888	עֶבְרָה	wrath, anger, fury (34)
889	עַוְלָה	iniquity, injustice, wickedness (34)
890	פָּרַח	(Q) to bud, sprout, bloom, shoot, break out, break open (34)
891	צָפַן	(Q) to hide, store (up), treasure (up), keep (34)
892	צָרַף	(Q) to smelt (metal), refine (by smelting), test (34)
893	קָנָא	(Pi) to envy, be envious of, jealous of, zealous for (34)
894	קָצַף	(Q) to be(come) angry or furious (34)
895	שְׂעֹרָה	barley; (fp) שְׂעֹרִים (34)
896	תְּשׁוּעָה	salvation, deliverance, victory (34)
897	אֵי	where? (33)
898	חָבַשׁ	(Q) to saddle, bind or buckle on, bind up (wound), wrap, twist (rope), imprison (33)
899	יְהַב	(Q) to give, come (33)
900	יוֹנָה	dove; (fp) יוֹנִים (33)
901	יְמָנִית	(fs adj) right, southern; (ms) יְמָנִי (33)
902	יָנַק	(Q) to suck; (Hi) suckle, nurse (33)
903	מַצֵּבָה	sacred stone, pillar (33)
904	עֵרֶךְ	value, assessment (33)
905	עֹרֶף	(back of) neck (33)

42

906	עֵשֶׂב	green plant, grass (33)
907	עִשָּׂרוֹן	tenth part; (mp) עֶשְׂרֹנִים (33)
908	צַד	side; (mp) צְדִּים (33)
909	צָמַח	(Q) to sprout, spring up, grow; (Hi) make grow or sprout (33)
910	קְלָלָה	curse (33)
911	רִמּוֹן	pomegranate, pomegranate tree (33)
912	רִנָּה	shout of joy or lament (33)
913	שֹׁרֶשׁ	root; (mp with 3ms suff) שָׁרָשָׁיו (33)
914	אַהֲבָה	love (32)
915	אֳנִיָּה	ship, boat (32)
916	אַרְמוֹן	palace, stronghold (32)
917	חַלּוֹן	(cs) window; (cp) חַלּוֹנוֹת and חַלּוֹנִים (32)
918	חִנָּם	without cause, without compensation, for nothing or in vain (32)
919	טַבָּח	guard, cook (32)
920	טוּב	goodness, well-being, happiness (32)
921	כָּחַד	(Ni) to be hidden, effaced; (Pi) hide, conceal (32)
922	כֶּלֶב	dog, male temple prostitute (32)
923	לְבוּשׁ	clothing, garment (32)
924	מְאוּמָה	(ms) something, anything (32)
925	מוּל	(Q) to circumcise; (Ni) be circumcised (32); cf מוּל (#847)
926	מִזְרָק	bowl; (mp) מִזְרָקוֹת (32)
927	מָחֳרָת	(the) next day (32); cf מָחָר (#627)
928	מֵעֶה	(ms) stomach, womb, entrails (32)
929	מַעֲשֵׂר	tithe, tenth (32)
930	נָוֶה	(ms) pasture, dwelling (32); cf נָוֶה (#1516)
931	נָשַׁק	(Q) to kiss (32)

932	לְעֻמַּת	(prep) beside, alongside, corresponding to; combination of prep לְ and עֻמָּה (32)
933	פְּנִימִי	(adj) inner; (fs) פְּנִימִית (32)
934	פְּקֻדָּה	appointment, service, watch, punishment (32)
935	תּוֹדָה	thanksgiving, song of thanksgiving, thank offering (32)
936	תִּקְוָה	hope, expectation (32)
937	אֶצְבַּע	(fs) finger, toe (31)
938	גָּג	roof; (mp) גַּגּוֹת (31)
939	גְּדוּד	band of raiders, military troops (31)
940	טַל	dew, light rain (31)
941	טָמַן	(Q) to hide (31)
942	יָלַל	(Hi) to howl, lament, wail (31)
943	כּוֹס	(fs) cup (31)
944	כָּזָב	lie, deception, falsehood (31)
945	כְּלָיוֹת	(fp) kidneys, place of thought or emotion (31)
946	כְּפִיר	young lion (31)
947	לְאֹם	people, nation; (mp) לְאֻמִּים (31)
948	מִין	kind, type, species (31)
949	נָאַף	(Q) to commit adultery; (metaphorically) commit idolatry; (Pi) commit adultery (31)
950	נָדַר	(Q) to make (perform) a vow, keep (make) a promise (31)
951	נָחָשׁ	serpent, snake (31)
952	סֻכָּה	booth, tabernacle (31)
953	עָב	cloud, clouds (31)
954	עָצוּם	(adj) mighty, numerous (31)
955	פֶּסֶל	idol, carved image (31)

956	צוּר	(Q) to tie up, bind, shut in, shut up, enclose, encircle, besiege (31); cf צוּר (#485)
957	שִׂמְלָה	garment, clothing (31); cf שַׂלְמָה (#1482)
958	שָׁטַף	(Q) to flood (over), overflow, rinse, wash (away) (31)
959	שְׁמִינִי	(adj) eighth; (fs) שְׁמִינִית (31)
960	אָוָה	(Pi) to wish, desire, want; (Hith) crave, wish for, long for (30)
961	אָמֵן	amen, surely, truly (30)
962	בְּכִי	weeping (30)
963	בֹּשֶׂם	spice, perfume (30)
964	גָּזַל	(Q) to tear off, tear away, seize, rob, take away by force (30)
965	דָּמָה	(Q) to be like, resemble; (Pi) liken, compare (30); cf דָּמָה (#1690)
966	הָדָר	majesty, glory, splendor (30); 20x in Isa, Pss
967	חִטָּה	wheat; (fp) חִטִּים (30)
968	יְרֵכָה	side, hip, far part, remote part (30)
969	כְּלִמָּה	insult, disgrace, humiliation (30)
970	מַאֲכָל	food (30)
971	נָהַג	(Q) to drive (flocks or herds), lead, guide; (Pi) lead or drive away (30)
972	סָפַד	(Q) to lament, wail, bewail, mourn for someone (30)
973	פִּנָּה	corner, cornerstone (30)
974	רַב	chief, captain, ruler (30); cf רַב (#119)
975	רָבַץ	(Q) to lie down, crouch (of animals), rest, stretch out (30)
976	רֶשַׁע	evil, wickedness, offense, injustice, wrong (30)
977	שְׁבוּעָה	oath; also spelled שְׁבֻעָה (30)
978	שָׁפֵל	(Q) to be(come) low, humble, humiliated; (Hi) bring down, overthrow, humiliate (30)

979	תְּנוּפָה	wave offering, consecrated gift (30)
980	בָּחַן	(Q) to test, put to the test, try, examine (29)
981	בָּרָד	hail (29)
982	הֵנָּה	(3fp pers pron) they; (fp dmstr pron and adj) those (29); cf הֵנָּה (#570)
983	זִמָּה	evil plan, shameful behavior (29)
984	חָלַם	(Q) to dream (29)
985	חֲצֹצְרָה	trumpet (29)
986	חֵרֶם	something set apart for destruction, devoted to destruction (29)
987	יָעַד	(Q) to designate, appoint; (Ni) meet, gather or assemble by appointment (29)
988	כֻּתֹּנֶת	tunic, garment, robe; also spelled כְּתֹנֶת (29)
989	לָבָן	(adj) white (29)
990	מִטָּה	couch, bed (29)
991	מָנַע	(Q) to withhold, hold back, retain, refuse, restrain (29)
992	מַעַל	unfaithfulness, infidelity (29); cf מַעַל (#292)
993	נֶגֶב	south, southward, Negev (29)
994	נִדָּה	menstrual flow, impurity, defilement (29)
995	סִיר	(cs) basin, pot, tub (29)
996	עֲשִׂירִי	(adj) tenth; (fs) עֲשִׂירִית (29)
997	עַתּוּד	male goat, leader (29)
998	פָּרָה	(Q) to bear fruit, be fruitful (29); cf פָּרָה (#1068)
999	קִרְיָה	city, town (29)
1000	רָעַשׁ	(Q) to quake, shake (29)
1001	שָׂרִיד	survivor (29)
1002	שְׁבוּת	captivity, exile, imprisonment (29)
1003	תָּלָה	(Q) to hang (up) (29)

1004	בָּשַׁל	(Q) to boil; (Pi) boil, cook, roast (28)
1005	חָבַר	(Q) to unite, ally oneself (with), join forces (28)
1006	חָכַם	(Q) to be(come) wise, act wisely (28)
1007	חָשַׂךְ	(Q) to withhold, keep back, refrain, spare, save, restrain (28)
1008	יָרָה	(Q, Hi) to throw, shoot, cast (lots) (28); cf יָרָה (#675)
1009	לִיץ	(Q) to boast (28)
1010	מָנָה	(Q) to count, number, reckon, assign, appoint (28); cf מָנָה (#1711)
1011	מְעִיל	robe, cloak (28)
1012	נֵבֶל	stringed instrument, harp (28); cf נֵבֶל (#1869)
1013	נָדַד	(Q) to flee, wander (about), depart, move, flutter (wings) (28)
1014	סוּף	reed, (coll) reeds; יַם־סוּף "Sea of Reeds" (or "Red Sea") (28)
1015	עָלַם	(Ni) to be concealed, hidden; (Hi) conceal, hide, cover up; (Hith) hide oneself (28)
1016	פֶּחָה	governor (28)
1017	פְּלֵיטָה	survivor, escape, deliverance (28)
1018	קֶצֶף	wrath, anger (28)
1019	קָשָׁה	(Q) to be heavy, hard or difficult; (Hi) make hard, harden, make stubborn or obstinate (28)
1020	רְכוּשׁ	goods, property, equipment (28)
1021	שָׂכָר	wages, payment, reward (28)
1022	שֵׂעָר	hair, hairiness (28)
1023	שִׁטָּה	acacia tree; (fp) שִׁטִּים (28)
1024	שָׁלֵם	(adj) whole, complete, safe (28); cf שָׁלֵם (#349)
1025	שִׁקּוּץ	abomination, detestable thing (28)
1026	שִׁשִּׁי	(adj) sixth; (fs) שִׁשִּׁית (28)
1027	תֵּבָה	ark, basket, box (28); 26x in Gen 6–9

1028	אַדִּיר	(adj) noble, majestic, mighty (27)
1029	בְּלִיַּעַל	(adj) useless, worthless; (n) worthlessness (27)
1030	בָּעַר	(Pi) to graze, sweep away, remove, get rid of, purge (27); cf בָּעַר (#558)
1031	חָקַר	(Q) to explore, search, spy out (27)
1032	חָרַשׁ	(Q) to plow, engrave, devise, plan (27); cf חָרַשׁ (#674)
1033	חָתַם	(Q) to seal (up), affix a seal (27)
1034	יוֹבֵל	ram's horn, trumpet, (year of) jubilee (27)
1035	יָצַת	(Q) to kindle, burn; (Hi) set on fire, set fire to (27)
1036	יָרֵחַ	moon (27)
1037	יָשַׁר	(Q) to be straight, upright or right, please (27)
1038	כַּפֹּרֶת	mercy seat, place of atonement, lid (27); 25x in Exod–Lev
1039	מוֹצָא	act of going forth, exit, source, spring (27)
1040	מוֹקֵשׁ	snare, trap (27)
1041	מְסִלָּה	highway, main road (27)
1042	נְקָמָה	vengeance, revenge (27)
1043	נָתַק	(Q) to pull off, tear away; (Ni) be drawn out or away, torn apart; (Pi) tear apart, tear to pieces (27)
1044	עוּף	(Q) to fly (27)
1045	פָּלַט	(Pi) to bring out, bring forth, bring to safety, save (27)
1046	פָּתָה	(Q) to be simple, inexperienced or gullible; (Pi) fool, deceive, persuade, seduce (27)
1047	צַר	(adj) narrow; (n) anxiety, distress (27); cf צַר (#490)
1048	קָטָן	(adj) small, young, insignificant, unimportant; (mp) קְטַנִּים (27); cf קָטֹן (#477)
1049	שׂוּשׂ	(Q) to rejoice; also spelled שִׂישׂ (27)
1050	שְׁמוּעָה	message, report, news (27)
1051	אֱוִיל	fool, idiot (26); 19x in Prov; cf אִוֶּלֶת (#1079)

48

1052	בָּצוּר	(adj) fortified, inaccessible (26)
1053	בֶּרֶךְ	(fs) knee (26)
1054	הוֹן	wealth, possessions (26)
1055	זָקֵן	(Q) to be(come) old, grow old (26); cf זָקֵן (#241)
1056	חָלַף	(Q) to pass on or away (quickly), pass by, vanish; (Hi) change, replace, substitute (26)
1057	טוּר	row, course (of stones) (26); 23x in Exod, 1 Kgs
1058	יָגַע	(Q) to toil, labor, struggle, grow or be weary (26)
1059	מָבוֹא	entrance, setting (of the sun), west (26)
1060	מַגֵּפָה	plague, slaughter (26)
1061	מַסֵּכָה	molten (metal) image, idol (26)
1062	נְדָבָה	freewill offering, voluntary gift (26)
1063	נָדִיב	(adj) noble, willing, generous (26)
1064	נֶשֶׁר	eagle, vulture (26)
1065	עִוֵּר	(adj) blind; (mp) עִוְרִים (26)
1066	עֶזְרָה	help, assistance, support (26)
1067	פָּרַד	(Ni) to divide, separate (intransitive), be scattered, separated (26)
1068	פָּרָה	cow (26); cf פָּרָה (#998)
1069	צוֹם	fast, (period of) fasting (26)
1070	צָרַר	(Q) to be hostile (toward), treat with hostility, attack (26); cf צָרַר (#681)
1071	קָדַם	(Pi) to be in front, confront, meet, go before, walk at the head, do something early or for the first time (26)
1072	קֵדְמָה	eastward, toward the east (26); קֶדֶם plus directional ה
1073	רָגַל	(Pi) to spy (out), scout (26)
1074	רָחַב	(Q) to open wide; (Hi) make wide or large, extend (26)
1075	רֶחֶם	womb (26)

1076   שָׂטָן   adversary, accuser, Satan (26)

1077   שְׁאָר   remnant, remainder (26); cf שְׁאֵרִית (#521)

1078   תַּאֲוָה   desire, longing (26)

1079   אִוֶּלֶת   folly, foolishness (25); 23x in Prov; cf אֱוִיל (#1051)

1080   אָפָה   (Q) to bake (25)

1081   בַּז   plunder, spoil (25)

1082   גָּבַר   (Q) to be strong, mighty, superior, excel, achieve, accomplish, prevail (25)

1083   דְּמוּת   likeness, form, image (25)

1084   הָגָה   (Q) to utter a sound, growl, moan, groan, coo (of a dove), speak, proclaim (25)

1085   חִיצוֹן   (adj) outer, external (25)

1086   חֹשֶׁן   breastplate (of the high priest) (25); 23x in Exod

1087   טָרַף   (Q) to tear (in pieces), rend (25)

1088   מְכוֹנָה   stand, base, support (25); 15x in 1 Kgs

1089   מָסָךְ   cover, curtain (25)

1090   מָרַד   (Q) to rebel, revolt (25)

1091   נוּד   (Q) to move to and fro, sway, wander, be(come) aimless, express grief or sympathy (by shaking the head) (25)

1092   נֵזֶר   consecration, dedication, crown (25)

1093   נֹכַח   (prep) in front of, opposite (25)

1094   נָסַךְ   (Q) to pour out, pour (cast) a metal image or statue; (Hi) pour out libations, offer a drink offering (25)

1095   סַף   threshold, doorframe (25)

1096   עֲגָלָה   cart, wagon (25)

1097   עָנָו   (adj) afflicted, oppressed, humble, meek (25)

1098   עָשָׁן   smoke (25)

1099   פַּח   snare, trap, net (25)

1100	פָּחַד	(Q) to tremble, shiver, be startled, in dread, in awe (25)
1101	פָּרֹכֶת	curtain (25)
1102	פִּתְאֹם	suddenly, unexpectedly (25)
1103	שֹׁד	violence, destruction (25)
1104	שׁוֹטֵר	officer, official (25)
1105	שָׁלַף	(Q) to draw out (sword), pull out, take out (25)
1106	שִׁלְשׁוֹם	day before yesterday, previously (25); תְּמוֹל שִׁלְשׁוֹם "yesterday and the day before;" cf תְּמוֹל (#1172)
1107	תּוֹצָאוֹת	end, limit, outermost area (25)
1108	תְּחִנָּה	plea, petition (for favor) (25)
1109	אֵבֶל	mourning, funeral ceremony (24)
1110	אוֹי	woe! alas! (24)
1111	אֵיד	disaster, calamity (24)
1112	אַרְבֶּה	(ms) locust (24)
1113	בָּשַׂר	(Pi) to bring good news, tell, announce (24)
1114	גָּוַע	(Q) to die, expire, pass away, perish (24)
1115	דִּין	(Q) to judge, minister or execute judgment, plead one's cause, contend with (24); cf דִּין (#1279)
1116	הוֹד	splendor, majesty (24)
1117	זִכָּרוֹן	memorial, remembrance (24)
1118	חוּס	(Q) to pity, look upon with compassion, spare (24)
1119	חֳלִי	illness, sickness (24)
1120	יָתֵד	(fs) tent peg, stake, pin (24)
1121	כָּבָה	(Q) to go out, be quenched, extinguished; (Pi) put out, quench, extinguish (24)
1122	כֵּן	(adj) honest, correct, right (24); cf כֵּן (#69, #1783)
1123	כֹּתֶרֶת	capital (top) of a pillar (24); 15x in 1 Kgs
1124	מְלוּכָה	kingship, royalty (24)

1125	נָאַץ	(Q) to spurn, despise; (Pi) treat disrespectfully or with irreverence (24)
1126	נָזָה	(Q) to spatter (blood); (Hi) sprinkle (24)
1127	נְשָׁמָה	breath (24)
1128	סוּג	(Q) to backslide, be disloyal; (Ni) turn back, withdraw, become disloyal (24)
1129	עֲלִילָה	deed, action (24)
1130	פִּקּוּדִים	precepts, directions, instructions (24); all in Pss, 21x in Ps 119
1131	רוּשׁ	(Q) to be poor (24)
1132	שָׁכַל	(Q) to become childless; (Pi) make someone childless, deprive of children, cause a miscarriage (24)
1133	תּוֹכַחַת	rebuke, correction (24)
1134	תּוּר	(Q) to spy out, reconnoiter, explore, investigate (24)
1135	תֵּימָן	(fs) south; (with directional ה) תֵּימָנָה (24)
1136	בַּד	linen cloth (23); cf בַּד (#782)
1137	בֶּצַע	unjust gain or profit (23)
1138	גָּלַח	(Pi) to shave (23)
1139	דִּמְעָה	(coll) tears (23)
1140	זֵכֶר	memory, remembrance (23)
1141	חֶלְקָה	piece (of land), portion (23)
1142	חָמַם	(Q) to be(come) warm (23)
1143	חָפַר	(Q) to dig, track, search (for), scout out, spy out (23); cf חָפַר (#1372)
1144	חָפַשׂ	(Q) to search (out), examine; (Pi) search thoroughly, track down; (Hith) disguise oneself (23)
1145	יָעַל	(Hi) to profit, gain profit, benefit (23)
1146	יִצְהָר	olive oil (23)
1147	כָּהַן	(Pi) to perform the duties of a priest, minister as a priest (23); cf כֹּהֵן (#66)

1148	כִּיּוֹר	wash basin, cooking pot (23)
1149	לוּ	if only, oh that (23)
1150	מִישׁוֹר	plain, level ground, fairness (23)
1151	מֶלַח	salt (23)
1152	מַס	forced labor (23)
1153	מַעְיָן	spring, fountain (23)
1154	מִקְרָא	summons, assembly (23); 20x in Exod–Num
1155	מְרִי	rebellion (23); 16x in Ezek
1156	נָגַשׂ	(Q) to oppress, force to work, be a slave driver or taskmaster, exact (contributions), collect (offerings) (23)
1157	עַז	(adj) strong, mighty (23)
1158	עֲטָרָה	crown, wreath; (fs cstr) עֲטֶרֶת (23)
1159	עָשִׁיר	(adj) rich, wealthy (23)
1160	פֶּסִיל	idol, cultic statue (23)
1161	צָהֳרַיִם	noon, midday (23)
1162	צָעִיר	(adj) little, small, young (23)
1163	רָבַב	(Q) to be(come) many, numerous, or great (23)
1164	שֹׁחַד	bribe, gift (23)
1165	שַׁחַר	dawn, daybreak (23)
1166	שַׁחַת	pit, grave (23)
1167	שֵׁכָר	intoxicating drink, beer (23)
1168	שֵׁנָה	sleep (23)
1169	שָׁקַל	(Q) to weigh (out) (23)
1170	תְּחִלָּה	beginning (23)
1171	תֹּם	integrity, innocence, perfection; (with 3ms suff) תֻּמּוֹ (23)
1172	תְּמוֹל	yesterday, previously (23); תְּמוֹל שִׁלְשׁוֹם "yesterday and the day before"; cf שִׁלְשׁוֹם (#1106)

1173	אֵיִל	pillar, doorpost (22); 21x in Ezek; cf אַיִל (#247)
1174	אֵפֶר	ashes, dust (22)
1175	גָּדַע	(Q) to cut off, cut down; (Ni) be cut off, cut down, cut into pieces; (Pi) cut down, cut to pieces (22)
1176	דָּת	law, decree (22); 20x in Esth
1177	הִין	liquid measurement, hin (22); 16x in Exod–Num
1178	זָהַר	(Hi) to warn (about), admonish, caution (22)
1179	זַעַם	anger, indignation, curse (22)
1180	חוֹל	sand (22)
1181	חָסֵר	(Q) to diminish, decrease, lack (22); cf חָסֵר (#1371)
1182	טֶרֶף	prey, food (22)
1183	כָּחַשׁ	(Pi) to deny, delude, deceive, lie, act deceptively, feign submission or obedience (22)
1184	כָּלָה	complete destruction, annihilation (22); cf כָּלָה (#218)
1185	מוֹלֶדֶת	relatives, offspring, descendants (22)
1186	מַחְתָּה	fire pan, censer (22); 18x in Exod–Num
1187	מָעַט	(Q) to be(come) few or too small; (Hi) make small or few, diminish, reduce, collect or gather little (22)
1188	מַעֲלֶה	ascent, stairs, rise (22); cf מַעֲלָה (#648)
1189	מִשְׁמָר	prison, guard(ing), custody, watch (22)
1190	מְתִים	(mp) men; מְתֵי מִסְפָּר few in number (22)
1191	נַעַל	(fs) sandal, shoe (22)
1192	נְקֵבָה	female, woman (22)
1193	סָקַל	(Q) to stone, put to death by stoning; (Ni) be stoned (to death) (22)
1194	פֶּגֶר	corpse, carcass (22)
1195	פָּשָׂה	(Q) to spread (the symptoms of disease) (22)
1196	קִיץ	(Hi) to awake, wake up (22)

1197	קָסַם	(Q) to practice divination, consult a spirit of the dead, predict (22)
1198	קָרָה	(Q) to encounter, meet, befall, happen to (22); cf קָרָא (#301)
1199	רֶגַע	moment, instant (22)
1200	רָדָה	(Q) to rule (over), have dominion over, govern (with the nuance of oppression), tread (in) the winepress (22)
1201	רֶשֶׁת	net, trap (22)
1202	שָׂשׂוֹן	joy, exultation (22)
1203	שְׁכֶם	shoulder; (with 3ms suff) שִׁכְמוֹ (22)
1204	שָׁעַן	(Ni) to lean (on or against), support oneself on, depend on (22)
1205	שָׁקַף	(Ni) to look down on (from above); (Hi) look down from above (22)
1206	תַּזְנוּת	prostitution, fornication (22); all in Ezek 16 and 23
1207	תָּעַב	(Pi) to abhor, loathe, commit an abomination (22)
1208	אֱלִיל	worthlessness, idol (21)
1209	אָתָה	(Q) to come; (Hi) bring (21)
1210	בָּרָק	lightning (21)
1211	גָּרַע	(Q) to shave, trim (a beard), diminish, restrain, withdraw (21)
1212	חָלִיל	far be it! never! (21); חָלִילָה לִּי "far be it from me!"
1213	חָמַד	(Q) to desire, take pleasure (delight) in, crave, covet (21)
1214	חֹתֵן	father-in-law (21)
1215	כַּעַס	anger, vexation (21)
1216	לְבוֹנָה	frankincense (21)
1217	לְחִי	(fs) jaw, cheek, chin (21)
1218	מְגִלָּה	scroll (21)

55

1219	מוּם	defect, blemish (21); 16x in Lev–Deut
1220	מוּשׁ	(Q) to withdraw (from a place), cease from, leave off, depart (21)
1221	מְנוּחָה	rest, resting place (21)
1222	מָסַס	(Ni) to melt (away), dissolve, become weak (21)
1223	מִשְׁחָה	anointing (21)
1224	נֵס	flag, banner (21); 15x in Isa, Jer
1225	נְתִיבָה	path, way (21)
1226	נָתַךְ	(Q) to gush forth, pour out; (Ni) gush forth, be poured (out or forth) (21)
1227	נָתַשׁ	(Q) to uproot, pull out, extract, pull up, remove, drive out (nations) (21)
1228	סוֹד	confidential conversation, circle of confidants (21)
1229	סָחַר	(Q) to pass through (of shepherds), travel about (conducting business); (Q ptc) trader, merchant (21)
1230	סֶרֶן	ruler, lord (21); 19x in Judg, 1 Sam
1231	עָוֶל	iniquity, injustice, wrong (21)
1232	פָּקַח	(Q) to open (the) eyes (21)
1233	פַּרְסָה	hoof (21)
1234	צוּם	(Q) to fast, abstain from food and drink (21)
1235	צְעָקָה	outcry, wailing (21)
1236	שָׂמֵחַ	(adj) joyful, glad, happy (21)
1237	שָׁאַג	(Q) to roar (21)
1238	שָׁבַר	(Q) to buy grain (for food) (21); cf שָׁבַר (#280)
1239	שָׁגָה	(Q) to stray (of sheep), go astray (morally), err, do or go wrong (unintentionally), stagger, reel (21)
1240	שַׁד	breast; (md) שָׁדַיִם (21)
1241	שָׁוַע	(Pi) to cry or call for help (21)
1242	שָׁזַר	(Hoph ptc) twisted; always spelled מָשְׁזָר (21); all in Exod 26–39

1243	שַׁחַק	layer of dust, cloud of dust, cloud (21)
1244	תָּמַךְ	(Q) to grasp, take hold of, hold, support (21)
1245	בְּרוֹשׁ	pine tree, juniper (20)
1246	חֶרֶשׂ	earthenware, potsherd (20)
1247	חָתָן	bridegroom, son-in-law (20)
1248	יָחַשׂ	(Hith) to be registered or enrolled in a genealogical list; (Hith inf as noun) genealogy, registration (20)
1249	יְסוֹד	foundation wall, base (20)
1250	מְהֵרָה	quickly, at once (20)
1251	מַחְסֶה	(ms) refuge, shelter (20)
1252	מָצוֹר	distress, siege, affliction (20)
1253	מִקְלָט	refuge, asylum (20)
1254	מַשָּׂא	oracle, pronouncement (20); cf מַשָּׂא (#719)
1255	נָבֵל	(Q) to fade, wither, decay, crumble away, wear out (20)
1256	עֲלִיָּה	upper room, roof chamber (20)
1257	עָרִיץ	(adj) ruthless, fierce, violent (20)
1258	עָתַר	(Q) to pray, plead, entreat; (Ni) be entreated; (Hi) pray, plead (20)
1259	צִנָּה	large shield (20)
1260	צָרַע	(Q) to be afflicted with a skin disease (usually leprosy); (Pu) be struck with a skin disease (20)
1261	קַיִץ	summer, summer fruit (20)
1262	רָחָב	(adj) wide, spacious (20)
1263	רָעֵב	(adj) hungry (20); cf רָעֵב (#1670)
1264	שָׂגַב	(Ni) to be high, exalted, inaccessible; (Pi) make high, make inaccessible, protect (20)
1265	שִׂיחַ	(Q) to consider, meditate, complain, lament, praise (20); cf שִׂיחַ (#1603)
1266	שָׂכַר	(Q) to hire (for wages) (20)

1267	שָׁבוּעַ	week, (period of) seven; (mp) שָׁבֻעִים and שָׁבֻעוֹת (20)
1268	שֶׁלֶג	snow (20)
1269	שְׁפֵלָה	foothills, Shephelah (20)
1270	תַּבְנִית	pattern, form (20)
1271	תֹּהוּ	emptiness, wasteland, formlessness (20)
1272	תִּמֹרָה	palm tree ornament; (fp) תִּמֹרִים and תִּמֹרוֹת (20); 14x in Ezek
1273	אוּלָם	but, however (19); cf אוּלָם (#552)
1274	אַשְׁמָה	guilt, blame (19)
1275	בִּקְעָה	valley, plain (19)
1276	גַּאֲוָה	pride, arrogance (19)
1277	גְּמוּל	recompense, requital (19)
1278	דָּג	fish (19); cf (fs) דָּגָה (#1499)
1279	דִּין	judgment, legal claim (19); cf דִּין (#1115)
1280	דָּמַם	(Q) to be silent, still, motionless, (struck) dumb, keep quiet, stand still (19)
1281	זָנַח	(Q) to reject, spurn (19)
1282	זְעָקָה	outcry, call for help (19)
1283	זָקָן	(cs) beard (19)
1284	חַטָּא	(adj) sinful; (n) sinner (19)
1285	חָקַק	(Q) to hew out or carve out (a grave), inscribe, engrave, enact, decree (19)
1286	יָנָה	(Q, Hi) to oppress, mistreat (19)
1287	יְפִי	beauty (19)
1288	לָאָה	(Q) to be(come) tired or weary; (Ni) tire (oneself) out, be tired of something; (Hi) make weary (19)
1289	לֶהָבָה	flame (19)
1290	לָחַץ	(Q) to squeeze, crowd, press, oppress, torment (19)

1291	מְזוּזָה	doorpost, doorframe (19)
1292	מְזִמָּה	purpose, plan, deliberation (19)
1293	מַטָּה	downward, beneath, below (19)
1294	מֵישָׁרִים	level path, uprightness, fairness (19)
1295	מַעֲרָכָה	row, battle line (19)
1296	מַשְׁקֶה	(ms) cupbearer, drink (19)
1297	נֹגַהּ	brightness, radiance (19)
1298	נָפַץ	(Q) to shatter, smash to pieces; (Pi) smash (19)
1299	נָקַב	(Q) to pierce, bore (through), stipulate, specify, designate, curse, slander (19)
1300	סָפָה	(Q) to take, sweep, snatch or carry away; (Ni) be carried, swept or snatched away (19)
1301	עֲבֹת	(cs) cord, rope; (cp) עֲבֹתֹת and עֲבֹתִים (19)
1302	עָלֶה	(ms) leaf, foliage (19)
1303	עָלַל	(Poel) to deal or act severely with, treat violently, glean (19)
1304	עֵנָב	grape (19)
1305	עַשְׁתֵּי	eleven, eleventh (19); always in the construction עַשְׁתֵּי־עָשָׂר or עַשְׁתֵּי־עֶשְׂרֵה
1306	פָּלִיט	fugitive, survivor (19)
1307	פֶּרֶץ	breach, gap (19)
1308	רִיק	(Hi) to empty out, pour out (19); cf רֵיק (#1738) and רִיק (#1601)
1309	רָמַס	(Q) to trample (down), tread (potter's clay or grapes), crush to pieces (19)
1310	רֹעַ	corruption, evil (19)
1311	רַעֲנָן	(adj) green, fresh, luxuriant (19)
1312	רָצַץ	(Q) to crush, oppress, mistreat (19)
1313	שֵׂיבָה	gray hair, old age (19)
1314	שָׁאַב	(Q) to draw water (19)

59

1315   שְׁגָגָה   error, accident (19)

1316   שׁוֹק   (fs) thigh, leg (19)

1317   שָׁכֵן   neighbor, resident (19)

1318   תַּחְתִּית   (fs adj) lower; (fp) תַּחְתִּיּוֹת (19)

1319   אָחַר   (Pi) to delay, detain, hesitate, linger (18)

1320   אָכְלָה   food, nourishment (18)

1321   אָפִיק   river, channel, stream bed (18)

1322   בָּאַשׁ   (Q) to stink, have a bad smell; (Hi) make odious, become hated (18)

1323   בִּירָה   citadel, fortress (18)

1324   גַּחֶלֶת   coal, burning charcoal (18)

1325   גַּל   heap, pile; (mp) גַּלִּים (18); cf גַּל (#1440)

1326   גָּלַל   (Q) to roll (away) (18)

1327   דָּכָא   (Pi) to crush, beat to pieces (18)

1328   זָרַח   (Q) to rise (sun), shine, come out, appear, break out (leprosy) (18)

1329   חוּשׁ   (Q) to hurry, make haste (18)

1330   חֵךְ   roof of the mouth, palate (18)

1331   יָאַל   (Hi) to be intent on something, be determined, show willingness or undertake to do something (18)

1332   יָבַל   (Hi) to bring (as gift or tribute), lead; (Hoph) be brought, led (18)

1333   כַּד   (fs) jar, pitcher; (fp) כַּדִּים (18)

1334   כַּפְתֹּר   decorative knob of a lampstand (18); 16x in Exod 25 and 37

1335   לָעַג   (Q, Hi) to mock, ridicule, deride (18)

1336   מָאוֹר   light, luminary, light-bearer (18); 15x in Gen–Num

1337   מִסְגֶּרֶת   rim, border, fortress, prison (18)

1338   מְצוּדָה   (mountain) stronghold, fortress (18); cf מְצָד (#1713)

1339	מָקוֹר	spring, fountain (18)
1340	מַקֵּל	(cs) rod, staff, branch; (cp) מַקְלוֹת (18)
1341	מֶרְחָק	distance, distant place (18)
1342	נָבָל	(adj) foolish, good-for-nothing; (n) fool (18)
1343	נָטַף	(Q) to drop, drip, secrete; (Hi) cause to drip, cause to flow (metaphorically, of prophetic speech) (18)
1344	נָשָׁה	(Q) to forget (18)
1345	סוּת	(Hi) to incite (against), stir up, provoke, instigate, seduce, mislead, lead astray (18)
1346	סְעָרָה	windstorm, tempest, gale (18)
1347	צְבִי	ornament, something beautiful, splendor (18); cf צְבִי (#1730)
1348	צַלְמָוֶת	(ms) shadow of death, deep darkness, gloom (18)
1349	קִינָה	lament, funeral song, dirge (18); 10x in Ezek
1350	רְבָבָה	ten thousand, great multitude, immense number (18)
1351	שָׂכִיר	(adj) hired worker; (n) day laborer (18)
1352	שָׁחַח	(Q) to cower, crouch, bow down (18)
1353	שָׁכַר	(Q) to be(come) drunk; (Pi, Hi) make (someone) drunk (18)
1354	תַּחֲנוּן	plea for mercy, supplication (for favor) (18)
1355	תָּכַן	(Q) to examine, consider, weigh; (Ni) be examined (18)
1356	תְּשִׁיעִי	(adj) ninth; (fs) תְּשִׁיעִית (18)
1357	אַבִּיר	(adj) mighty, strong, powerful (17)
1358	אֶזְרָח	native, citizen (17)
1359	אֵיכָה	how? where? (17)
1360	אֵימָה	terror, fright, horror (17)
1361	אַיִן	wherefrom? whence? (17); cf אַיִן (#60)
1362	אָכֵן	surely, truly, however (17)

1363	בִּכּוּרִים	firstfruits, early harvest (17)
1364	בִּלְעֲדֵי	(prep) apart from, except for, without (17)
1365	בְּרֵכָה	pool, pond, reservoir (17)
1366	גֹּבַהּ	(ms) height, pride (17)
1367	גַּנָּב	thief, kidnapper (17); 13x in Ezek
1368	דָּרוֹם	south, south wind (17)
1369	חִידָה	riddle, difficult or enigmatic question (17)
1370	חֹמֶר	mud, clay, mortar (17); cf חֹמֶר (#1629)
1371	חָסֵר	(adj) lacking, wanting; (ms cstr) חֲסַר (17); cf חָסֵר (#1181)
1372	חָפֵר	(Q) to be ashamed (17); cf חָפַר (#1143)
1373	חָפְשִׁי	(adj) free, exempt (17)
1374	חָצִיר	grass (17)
1375	חָשַׁךְ	(Q) to be(come) dark, grow dim (eyes) (17)
1376	יָצַג	(Hi) to set, place, establish, take one's stand (17)
1377	יְקָר	precious thing, something valuable, honor, respect (17)
1378	כָּלָא	(Q) to shut up, restrain, withhold, keep back (17)
1379	כְּתָב	writing, document, register (17)
1380	כָּתַת	(Q) to beat, crush fine, hammer (into pieces); (Pi) beat, hammer, crush to pieces (17)
1381	לוּן	(Ni, Hi) to murmur (against), grumble (17)
1382	מָדוֹן	strife, dispute, quarrel (17)
1383	מוּג	(Q) to waver, melt; (Ni) wave, sway back and forth, undulate (17)
1384	מָטַר	(Hi) to cause rain to fall, send rain (17)
1385	מָכוֹן	place, site, foundation, support (17)
1386	מֶמְשָׁלָה	rule, dominion, authority (17)
1387	מָעוֹן	dwelling place, habitation, refuge (17)

1388	מִשְׂגָּב	fortress, refuge, high point (17)
1389	מָשַׁל	(Q) to use a proverb, to speak in parables or poetry; (Ni) be(come) like, similar or the same as (17); cf מָשַׁל (#438)
1390	מַתָּנָה	gift, present (17)
1391	נָדַב	(Q) to incite, instigate; (Hith) volunteer, make a voluntary decision, offer voluntarily, give a freewill offering (17)
1392	נֶזֶם	earring, nose-ring (17)
1393	נָקָם	vengeance, revenge (17)
1394	נָקַף	(Hi) to surround, go around, encircle, encompass, enclose (17)
1395	נָתִין	temple servant (17)
1396	סְגָן	official, ruler (17)
1397	סָרַר	(Q) to be stubborn or rebellious (17)
1398	עָוָה	(Q) to do wrong; (Ni) be disturbed or irritated; (Hi) twist, pervert, do wrong (17)
1399	עֹז	refuge, protection (17); cf עֹז (#463)
1400	עֵזֶר	help, assistance (17)
1401	עָיֵף	(adj) tired, exhausted, weary (17)
1402	עָלַז	(Q) to exult, triumph (17)
1403	עָמֹק	(adj) deep, unfathomable, mysterious; (fs) עֲמֻקָּה (17)
1404	עָצָב	idol, image, false god; (always mp) עֲצַבִּים (17)
1405	עָצַם	(Q) to be vast, mighty, powerful, or numerous (17)
1406	עָרַב	(Q) to stand as surety for, pledge oneself (as surety for debts), be responsible for someone, conduct trade, barter (17)
1407	עָשַׁר	(Q) to be(come) rich; (Hi) make rich, gain riches (17)
1408	פֶּרַח	blossom, bud, flower (17)
1409	פֶּתִי	naïve person, simpleton; (mp) פְּתָאִים (17); 13x in Prov

63

1410	צוּד	(Q) to hunt (17)
1411	צָמָא	thirst (17); cf צָמֵא (#1889)
1412	קָדַר	(Q) to be(come) dark, dirty, untidy, dressed in the clothes of mourning (17)
1413	קָלוֹן	shame, dishonor (17)
1414	קְעָרָה	dish, bowl, platter (17)
1415	רָכַל	(Q ptc) to go about as a trader (tradesman), merchant (17)
1416	רָמַשׂ	(Q) to crawl, creep, swarm, teem (17)
1417	רֶמֶשׂ	creeping thing, animal that creeps upon the earth (17); 10x in Gen
1418	רַעַשׁ	earthquake, clatter, commotion (17)
1419	רָקִיעַ	expanse, firmament (17)
1420	שְׂבָכָה	network, lattice, grid (17)
1421	שִׂנְאָה	hatred, enmity, malice (17)
1422	שָׁאוֹן	noise, uproar, tumult (17)
1423	שׁוּשַׁן	lily, lotus flower; also spelled שׁוֹשָׁן (17)
1424	שָׁלִישׁ	officer, third man in a chariot (17)
1425	שֵׁמַע	report, news, rumor (17)
1426	שָׁפָל	(adj) low, lowly, humble, deep (17)
1427	תָּא	chamber, guardroom (17); 15x in Ezek
1428	תֶּבֶן	straw, chaff (17)
1429	תֹּף	tambourine, hand drum; (mp) תֻּפִּים (17)
1430	אוֹב	medium, necromancer, ghost (16)
1431	אוֹן	strength, vigor, manhood, wealth (16)
1432	אָזַר	(Q) to gird (on), equip (16)
1433	בֹּהֶן	thumb, big toe (16)
1434	בָּלָה	(Q) to be(come) worn out, used up or exhausted (16)

1435	בָּעַל	(Q) to rule over, be(come) lord or husband of, marry, own (take someone into possession as betrothed) (16)
1436	בָּעַת	(Pi) to terrify, frighten, startle (16)
1437	בָּצַע	(Q) to cut off, sever, break off (away), make profit (16)
1438	בָּרַר	(Q) to purify, purge, sort, choose, select (16)
1439	גְּדִי	young goat, kid (16)
1440	גַּל	wave (16); cf גָּל (#1325)
1441	דְּבִיר	inner sanctuary, most holy place (16); 11x in 1 Kgs
1442	דּוּשׁ	(Q) to tread on, trample down (out), thresh, exterminate, destroy; also spelled דִּישׁ (16)
1443	הָלְאָה	beyond, far away, out there (16)
1444	זוּלָה	except, only (16)
1445	חָגַג	(Q) to stagger, reel, celebrate a pilgrimage festival (16)
1446	חֹזֶה	(ms) seer (16)
1447	חֶמְדָּה	something desirable, precious, or valuable (16)
1448	חָצַב	(Q) to quarry, hew (out), dig, dress (stones) (16)
1449	חֹרֶב	dryness, drought, heat, waste (16)
1450	חָשָׁה	(Q) to be silent; (Hi) be silent, order (someone) to be silent, hesitate, delay (16)
1451	טָבַל	(Q) to dip (something into) (16)
1452	יְגִיעַ	labor, work, product of labor, gain (16)
1453	יֶקֶב	wine vat, winepress (16)
1454	יָשֵׁן	(Q) to sleep, go to sleep, be asleep (16)
1455	כָּזַב	(Pi) to lie, deceive (16)
1456	מַחֲצִית	half, middle (16)
1457	מַטָּרָה	guard, prison, (archery) target (16)
1458	מַכְאוֹב	pain, suffering (16)

1459	מִכְסֶה	(ms) cover, covering (16)
1460	מִסְפֵּד	wailing, mourning, funeral ceremony (16)
1461	מָרַר	(Q) to be bitter (of taste, experience, or attitude), desperate; (Hi) embitter, cause bitterness or grief (16)
1462	מָשׂוֹשׂ	joy, delight (16)
1463	נָזִיר	one who is devoted or consecrated, a Nazirite (16)
1464	נָזַל	(Q) to trickle, drip down, flow (16)
1465	סָכַךְ	(Q) to overshadow, cover (protectively), protect (16)
1466	סַם	perfume, spices (16)
1467	עָנָה	(Q) to sing (16); cf עָנָה (#152, #449)
1468	עָרוֹם	(adj) naked (16)
1469	עָרְלָה	foreskin (16)
1470	עָשׂוֹר	ten, tenth (day) (16)
1471	פָּרַע	(Q) to let go, loose or free, let the hair of the head hang loose, allow to run wild, leave unattended (16)
1472	פֵּשֶׁת	linen, flax; (fp) פִּשְׁתִּים (16)
1473	צִיָּה	desert, dry land (16)
1474	צֶמֶר	wool (16)
1475	קֶלַע	curtain (16)
1476	קַשׁ	stubble, chaff (16)
1477	קֶשֶׁר	alliance, conspiracy, treason (16)
1478	רָגַם	(Q) to stone, kill by stoning (16)
1479	רֵיקָם	empty-handed, without success (16)
1480	רַךְ	(adj) tender, frail, weak, soft (16)
1481	שֵׂכֶל	insight, understanding, success; also spelled שֶׂכֶל (16)
1482	שַׂלְמָה	garment, clothing (16); cf שִׂמְלָה (#957)
1483	שְׁאֵר	flesh, meat, food, blood relative (16)
1484	שִׁבֹּלֶת	ear of grain; (fp) שִׁבֳּלִים (16)

1485	שָׁוָה	(Q) to be(come) like or similar to, be the equal of, resemble; (Pi) make like, make level (16)
1486	שֶׁפֶט	act of judgment, punishment (16)
1487	אֲהָהּ	ah! alas! (15)
1488	אָמַל	(Pulal) to dry up, waste away, languish (15)
1489	אַמְתַּחַת	sack, bag (15); all in Gen 42–44
1490	אֵפוֹא	then, so; also spelled אֵפֹו (15)
1491	אָרֵךְ	(adj) long, slow (15); 13x אֶרֶךְ־אַפַּיִם (lit) "long of nose;" (idiom) slow to anger or patient
1492	גְּבִירָה	mistress, lady, queen mother (15)
1493	גָּדֵר	wall (of stone) (15)
1494	גָּזַז	(Q) to shear, cut (15)
1495	גֻּלָּה	bowl, basin (15)
1496	גָּלוּת	exile, exiles (15)
1497	גְּעָרָה	rebuke, threat (15)
1498	גָּרָה	(Hith) to strive (against), oppose, battle (15)
1499	דָּגָה	fish (15); cf (ms) דָּג (#1278)
1500	דֶּשֶׁן	fat, fat-soaked ashes (15)
1501	הָלַל	(Q) to be infatuated, deluded; (Hithpolel) be mad, act like a madman (15); cf הָלַל (#282)
1502	הָרֶה	(fs adj) pregnant (15); cf הָרָה (#728)
1503	זוּ	(dmstr pron and adj) this; (rel pron) who, that, which (15)
1504	חָבֵר	associate, companion, friend (15)
1505	חָצָה	(Q) to divide (into) (15)
1506	כָּבַשׁ	(Q) to subdue, subjugate, make subservient, bring into bondage, violate (rape) a woman; (Ni) be subdued, be subjugated (15)
1507	כָּלִיל	(adj) entire, whole, complete (15)
1508	כַּרְמֶל	fertile field, orchard, plantation (15)

1509	מֹאזְנַיִם	balances, scales (15)
1510	מִבְטָח	confidence, trust, security (15)
1511	מְחִיר	price, payment, money (15)
1512	מִלֻּאִים	consecration, ordination (of a priest), setting (of stones) (15)
1513	מִקְנָה	purchase, acquisition (15)
1514	מַשְׂאֵת	gift, tribute (15)
1515	נָגַן	(Pi) to play a stringed instrument (15)
1516	נָוֶה	pasture, dwelling; (fp cstr) נְאוֹת (15); cf נָוֶה (#930)
1517	סוּפָה	wind (of a storm), tempest, gale (15)
1518	סַל	basket (15)
1519	עָצַב	(Q) to hurt, pain, rebuke, grieve; (Ni) be pained for, in grieving for, worried, distressed (15)
1520	עֵקֶב	because, on account of; (n) result, wages (15)
1521	עָרָה	(Pi) to uncover, reveal, expose, lay bare, empty; (Hi) uncover, make naked, expose (15)
1522	עֲרָפֶל	thick darkness, gloom (15)
1523	עָרַץ	(Q) to tremble, be terrified, in dread, startled, alarmed; (Hi) terrify, strike (inspire) with awe (15)
1524	עֹשֶׁק	oppression, extortion (15)
1525	פָּצָה	(Q) to open (the mouth), speak (15)
1526	צֶלֶם	image, idol (15)
1527	צֶמֶד	pair, team (15)
1528	צָמַת	(Hi) to silence, exterminate, annihilate (15)
1529	קָדַד	(Q) to bow down, kneel down (15)
1530	רֹמַח	spear, lance (15)
1531	רְמִיָּה	laziness, slackness, deceit, treachery (15)
1532	רִשְׁעָה	wickedness, guilt (15)
1533	שׁוּר	(Q) to behold, regard (15)

1534	שָׁנָה	(Q) to change; (Pi) change, alter, pervert (15); cf שָׁנָה (#51)
1535	שֶׁרֶץ	swarming things (15); 12x in Lev
1536	תֹּאַר	form, shape, appearance (15)
1537	תָּם	(adj) blameless, complete, perfect; (mp) תַּמִּים (15)
1538	תַּן	(cs) jackal; (cp) תַּנִּים (15)
1539	תַּנּוּר	(cs) oven, firepot, furnace (15)
1540	תַּנִּין	serpent, dragon, monster (15)
1541	תְּרָפִים	images, statues, idols (15)
1542	אֵזוֹר	loincloth, girdle (14)
1543	אֵיתָן	(adj) everflowing, constant, enduring; (mp) אֵתָנִים (14)
1544	אָנַף	(Q) to be angry (14)
1545	אָסִיר	prisoner (14)
1546	בּוּז	(Q) to show contempt (for), despise (14); cf בּוּז (#1755)
1547	בַּר	grain, corn, wheat (14)
1548	בָּרִיא	(adj) fat, well fed (14)
1549	גְּאֻלָּה	right of redemption, next-of-kin (14)
1550	גָּבִיעַ	cup, bowl (14)
1551	גָּעַר	(Q) to rebuke, reproach (14)
1552	דֶּגֶל	division of a tribe, banner, standard (14); 13x in Num
1553	דַּק	(adj) thin, lean, skinny; (fp) דַּקּוֹת (14)
1554	דֶּשֶׁא	grass, vegetation (14)
1555	חוֹתָם	seal, signet ring (14)
1556	חָכָה	(Pi) to wait (for), tarry, long for, be patient (14)
1557	חַלָּה	cake, ring-shaped bread (14)
1558	טוּל	(Hi) to throw (far), cast, hurl; (Hoph) be thrown, hurled (14)

1559	יַבָּשָׁה	dry land, dry ground (14)
1560	יָגוֹן	grief, sorrow, agony (14)
1561	יְרֻשָּׁה	possession, inheritance (14)
1562	יֹשֶׁר	uprightness, honesty, straightness (14)
1563	כָּבֵד	(fs) liver (14); cf כָּבֵד (#353, #773)
1564	כְּהֻנָּה	priesthood (14)
1565	כָּרָה	(Q) to dig, excavate, hollow out (14)
1566	לָוָה	(Q) to borrow; (Hi) lend to (14); cf לָוָה (#1706)
1567	לוּלֵי	if not, unless, except; also spelled לוּלֵא (14)
1568	לַפִּיד	torch, lightning (14)
1569	מוּר	(Hi) to change, alter, exchange (14)
1570	מָחַץ	(Q) to smash, shatter, beat to pieces, smite (14)
1571	מִכְשׁוֹל	stumbling block, obstacle, offense (14)
1572	מַעֲרָב	west, sunset (14)
1573	מָרַט	(Q) to make smooth, bare, bald, polish, scour, pull out (hair), sharpen (sword); (Pu) be polished, smooth, bare (14)
1574	מַשְׂכִּיל	uncertain technical term, perhaps indicating a song of wisdom or insight (14); all in psalm titles
1575	נְגִינָה	music of a stringed instrument, song of mockery (14)
1576	נָשָׁא	(Hi) to deceive, cheat, trick (14)
1577	נֶתֶק	skin disease, scab (14); all in Lev
1578	עֲדִי	ornament, jewelry; (with 3ms suff) עֶדְיוֹ (14)
1579	עָכַר	(Q) to disturb, trouble, confuse, bring disaster (ruin); be stirred up, ruined, cut off (14)
1580	עָצֵל	(adj) low, lazy; (n) sluggard (14); all in Prov
1581	עָקֵב	heel, footprint, rear guard (of an army) (14)
1582	פָּגַשׁ	(Q) to meet, encounter, confront (14)
1583	פְּנִימָה	inside, within (14)

1584	פִּסֵחַ	(adj) lame, crippled (14)
1585	פְּעֻלָּה	work, deed, reward, payment (14)
1586	פֶּרֶד	mule (14)
1587	פָּרַס	(Q) to break; (Hi) have a divided hoof (14)
1588	פַּת	piece, scrap, morsel; (fp) פִּתִּים (14)
1589	צָבָא	(Q) to wage war, go to war, fight against (14); cf צָבָא (#107)
1590	צַיִד	game, hunting, hunter (14)
1591	צִיץ	flower, blossom; (mp) צִצִּים (14)
1592	צַעַד	step, pace (14)
1593	קָבַב	(Q) to curse (14)
1594	קְבוּרָה	grave, burial (14)
1595	קִבֵּל	(Pi) to take, receive, accept (14)
1596	קֶמַח	flour (14)
1597	קָצַץ	(Q) to cut (chop) off, trim; (Pi) cut (chop) off, cut in pieces (14)
1598	קָצַר	(Q) to be(come) short, shortened, impatient (14); cf קָצַר (#855)
1599	רָוָה	(Q) to drink one's fill; (Pi, Hi) drink abundantly, water thoroughly, drench, saturate (14)
1600	רָוַח	(Q) to get relief; (Pu) be wide or spacious; (Hi) smell (14)
1601	רֵיק	(adj) empty, vain (14); cf רִיק (#1308)
1602	שְׂחוֹק	laughter, laughingstock, mockery (14)
1603	שִׂיחַ	complaint, lament (14); cf שִׂיחַ (#1265)
1604	שָׁאַף	(Q) to gasp, pant (for or after), long for (14)
1605	שְׁבִית	captivity (14)
1606	שָׁלַל	(Q) to plunder, spoil, capture, rob (14)
1607	שָׁרַץ	(Q) to swarm, teem (with), be innumerable (14)

71

1608	תּוֹר	(fs) turtledove; (fp) תֹּרִים (14)
1609	תּוֹשָׁב	resident alien, stranger, sojourner (14)
1610	תַּחַשׁ	porpoise, dolphin, leather (14)
1611	אֵלָה	oak, terebinth, large tree (13)
1612	אָנָּא	please! I ask you!; also spelled אָנָּה (13)
1613	אָנַח	(Ni) to sigh, groan (13)
1614	אָרַג	(Q) to weave; (Q ptc) weaver (13)
1615	בָּחִיר	(adj) chosen, elect (13)
1616	בַּת	(ms) liquid measurement, bath; (mp) בַּתִּים (13); cf בַּת (#82)
1617	גְּדוּלָּה	greatness, great deed (13)
1618	גֹּדֶל	greatness, arrogance (13)
1619	גְּוִיָּה	body, corpse (13)
1620	הַוָּה	destruction, ruin (13)
1621	הָמַם	(Q) to make (a) noise, confuse, bring into motion and confusion (army), discomfit, disturb (13)
1622	וָו	hook, nail, peg (13); all in Exod
1623	זֵד	(adj) proud, insolent, presumptuous (13)
1624	זוֹב	discharge (of body fluid), hemorrhage (13); all in Lev
1625	זָמַם	(Q) to consider, think, ponder, devise, plan (evil), purpose (13)
1626	חָבַל	(Q) to take, hold or seize (something) in pledge, exact a pledge from someone, bind by taking a pledge (13); cf חָבַל (#1766)
1627	חָבַק	(Q) to embrace, fold the hands (in idleness); (Pi) embrace (13)
1628	חָזֶה	(ms) breast (of sacrificial animal) (13)
1629	חֹמֶר	dry measurement, heap, pile, homer (13); cf חֹמֶר (#1370)
1630	חַנּוּן	(adj) gracious, merciful (13)

1631	חָנֵף	(adj) godless, profane (13)
1632	חָפֵץ	delighting (in), desiring (13); cf חָפֵץ (#471)
1633	חֹר	noble, free person (13)
1634	טָהֳרָה	purification, purity, ceremonial cleanness (13)
1635	טִיט	mud, mire, clay (13)
1636	טַעַם	taste, sense, discernment (13)
1637	יְבוּל	produce, harvest, crop (13)
1638	יָלִיד	(adj) born (of); (n) son, slave (13)
1639	יְשִׁימוֹן	desert, wilderness, wasteland (13)
1640	כֹּפֶר	ransom, bribe (13)
1641	כֶּשֶׂב	young ram, lamb (13)
1642	לֻלָאֹת	(fp) loops, knots (13); all in Exod
1643	מַבּוּל	flood, deluge (13); 12x in Gen 7–11
1644	מַחְמָד	something desirable, precious thing (13)
1645	מַחְסוֹר	need, lack, poverty (13)
1646	מָן	manna (13)
1647	מַעְגָּל	path, wagon track (13)
1648	מֵצַח	forehead, brow (13)
1649	מְצִלְתַּיִם	(cd) cymbals (13)
1650	מְרַאֲשׁוֹת	(fp) at the head of, headrest (13)
1651	מִרְעֶה	(ms) pasture, place of grazing (13)
1652	מַרְפֵּא	healing, cure, remedy (13)
1653	מְשׁוּבָה	backsliding, falling away, apostasy (13)
1654	נְבָלָה	outrage, disgrace, stupidity (13)
1655	נָעִים	(adj) pleasant, lovely, delightful (13)
1656	נֵתַח	piece of meat (13)
1657	סָכַן	(Q) to be of use or service; (Hi) be accustomed to, familiar (acquainted) with, in the habit of (13)

1658	סָתַם	(Q) to plug or stop up, shut up, close, hide, keep secret, disguise (13)
1659	עָטָה	(Q) to wrap, cover or envelop (oneself) with (13)
1660	פָּאַר	(Pi) to glorify, exalt, beautify; (Hith) show or manifest one's glory, glorify oneself, be glorified, boast (13)
1661	פֶּלֶא	wonder, miracle, something extraordinary (13)
1662	פָּקִיד	leader, overseer, officer (13)
1663	צָחַק	(Q) to laugh; (Pi) joke (with), play (with), amuse oneself, fondle (13)
1664	צְפַרְדֵּעַ	(fs) frog; (fp) צְפַרְדְּעִים (13); 11x in Exod
1665	קַו	measuring line (13)
1666	קַל	(adj) light, swift, agile (13)
1667	קֵן	nest, nestlings (13)
1668	רָגַע	(Q) to crust over or become hard (of skin), stir up (sea); (Hi) give rest to, come to rest, make peace, linger (13)
1669	רַחוּם	(adj) compassionate (13)
1670	רָעֵב	(Q) to be hungry, suffer famine (13); cf רָעָב (#1263)
1671	שְׂרֵפָה	burning, fire (13)
1672	שְׁאֵלָה	request, petition (13)
1673	שׁוּט	(Q) to roam (around), go (rove) about, row (across water); (Polel) roam about (around) (13)
1674	שְׁחִין	boil, blister, skin ulcer (13)
1675	שִׁירָה	song (13); cf שִׁיר (#418, #455)
1676	שִׁכּוֹר	(adj) drunk; (n) drunkard (13)
1677	שָׁעָה	(Q) to gaze at, look at, look (regard) with favor, be concerned about (13)
1678	תַּחְתּוֹן	(adj) lower, lowest (13)
1679	תַּעַר	razor, knife, sheath (13)

1680	אַדֶּרֶת	cloak, robe (12)
1681	בַּהֶרֶת	white spot on the skin (12); all in Lev
1682	בּוּס	(Q) to tread down, trample under foot (12)
1683	בִּי	please, with your permission (12)
1684	בְּכֹרָה	birthright, right of the firstborn (12)
1685	גַּב	something curved, back, eyebrow, rim (of a wheel) (12)
1686	גְּזַר	(Q) to cut (in two, in pieces), divide, cut down, decide; (Ni) be cut off (from), decided (12)
1687	גֻּלְגֹּלֶת	head, skull (12)
1688	גַּנָּה	garden, orchard (12)
1689	דֹּב	bear (12)
1690	דָּמָה	(Ni) to be destroyed, ruined (12); cf דָּמָה (#965)
1691	דָּקַק	(Q) to crush, become fine through grinding; (Hi) crush fine, pulverize; (Hoph) be crushed fine (12)
1692	הֶאָח	aha! (12)
1693	הֲלֹם	here, to here (12)
1694	זְנוּנִים	prostitution, fornication (12)
1695	זָעַם	(Q) to curse, scold, denounce (12)
1696	חֲלִיפָה	change, shift, relief; (fp) חֲלִיפוֹת (12)
1697	חָפָה	(Q) to cover; (Pi) overlay (with) (12)
1698	חֵקֶר	searching, something searched out (12)
1699	טֶבַח	slaughtering, slaughter (12)
1700	יָחִיד	(adj) only (child), lonely, solitary (12)
1701	יֶרַח	month (12)
1702	כַּר	ram, battering ram; (mp) כָּרִים (12)
1703	לָבִיא	(cs) lion, lioness (12)
1704	לְבֵנָה	brick, tile, paving-stone; (fp) לְבֵנִים (12)
1705	לַהַב	flame, blade (of a sword) (12)

1706	לָוָה	(Ni) to join oneself to (12); cf לָוָה (#1566)
1707	לַחַץ	oppression, affliction (12)
1708	מִבְחָר	choicest, finest, best (people or things) (12)
1709	מְהוּמָה	confusion, dismay, panic (12)
1710	מוֹטָה	yoke, bar, carrying pole (12); 10x in Isa, Ezek
1711	מָנָה	part, portion, share (12); cf מָנָה (#1010)
1712	מַסַּע	breaking camp, setting out, journey (12)
1713	מְצָד	(fs) stronghold, fortress (12); cf מְצוּדָה (#1338)
1714	מִצְנֶפֶת	turban, headband, diadem (12); 11x in Exod, Lev
1715	מִקְצוֹעַ	corner, angle (12)
1716	מֹר	myrrh, myrrh oil (12)
1717	מַרְאָה	appearance, vision (12)
1718	מָתוֹק	(adj) sweet, pleasant (12)
1719	נָפַח	(Q) to breathe, blow, blow fire upon, set aflame, gasp, pant (12)
1720	נְצִיב	pillar, post, military garrison (12)
1721	נֶשֶׁךְ	interest, usury (12)
1722	נֶשֶׁף	twilight, dusk (12)
1723	סָלַל	(Q) to pile up, heap up, lift up, exalt, praise (12)
1724	סָעַד	(Q) to support, sustain, strengthen (with food), uphold (12)
1725	עֶגְלָה	heifer, young cow (12)
1726	עָוַת	(Q) to bend, make crooked, pervert (justice), falsify (balances), suppress (12)
1727	עָמִית	(ms) neighbor, friend, community (12)
1728	עָמַל	(Q) to labor, toil, exert oneself (12)
1729	עָקָר	(adj) barren, childless (12)
1730	צְבִי	gazelle (12); cf צְבִי (#1347)
1731	צוּק	(Hi) to oppress, press hard, harass, constrain (12)

1732	צֶמַח	growth, sprout, branch (12)
1733	קָצִין	commander, leader, ruler (12)
1734	קָרֵב	approaching, drawing near (12)
1735	רֹאשׁ	poisonous herb, venom (12); cf רֹאשׁ (#80)
1736	רָבַע	(Q) to provide with four corners, make square (12)
1737	רַגְלִי	(one who goes) on foot, pedestrian, foot soldier (12)
1738	רִיק	emptiness, vanity (12); cf רֵיק (#1308)
1739	רִקְמָה	(something) embroidered, woven garment (12)
1740	שׁוֹאָה	trouble, ruin, storm (12)
1741	שָׁחַר	(Pi) to seek eagerly for, look diligently for, be intent on (12)
1742	שָׁקַד	(Q) to (keep) watch, be wakeful, vigilant, concerned about, watch over (12)
1743	שָׁרַק	(Q) to hiss, whistle (12)
1744	תּוּשִׁיָּה	wisdom, success (12)
1745	אֲבָל	but, however, indeed, truly (11)
1746	אֹדוֹת	because, on account of; (always with prep עַל (עַל אֹדוֹת (11)
1747	אַיָּל	(male) deer, stag (11)
1748	אַיָּלָה	(female) deer, doe (11)
1749	אֶלֶף	clan, tribe, region (11); cf אֶלֶף (#101)
1750	אֲנָחָה	sighing, groaning (11)
1751	אִסָּר	obligation, pledge, vow; also spelled אֱסָר (11); all in Num 30
1752	אָרַשׂ	(Pi) to betroth, be engaged; (Pu) be(come) betrothed or engaged (11)
1753	אֶתְנַן	wages, payment, gift (11)
1754	בָּדָד	alone, by oneself (11)
1755	בּוּז	contempt (11); cf בּוּז (#1546)

1756	גָּאַל	(Ni, Pu) to be defiled, become impure; (Hith) defile oneself (11); cf גָּאַל (#372)
1757	גָּזִית	cut stone (11)
1758	גֵּרָה	cud (11); all in Lev 11 and Deut 14
1759	דָּקַר	(Q) to pierce (through), run through; (Pu) be pierced through (11)
1760	דָּשֵׁן	(Pi) to refresh, revive, clean away fat ashes; (Pu) be made fat (11)
1761	הָדַף	(Q) to thrust (away, out), push (away), drive away (out), shove (11)
1762	זָדוֹן	arrogance, presumption (11)
1763	זֹה	(dmstr adj) this (11); alternate form of זֹאת (#79)
1764	זַךְ	(adj) pure, clean (11)
1765	זָנָב	tail (11)
1766	חָבַל	(Q) to act corruptly or ruinously; (Pi) ruin, destroy (11); cf חָבַל (#1626)
1767	חוֹחַ	thorn, thornbush (11)
1768	חַיָּה	life; (with 3ms suff) חַיָּתוֹ (11); cf חַיָּה (#390)
1769	חֲלָצַיִם	(md) loins, stomach, waist (11)
1770	חָמוֹת	mother-in-law (11)
1771	חָמֵץ	leaven, something leavened (11)
1772	חָנַף	(Q) to be godless (of a priest or prophet), defiled (of land); (Hi) defile, pollute (11)
1773	חַרְטֹם	magician, soothsayer priest; (mp) חַרְטֻמִּים (11)
1774	חָשַׁק	(Q) to be attached to, cling to, love (11)
1775	חָתַן	(Hith) to intermarry with, become related by marriage, become a son-in-law (11)
1776	טָבַח	(Q) to slaughter, butcher, slay (11)
1777	טוּחַ	(Q) to plaster (wall of a house), coat, overlay (11)
1778	טָעַם	(Q) to taste, eat, savor food (11)

1779	יִדְּעֹנִי	soothsayer (11)
1780	יָקַץ	(Q) to awake, wake up, become active (11)
1781	יָקַר	(Q) to be difficult, precious, prized, highly valued, esteemed, honored, costly or rare (11)
1782	יֹתֶרֶת	covering, lobe (of an animal's liver) (11)
1783	כֵּן	base, stand; (with 3ms suff) כַּנּוֹ (11); cf כֵּן (#69, #1122)
1784	כָּנַס	(Q) to gather, collect, amass; (Pi) gather, assemble (11)
1785	מָגוֹר	place of residence, temporary dwelling; (mp cstr) מְגוּרֵי (11)
1786	מַד	garment, clothes (11)
1787	מוֹרָא	fear, terror (11)
1788	מְחִתָּה	terror, ruin, destruction (11)
1789	מִשְׁעֶנֶת	staff, stick, support (11)
1790	נָבַע	(Hi) to make (something) gush or bubble (forth), pour out or ferment (11)
1791	נָגַח	(Q) to gore (ox as subject); (Pi) push, butt, thrust, knock down (11)
1792	נָחַשׁ	(Pi) to practice divination, seek and give omens, observe signs, foretell, predict (11)
1793	נָעַר	(Q, Pi) to shake (out or off); (Ni) be shaken (out or off) (11)
1794	נָשַׁךְ	(Q, Pi) to bite (11)
1795	סֹלְלָה	mound, siege ramp (11)
1796	סַפִּיר	sapphire, lapis lazuli (11)
1797	עוֹלֵל	child (11)
1798	עָזַז	(Q) to be strong, prevail (against), defy (11)
1799	עָטַף	(Q) to be(come) weak, feeble or faint; (Hith) feel weak or faint (11)
1800	עָנַן	(Polel) to practice soothsaying, conjure up (spirits), interpret signs (11)

1801	עֲצָרָה	assembly, celebration; also spelled עֲצֶרֶת (11)
1802	עָרוּם	(adj) crafty, cunning, clever, prudent (11)
1803	עֲרֵמָה	heap, mound (of grain) (11)
1804	פֶּטֶר	firstborn (11)
1805	פִּתּוּחַ	engraving, inscription (11)
1806	פָּתִיל	cord, thread (11)
1807	צֶאֱצָאִים	offspring, descendants (11)
1808	קָדְקֹד	crown of the head, skull (11)
1809	קָדֵשׁ	cult or temple prostitute (11)
1810	קוֹץ	thorn, thornbush (11)
1811	קֶסֶם	divination, prediction (11)
1812	קָרְחָה	baldness, bald spot (11)
1813	רֹאֶה	seer (11)
1814	רִבּוֹא	(fs) ten thousand, countless number; also spelled רִבּוֹ (11)
1815	רָעַם	(Q) to rage, roar (sea), thunder, storm; (Hi) thunder, storm (11)
1816	רָקַע	(Q) to stamp (down or out), trample, spread out; (Pi) beat out, hammer out (11)
1817	שַׁבָּתוֹן	day of rest, Sabbath, feast (11)
1818	שֹׁהַם	precious stone, carnelian (11)
1819	שׁוּל	hem, skirt (of robe) (11)
1820	שַׁוְעָה	cry for help (11)
1821	שָׁסָה	(Q) to plunder, spoil (11)
1822	שֶׁקֶץ	detestable thing, abomination (11)
1823	תִּיכוֹן	(adj) middle, center (11)
1824	אִגֶּרֶת	letter, document; (fp) אִגְּרוֹת (10)
1825	אָדַם	(Q) to be red; (Pu) be reddened, dyed red (10)
1826	אוּץ	(Q) to urge, press, be in a hurry, pressed (10)

1827	אֵזוֹב	hyssop (10)
1828	אֵיפֹה	where? (10)
1829	אַלּוֹן	large (oak) tree (10)
1830	אֲפֵלָה	darkness, gloominess (10)
1831	אָשַׁר	(Pi) to call or consider blessed, fortunate, or happy; (Pu) be called blessed, fortunate or happy (10)
1832	בִּגְלַל	because of, on account of (10)
1833	בֶּדֶק	damage, breach, crack (10)
1834	בִּזָּה	spoil, plunder (10)
1835	בַּלָּהָה	sudden terror, horror (10)
1836	בְּמוֹ	(prep) in, at, with, by, against; alternate (poetic) form of prep בְּ (10)
1837	בְּתוּלִים	virginity, evidence of virginity (10)
1838	גָּדַר	(Q) to build a wall, block a road (10)
1839	גּוּר	(Q) to be afraid, dread, stand in awe (10); cf גּוּר (#430)
1840	גָּעַל	(Q) to loathe, abhor, feel disgust (10)
1841	גָּעַשׁ	(Q) to shake (10)
1842	זִיד	(Q) to act insolently; (Hi) boil or cook, become hot (with anger), behave arrogantly (10)
1843	זֵר	frame, border, molding (10); all in Exod
1844	חָדַשׁ	(Pi) to make new, renew, restore (10)
1845	חוּל	(Q) to go around, whirl (about), dance, writhe; also spelled חִיל (10); cf חִיל (#661)
1846	חָלָק	(adj) smooth, slippery, flattering (10)
1847	חֹם	heat, warmth (10)
1848	חֶמְאָה	butter, cream, curdled milk (10)
1849	חָפַז	(Q) to be in a hurry, hurry away (in alarm or fear), hasten in alarm; (Ni) run away in alarm (10)
1850	חָרֵב	(adj) dry, desolate, wasted (10); cf חָרֵב (#840)

81

1851	חָרַץ	(Q) to decide, cut (10)
1852	חָשַׂף	(Q) to strip, strip off, bare, skim or scoop off (10)
1853	טָבַע	(Q) to sink, penetrate; (Hoph) be sunk, settled, or planted (10)
1854	יִתְרוֹן	advantage, profit (10); all in Eccl
1855	כַּבִּיר	(adj) mighty, strong, powerful (10)
1856	כֶּלֶא	prison, confinement (10)
1857	לָהַט	(Q) to blaze, burn; (Pi) set ablaze, devour (with fire), scorch (10)
1858	מָדוֹן	contention, quarrel (10)
1859	מִמְכָּר	something sold, merchandise, sale (10)
1860	מִסְתָּר	secret place, hiding place (10)
1861	מַעֲרֶכֶת	row (of bread), consecrated bread (10)
1862	מַצָּב	military garrison, station (10)
1863	מָקַק	(Ni) to rot (away), fester (wounds), dwindle or waste away, decay, melt, dissolve (10)
1864	מִקְרֶה	(ms) accident, chance, fate (10)
1865	מַרְעִית	pasture, place of grazing (10)
1866	מַשְׁחִית	destroyer, destruction (10)
1867	מָשַׁשׁ	(Q) to feel, touch; (Pi) feel (over, through), grope, search, rummage through (10)
1868	נָאוֶה	(adj) lovely, beautiful, desirable, suitable (10)
1869	נֵבֶל	jar, bottle (10); cf נֶבֶל (#1012)
1870	נָגַר	(Ni) to flow, gush forth, be poured (out), spilled, stretched out (hands); (Hi) pour (out, down) (10)
1871	נָהַל	(Pi) to lead, guide, escort, provide (with food) (10)
1872	נָזַר	(Ni) to devote, dedicate or consecrate oneself to (a deity), treat with awe, deal respectfully with; (Hi) restrain from, abstain from, live as a Nazirite (10)
1873	נְחוּשָׁה	copper, bronze (10)

1874	סוּךְ	(Q) to grease (oneself) with oil, anoint (10)
1875	עֵירֹם	(adj) naked; (n) nakedness (10)
1876	עָנַג	(Hith) to pamper oneself, take delight (pleasure) in, refresh oneself (10)
1877	עַפְעַפַּיִם	(md) eyelids, eyes (10)
1878	עִקֵּשׁ	(adj) perverted, crooked, false (10)
1879	עֹרֵב	raven (10)
1880	עֶרֶשׂ	(fs) couch, bed (10)
1881	עָשַׂר	(Q) to exact a tithe, take a tenth part of; (Pi) give, pay or receive a tenth, tithe (10)
1882	פּוּחַ	(Hi) to testify (10)
1883	פִּזַּר	(Pi) to scatter, disperse (10)
1884	פַּחַת	pit, ravine (10)
1885	פֶּלֶג	water channel, canal (10)
1886	פֶּרֶא	wild donkey (10)
1887	פָּרַק	(Q) to tear away, pull away, rescue; (Pi) pull or tear off; (Hith) pull or tear off from oneself, be pulled or torn off (10)
1888	צֵידָה	food, provisions (10)
1889	צָמֵא	(Q) to thirst, be thirsty (10); cf צָמָא (#1411)
1890	קַדְמֹנִי	(adj) eastern, former, past (10)
1891	קָמָה	standing grain (10)
1892	קִנְיָן	property, possessions (10)
1893	קֶרֶס	(curtain) hook, clasp (10); all in Exod
1894	רַעְיָה	darling, beloved (10); 9x in Song
1895	שָׂבֵעַ	(adj) satisfied, full (10)
1896	שַׁאֲנָן	(adj) at ease, secure, untroubled; (fp) שַׁאֲנַנּוֹת (10)
1897	שָׁמַט	(Q) to let loose, let fall, let drop, release, abandon, leave fallow (10)

1898   שָׁמֵן   (adj) fat, rich (10)

1899   שְׁפִי   barren height; (mp) שְׁפָיִים and שְׁפָיִם (10)

1900   שְׁרִרוּת   stubbornness, hardness (10)

1901   שָׁתַל   (Q) to plant, transplant (10)

1902   תַּהְפּוּכָה   perversity, perverse thing (10)

1903   תְּמוּנָה   form, likeness, image (10)

Hebrew Words
Arranged by Common Root
Listed Alphabetically

The following word list contains Hebrew words that occur at least 10 times and share a common root. Note that most of the cognate groupings begin with a verb. Following the verb (if any), entries are arranged by frequency. The words in this list also appear in the Frequency list (beginning on page 2), but not all words that appear in the Frequency list will appear in this list.

אבל

    אָבַל (Q) to mourn, lament; (Hith) observe mourning rites (36)

    אֵבֶל mourning, funeral ceremony (24)

אדר

    אַדִּיר (adj) noble, majestic, mighty (27)

    אַדֶּרֶת cloak, robe (12)

אהב

    אָהַב (Q) to love (of human and divine love); (Pi ptc) lover (217)

    אַהֲבָה love (32)

אוה

    אָוָה (Pi) to wish, desire, want; (Hith) crave, wish for, long for (30)

    תַּאֲוָה desire, longing (26)

אור

    אוֹר (Hi) to give light, shine, illuminate, light up (44)

    אוֹר (cs) light, daylight, sunshine (120)

    מָאוֹר light, luminary, light-bearer (18); 15x in Gen–Num

אזן

    אָזַן (Hi) to give ear to, listen (to), hear, heed (41)

    אֹזֶן (fs) ear; (fd cstr) אָזְנֵי (188)

אזר

    אָזַר (Q) to gird (on), equip (16)

    אֵזוֹר loincloth, girdle (14)

אחז

    אָחַז (Q) to seize, grasp, take hold (of), hold fast (63)

    אֲחֻזָּה property, possession (66)

אחר

    אָחַר (Pi) to delay, detain, hesitate, linger (18)

    אַחֲרֵי (prep) after, behind; also spelled (97x) אַחַר (718)

    אַחֵר (adj) other, another; (fs) אַחֶרֶת (166)

    אַחֲרִית end, extremity, last (61)

    אַחֲרוֹן (adj) last, behind, west (51)

אכל

אָכַל   (Q) to eat, consume; (Ni) be eaten, consumed; (Hi) feed (820)

אֹכֶל   food (38)

מַאֲכָל   food (30)

אָכְלָה   food, nourishment (18)

אמן

אָמַן   (Ni) to be reliable, faithful or trustworthy; (Hi) believe (in), trust, have trust in, put trust in (97)

אֱמֶת   truth, fidelity; (with 2ms suff) אֲמִתֶּךָ (127)

אֱמוּנָה   faithfulness, reliability (49)

אָמֵן   amen, surely, truly (30)

אמר

אָמַר   (Q) to say; (Ni) be said, called; (Hi) declare, proclaim (5,316)

אֹמֶר   word, saying, speech (48)

אִמְרָה   word, saying (36)

אנח

אָנַח   (Ni) to sigh, groan (13)

אֲנָחָה   sighing, groaning (11)

אנף

אָנַף   (Q) to be angry (14)

אַף   nostril, nose; (metaphorically) anger; (md) אַפַּיִם (277)

אסר

אָסַר   (Q) to tie, bind, fetter, imprison (73)

אָסִיר   prisoner (14)

אִסָּר   obligation, pledge, vow; also spelled אֱסָר (11); all in Num 30

ארך

אָרַךְ   (Hi) to make long, lengthen, extend (34)

אֹרֶךְ   length (95)

אָרֵךְ   (adj) long, slow (15); 13x אֶרֶךְ־אַפַּיִם (lit) "long of nose;" (idiom) slow to anger or patient

אשם

אָשַׁם (Q) to be(come) guilty, commit an offense (35)

אָשָׁם guilt, guilt offering (46); 27x in Lev

אַשְׁמָה guilt, blame (19)

אשר

אָשַׁר (Pi) to call or consider blessed, fortunate, or happy; (Pu) be called blessed, fortunate, or happy (10)

אַשְׁרֵי blessed, happy (44); 26x in Pss

בוא

בּוֹא (Q) to go in, enter, come to, come upon; (Hi) bring (in), come (in); (Hoph) be brought (2,592)

תְּבוּאָה produce, harvest (43)

מָבוֹא entrance, setting (of the sun), west (26)

בוז

בּוּז (Q) to show contempt (for), despise (14)

בּוּז contempt (11)

בוש

בּוֹשׁ (Q) to be ashamed; (Hi) put to shame (125)

בֹּשֶׁת shame, disgrace (41)

בזז

בָּזַז (Q) to plunder, spoil (43)

בַּז plunder, spoil (25)

בִּזָּה spoil, plunder (10)

בחר

בָּחַר (Q) to choose, test, examine (172)

בָּחִיר (adj) chosen, elect (13)

מִבְחָר choicest, finest, best (people or things) (12)

בטח

בָּטַח (Q) to trust, rely upon (118)

בֶּטַח security, safety (42)

מִבְטָח confidence, trust, security (15)

בִּין

בִּין (Q) to understand, perceive, consider, give heed to; (Ni) be discerning, have understanding; (Hi) understand, teach; (Hith) show oneself perceptive (171)

תְּבוּנָה understanding, skill (42); 19x in Prov

בִּינָה understanding, insight (38)

בכה

בָּכָה (Q) to weep (in grief or joy), weep for (114)

בְּכִי weeping (30)

בכר

בְּכוֹר firstborn, oldest offspring (120)

בִּכּוּרִים firstfruits, early harvest (17)

בְּכֹרָה birthright, right of the firstborn (12)

בלה

בָּלָה (Q) to be(come) worn out, used up or exhausted (16)

בְּלִי without, nothing (59)

בנה

בָּנָה (Q) to build (up), rebuild, build (establish) a family; (Ni) be built, have a child (by or from) (377)

תַּבְנִית pattern, form (20)

בעל

בָּעַל (Q) to rule over, be(come) lord or husband of, marry, own (take someone into possession as betrothed) (16)

בַּעַל owner, master, husband, (divine title) Baal (161)

בצע

בָּצַע (Q) to cut off, sever, break off (away), make profit (16)

בֶּצַע unjust gain or profit (23)

בקע

בָּקַע (Q) to cleave, split, breach, break open; (Ni) be cleft, split (open); (Pi) split, rip open (51)

בִּקְעָה valley, plain (19)

בְּרֵךְ

    בָּרַךְ (Q Pass ptc) blessed, praised, adored; (Pi) bless, praise (327)

    בְּרָכָה blessing, gift (71)

בתל

    בְּתוּלָה virgin (50)

    בְּתוּלִים virginity, evidence of virginity (10)

גאל

    גָּאַל (Q) to redeem, act as kinsman (perform the responsibilities of the next-of-kin), avenge (104)

    גְּאֻלָּה right of redemption, next-of-kin (14)

גבה

    גָּבַה (Q) to be high, tall, lofty, exalted, or haughty; (Hi) make high, exalt (34)

    גָּבֹהַּ (adj) high, exalted; (fs) גְּבֹהָה (41)

    גֹּבַהּ (ms) height, pride (17)

גבר

    גָּבַר (Q) to be strong, mighty, superior, excel, achieve, accomplish, prevail (25)

    גִּבּוֹר (adj) mighty, valiant, heroic; (n) hero (160)

    גֶּבֶר strong man, young man, hero (66)

    גְּבוּרָה power, strength; (fp) גְּבוּרֹת mighty deeds (62)

    גְּבִירָה mistress, lady, queen mother (15)

גדל

    גָּדַל (Q) to grow up, be(come) great, strong, wealthy, important; (Pi) bring up (children), make great, extol; (Hi) make great, magnify, do great things (117)

    גָּדוֹל (adj) great, big, large (527)

    מִגְדָּל tower; (mp) מִגְדָּלִים and מִגְדָּלוֹת (45)

    גֹּדֶל greatness, arrogance (13)

    גְּדוּלָּה greatness, great deed (13)

גדר

    גָּדַר (Q) to build a wall, block a road (10)

    גָּדֵר wall (of stone) (15)

גור

גּוּר   (Q) to sojourn, dwell (stay) as a foreigner or alien (82)

גֵּר   stranger, sojourner, alien (92)

מָגוֹר   place of residence, temporary dwelling; (mp cstr)
     מְגוּרֵי (11)

גלה

גָּלָה   (Q) to uncover, reveal, disclose; (Ni) uncover, reveal
     oneself, be revealed, exposed; (Pi) uncover, reveal,
     disclose; (Hi) take (carry away) into exile (187)

גּוֹלָה   captivity, exiles (42)

גָּלוּת   exile, exiles (15)

גלל

גָּלַל   (Q) to roll (away) (18)

מְגִלָּה   scroll (21)

גמל

גָּמַל   (Q) to complete, finish, wean, ripen, render;
     recompense, requite (37)

גְּמוּל   recompense, requital (19)

גנב

גָּנַב   (Q) to steal, deceive (40)

גַּנָּב   thief, kidnapper (17); 13x in Ezek

גער

גָּעַר   (Q) to rebuke, reproach (14)

גְּעָרָה   rebuke, threat (15)

דבר

דָּבַר   (Q) to speak (rare in Q); (Pi) speak (1,136)

דָּבָר   word, matter, thing (1,454)

דין

דִּין   (Q) to judge, minister or execute judgment, plead
     one's cause, contend with (24)

דִּין   judgment, legal claim (19)

מָדוֹן   strife, dispute, quarrel (17)

דקק

דָּקַק (Q) to crush, become fine through grinding; (Hi) crush fine, pulverize; (Hoph) be crushed fine (12)

דַּק (adj) thin, lean, skinny; (fp) דַּקּוֹת (14)

דרך

דָּרַךְ (Q) to tread (often in the sense of pressing for wine or oil), march, draw a bow; (Hi) cause to tread, march or walk (63)

דֶּרֶךְ (cs) way, road, journey (712)

דשן

דָּשֵׁן (Pi) to refresh, revive, clean away fat ashes; (Pu) be made fat (11)

דֶּשֶׁן fat, fat-soaked ashes (15)

הלל

הָלַל (Pi) to praise, sing hallelujah; (Pu) be praised, praiseworthy; (Hith) boast (146); cf הָלַל (#1501)

תְּהִלָּה praise, song of praise (58)

המה

הָמָה (Q) to make (a) noise, make a sound, roar, growl, moan, groan, be boisterous (34)

הָמוֹן multitude, crowd, sound, roar (85)

הפך

הָפַךְ (Q) to turn, overturn, overthrow, destroy; (Ni) be destroyed, turned into, changed (95)

תַּהְפּוּכָה perversity, perverse thing (10)

הרה

הָרָה (Q) to conceive, be(come) pregnant (43)

הָרָה (fs adj) pregnant (15)

זבח

זָבַח (Q) to slaughter (for sacrifice), sacrifice; (Pi) offer sacrifice, sacrifice (134)

מִזְבֵּחַ altar; (mp) מִזְבְּחוֹת (403)

זֶבַח sacrifice (162)

92

זוב

זוּב (Q) to flow (away), suffer a discharge (42)

זוֹב discharge (of body fluid), hemorrhage (13); all in Lev

זיד

זִיד (Q) to act insolently; (Hi) boil or cook, become hot (with anger), behave arrogantly (10)

זֵד (adj) proud, insolent, presumptuous (13)

זָדוֹן arrogance, presumption (11)

זכר

זָכַר (Q) to remember; (Ni) be remembered, thought of; (Hi) remind (235)

זִכָּרוֹן memorial, remembrance (24)

זֵכֶר memory, remembrance (23)

זמם

זָמַם (Q) to consider, think, ponder, devise, plan (evil), purpose (13)

מְזִמָּה purpose, plan, deliberation (19)

זמר

זָמַר (Pi) to sing, praise, make music, play an instrument (45)

מִזְמוֹר psalm, song (57); all in Pss

זנה

זָנָה (Q) to commit fornication, be a harlot (prostitute), be unfaithful (60)

זוֹנָה prostitute, harlot (34)

תַּזְנוּת prostitution, fornication (22); all in Ezek 16 and 23

זְנוּנִים prostitution, fornication (12)

זעם

זָעַם (Q) to curse, scold, denounce (12)

זַעַם anger, indignation, curse (22)

זעק

זָעַק (Q) to cry (out), call for help, summon (73)

זְעָקָה outcry, call for help (19)

93

זקן

זָקֵן (Q) to be(come) old, grow old (26)
זָקֵן (adj) old; (n) elder, old man (180)
זָקָן (cs) beard (19)

זרח

זָרַח (Q) to rise (sun), shine, come out, appear, break out (leprosy) (18)
מִזְרָח east, sunrise (74)

זרע

זָרַע (Q) to sow, scatter seed (56)
זֶרַע seed, offspring, descendants (229)

זרק

זָרַק (Q) to toss, throw, scatter, sprinkle (34)
מִזְרָק bowl; (mp) מִזְרָקוֹת (32)

חבר

חָבַר (Q) to unite, ally oneself (with), join forces (28)
חָבֵר associate, companion, friend (15)

חגג

חָגַג (Q) to stagger, reel, celebrate a pilgrimage festival (16)
חַג feast, festival, procession; also spelled חָג; (mp) חַגִּים (62)

חדש

חָדַשׁ (Pi) to make new, renew, restore (10)
חֹדֶשׁ month, new moon (283)
חָדָשׁ (adj) new, fresh (53)

חזה

חָזָה (Q) to see, behold, perceive (55)
חָזוֹן vision, revelation (35)
חֹזֶה (ms) seer (16)

חזק

חָזַק (Q) to be(come) strong, have courage; (Pi) make strong, strengthen; (Hi) strengthen, seize, grasp, take hold of; (Hith) strengthen oneself, show oneself as strong or courageous (290)

חָזָק (adj) strong, mighty, hard (57)

חטא

חָטָא (Q) to miss (a goal or mark), sin, commit a sin; (Pi) make a sin offering; (Hi) cause to sin (240)

חַטָּאת sin, sin offering; (fs cstr) חַטַּאת; (fp cstr) חַטֹּאות and חַטֹּאת (298)

חֵטְא sin (34)

חַטָּא (adj) sinful; (n) sinner (19)

חיה

חָיָה (Q) to live, be alive, revive, restore to life; (Pi) preserve alive, let live, give life; (Hi) preserve, keep alive, revive, restore to life (283)

חַי (adj) living, alive; (mp) חַיִּים (254)

חַיִּים life, lifetime (140)

חַיָּה animal, beast, living thing (96)

חַיָּה life; (with 3ms suff) חַיָּתוֹ (11)

חכם

חָכַם (Q) to be(come) wise, act wisely (28)

חָכְמָה wisdom, skill (153)

חָכָם (adj) wise, skillful, experienced (138)

חלה

חָלָה (Q) to be(come) weak or tired, be(come) sick; (Ni) be exhausted; (Pi) appease, flatter (75)

חֳלִי illness, sickness (24)

חלל

חָלַל (Ni) to be defiled, profaned, defile oneself; (Pi) profane, pollute, defile; (Hi) let something be profaned (135)

חָלָל (adj) pierced, slain, defiled (94)

חלם

    חָלַם (Q) to dream (29)

    חֲלוֹם dream (65)

חלף

    חָלַף (Q) to pass on or away (quickly), pass by, vanish; (Hi) change, replace, substitute (26)

    חֲלִיפָה change, shift, relief; (fp) חֲלִיפוֹת (12)

חלק

    חָלַק (Q) to divide, share (with or in), apportion, distribute; (Pi) divide (in pieces), apportion, scatter (55)

    חֵלֶק portion, share (66)

    מַחֲלֹקֶת division, portion (42)

    חֶלְקָה piece (of land), portion (23)

חמד

    חָמַד (Q) to desire, take pleasure (delight) in, crave, covet (21)

    חֶמְדָּה something desirable, precious, or valuable (16)

    מַחְמָד something desirable, precious thing (13)

חמם

    חָמַם (Q) to be(come) warm (23)

    חֵמָה wrath, heat, poison (125)

    חֹם heat, warmth (10)

חנה

    חָנָה (Q) to decline, camp, encamp, pitch camp, lay siege to (143)

    מַחֲנֶה (cs) camp, army; (cp) מַחֲנוֹת and מַחֲנִים (215)

חנן

    חָנַן (Q) to be gracious to, show favor to, favor; (Hith) plead for grace, favor or compassion (77)

    חֵן favor, grace, charm (69)

    תְּחִנָּה plea, petition (for favor) (25)

    תַּחֲנוּן plea for mercy, supplication (for favor) (18)

    חַנּוּן (adj) gracious, merciful (13)

חנף

חָנַף   (Q) to be godless (of a priest or prophet), defiled (of land); (Hi) defile, pollute (11)

חָנֵף   (adj) godless, profane (13)

חסה

חָסָה   (Q) to seek or take refuge (37)

מַחְסֶה   (ms) refuge, shelter (20)

חסר

חָסֵר   (Q) to diminish, decrease, lack (22)

חָסֵר   (adj) lacking, wanting; (ms cstr) חֲסַר (17)

מַחְסוֹר   need, lack, poverty (13)

חפץ

חָפֵץ   (Q) to delight in, take pleasure in, desire, be willing (74)

חֵפֶץ   delight, desire, pleasure, joy (38)

חָפֵץ   delighting (in), desiring (13); cf חָפֵץ (#471)

חצה

חָצָה   (Q) to divide (into) (15)

חֲצִי   half, middle (125)

מַחֲצִית   half, middle (16)

חקק

חָקַק   (Q) to hew out or carve out (a grave), inscribe, engrave, enact, decree (19)

חֹק   statute, appointed time, portion; (mp) חֻקִּים (131)

חֻקָּה   statute, ordinance (104)

חקר

חָקַר   (Q) to explore, search, spy out (27)

חֵקֶר   searching, something searched out (12)

חרב

חָרֵב   (Q) to dry up (intransitive), lie in ruins; (Hi) cause to dry up, lay waste, make desolate (36)

חֹרֶב   dryness, drought, heat, waste (16)

חָרֵב   (adj) dry, desolate, wasted (10)

97

חרה

חָרָה (Q) to be(come) hot, burn with anger, become angry (93)

חָרוֹן anger, fury, burning (41)

חרם

חָרַם (Hi) to devote to the ban, dedicate to destruction, exterminate (50)

חֵרֶם something set apart for destruction, devoted to destruction (29)

חרף

חָרַף (Q) to taunt, reproach; (Pi) taunt, reproach, revile (38)

חֶרְפָּה reproach, disgrace, shame (73)

חרשׁ

חָרַשׁ (Q) to plow, engrave, devise, plan (27)

חָרָשׁ craftsman (36)

חשׁב

חָשַׁב (Q) to think, consider, devise, plan, value, reckon; (Ni) be reckoned, accounted, considered (as); (Pi) think, consider, devise, plan (124)

מַחֲשָׁבָה thought, plan, scheme (56)

חשׁך

חָשַׁךְ (Q) to be(come) dark, grow dim (eyes) (17)

חֹשֶׁךְ darkness (80)

חתם

חָתַם (Q) to seal (up), affix a seal (27)

חוֹתָם seal, signet ring (14)

חתן

חָתַן (Hith) to intermarry with, become related by marriage, become a son-in-law (11)

חֹתֵן father-in-law (21)

חָתָן bridegroom, son-in-law (20

חתת

חָתַת (Q) to be shattered, dismayed, filled with terror (55)

מְחִתָּה terror, ruin, destruction (11)

טבח

טָבַח   (Q) to slaughter, butcher, slay (11)

טַבָּח   guard, cook (32)

טֶבַח   slaughtering, slaughter (12)

טהר

טָהֵר   (Q) to be clean (ceremonially), pure (morally); (Pi) cleanse, purify, pronounce clean; (Hith) purify or cleanse oneself (94)

טָהוֹר   (adj) clean, pure (96)

טָהֳרָה   purification, purity, ceremonial cleanness (13)

טוב

טוֹב   (Q) to be good, pleasing, pleasant, joyful, well with (44); cf טוֹב (#92) and יָטַב (#343)

טוֹב   (adj) good, pleasant (530)

טוּב   goodness, well-being, happiness (32)

טמא

טָמֵא   (Q) to be(come) unclean; (Ni) defile oneself; (Pi) defile, pronounce or declare unclean; (Hith) defile oneself, become unclean (162)

טָמֵא   (adj) unclean (88)

טֻמְאָה   uncleanness, impurity (36)

טעם

טָעַם   (Q) to taste, eat, savor food (11)

טַעַם   taste, sense, discernment (13)

טרף

טָרַף   (Q) to tear (in pieces), rend (25)

טֶרֶף   prey, food (22)

יבל

יָבַל   (Hi) to bring (as gift or tribute), lead; (Hoph) be brought, led (18)

יְבוּל   produce, harvest, crop (13)

יבשׁ

יָבֵשׁ (Q) to dry up, be(come) dry, wither; (Hi) make dry (up), make wither (59)

יַבָּשָׁה dry land, dry ground (14)

יגע

יָגַע (Q) to toil, labor, struggle, grow or be weary (26)

יְגִיעַ labor, work, product of labor, gain (16)

ידה

יָדָה (Hi) to thank, praise, confess; (Hith) confess (111)

תּוֹדָה thanksgiving, song of thanksgiving, thank offering (32)

ידע

יָדַע (Q) to know, know sexually (have intercourse with); (Ni) be(come) known, reveal oneself; (Hi) make known, inform (956)

דַּעַת knowledge, understanding, ability (88)

יִדְּעֹנִי soothsayer (11)

יחד

יַחְדָּו together, at the same time (96)

יַחַד together, along with (46)

יכח

יָכַח (Hi) to reprove, rebuke, reproach, chasten, punish, decide, mediate, arbitrate (59)

תּוֹכַחַת rebuke, correction (24)

ילד

יָלַד (Q) to bear (children), give birth, bring forth, beget; (Ni) be born; (Pi) help at birth, serve as midwife; (Pu) be born; (Hi) become the father of, beget (499)

יֶלֶד child, boy, youth (89)

יָלִיד (adj) born (of); (n) son, slave (13)

מוֹלֶדֶת relatives, offspring, descendants (22)

תּוֹלְדוֹת (fp) generations, descendants; (fp cstr) תּוֹלְדֹת and תֹּלְדוֹת (39)

יסד

יָסַד֫ (Q) to found, establish, appoint, destine, allocate; (Pi) found, appoint, establish (41)

יְסוֹד foundation wall, base (20)

יסר

יִסַּר֫ (Pi) to teach, discipline, correct, chastise, rebuke (41)

מוּסָר discipline, correction, instruction (50)

יעד

יָעַד֫ (Q) to designate, appoint; (Ni) meet, gather or assemble by appointment (29)

מוֹעֵד appointed time (of feast), meeting place, assembly (223)

עֵדָה congregation, assembly (171)

יעץ

יָעַץ֫ (Q) to advise, counsel, plan, decide; (Ni) consult (take counsel) together (80)

עֵצָה counsel, plan, advice (87)

יפה

יָפֶה (adj) beautiful; (fs) יָפָה (42)

יֳפִי beauty (19)

יצא

יָצָא֫ (Q) to go or come out; (Hi) cause to go or come out, lead out, bring out (1,076)

מוֹצָא act of going forth, exit, source, spring (27)

תּוֹצָאוֹת end, limit, outermost area (25)

צֶאֱצָאִים offspring, descendants (11)

יקר

יָקַר֫ (Q) to be difficult, precious, prized, highly valued, esteemed, honored, costly, or rare (11)

יָקָר (adj) precious, valuable (36)

יְקָר precious thing, something valuable, honor, respect (17)

יָרָא

יָרֵא   (Q) to fear, be afraid, be in awe of, reverence; (Ni) be feared, held in honor (317); cf יָרֵא (#539)

יָרֵא   (adj) fearful (63)

יִרְאָה   fear; (fs cstr) יִרְאַת (44); יִרְאַת יְהוָה "the fear of Yahweh"

מוֹרָא   fear, terror (11)

יָרה

יָרָה   (Hi) to instruct, teach (47)

תּוֹרָה   law, instruction, teaching (223)

יָרח

יָרֵחַ   moon (27)

יֶרַח   month (12)

יָרש

יָרַשׁ   (Q) to inherit, take possession of, dispossess, impoverish; (Hi) cause to possess or inherit, dispossess (232)

יְרֻשָׁה   possession, inheritance (14)

יָשׁב

יָשַׁב   (Q) to sit (down), dwell, inhabit; (Hi) cause to sit or dwell, settle (a city) (1,088)

מוֹשָׁב   dwelling, settlement, seat; (mp) מוֹשָׁבוֹת (44)

תּוֹשָׁב   resident alien, stranger, sojourner (14)

יָשׁן

יָשֵׁן   (Q) to sleep, go to sleep, be asleep (16)

שֵׁנָה   sleep (23)

יָשׁע

יָשַׁע   (Ni) to be delivered, victorious, receive help; (Hi) help, save, deliver, rescue, come to the aid of (205)

יְשׁוּעָה   salvation, help, deliverance (78)

יֵשַׁע   salvation, deliverance, help; (with 1cs suff) יִשְׁעִי (36)

תְּשׁוּעָה   salvation, deliverance, victory (34)

יָשַׁר

יָשַׁר (Q) to be straight, upright or right, please (27)

יָשָׁר (adj) upright, just (119)

מִישׁוֹר plain, level ground, fairness (23)

מֵישָׁרִים level path, uprightness, fairness (19)

יֹשֶׁר uprightness, honesty, straightness (14)

יתר

יָתַר (Ni) to be left over, remain; (Hi) have (something) left over or remaining (106)

יֶתֶר rest, remainder, excess (97)

יִתְרוֹן advantage, profit (10); all in Eccl

כבד

כָּבֵד (Q) to be heavy, weighty, honored; (Ni) be honored; (Pi) honor; (Hi) make heavy, dull, or insensitive, harden (heart) (114); cf כָּבֵד (#773, #1563)

כָּבוֹד glory, splendor, honor, abundance (200); כְּבוֹד יְהוָה "the glory of Yahweh"

כָּבֵד (adj) heavy, severe, important (41)

כהן

כָּהַן (Pi) to perform the duties of a priest, minister as a priest (23)

כֹּהֵן priest; (mp) כֹּהֲנִים (750)

כְּהֻנָּה priesthood (14)

כון

כּוּן (Ni) to be established, steadfast, ready, arranged, stand firm; (Hi) establish, set up, prepare, make ready, make firm; (Polel) set up, establish (219)

מְכוֹנָה stand, base, support (25); 15x in 1 Kgs

כֵּן (adj) honest, correct, right (24)

מָכוֹן place, site, foundation, support (17)

כֵּן base, stand; (with 3ms suff) כַּנּוֹ (11)

כזב

כָּזַב (Pi) to lie, deceive (16)

כָּזָב lie, deception, falsehood (31)

103

כלא

כָּלָא (Q) to shut up, restrain, withhold, keep back (17)

כֶּלֶא prison, confinement (10)

כלה

כָּלָה (Q) to be complete, finished, at an end, accomplished, spent, exhausted, come to an end; (Pi) complete, finish, bring to an end (207); cf כָּלָה (#1184)

כֹּל all, each, every; (cstr) כָּל־ (5,415)

כָּלָה complete destruction, annihilation (22)

כָּלִיל (adj) entire, whole, complete (15)

כלם

כָּלַם (Ni) to be hurt, humiliated, ashamed, disgraced; (Hi) put to shame, humiliate, disgrace (38)

כְּלִמָּה insult, disgrace, humiliation (30)

כסה

כָּסָה (Q) to cover, conceal, hide; (Pi) cover (up), conceal, clothe (153)

מִכְסֶה (ms) cover, covering (16)

כעס

כָּעַס (Q) to be angry, vexed; (Hi) vex, provoke, provoke (God) to anger (55)

כַּעַס anger, vexation (21)

כפר

כָּפַר (Pi) to cover (over), atone (for), make atonement (102)

כַּפֹּרֶת mercy seat, place of atonement, lid (27); 25x in Exod–Lev

כֹּפֶר ransom, bribe (13)

כשל

כָּשַׁל (Q) to stumble, totter, stagger; (Ni) be caused to stumble, stumble (65)

מִכְשׁוֹל stumbling block, obstacle, offense (14)

כתב

כָּתַב (Q) to write (upon), register, record; (Ni) be written (225)

כְּתָב writing, document, register (17)

לבש

לָבַשׁ (Q) to put on a garment, clothe, be clothed; (Hi) clothe (112)

לְבוּשׁ clothing, garment (32)

להב

לֶהָבָה flame (19)

לַהַב flame, blade (of a sword) (12)

לחם

לָחַם (Q, Ni) to fight, do battle with (rare in Q) (171)

מִלְחָמָה war, battle, struggle (319)

לחץ

לָחַץ (Q) to squeeze, crowd, press, oppress, torment (19)

לַחַץ oppression, affliction (12)

מדד

מָדַד (Q) to measure, measure off (distance or expanse), measure out (grain) (52)

מִדָּה measure, measurement (55)

מהר

מִהַר (Pi) to hasten, hurry, go or come quickly (81)

מְהֵרָה quickly, at once (20)

מוט

מוֹט (Q) to totter, shake, sway, stagger; (Ni) be made to stagger, stumble, or totter (39)

מוֹטָה yoke, bar, carrying pole (12); 10x in Isa, Ezek

מות

מוּת (Q) to die; (Hi) kill, put to death; (Hoph) be killed (845)

מָוֶת death, dying; (ms cstr) מוֹת (153)

מחר

מָחָר tomorrow (52)

מָחֳרָת (the) next day (32)

מטר

מָטַר (Hi) to cause rain to fall, send rain (17)

מָטָר rain (38)

מכר

מָכַר (Q) to sell, hand over; (Ni) be sold, sell oneself (into slavery) (80)

מִמְכָּר something sold, merchandise, sale (10)

מלא

מָלֵא (Q) to be full, fill (up); (Ni) be filled (with); (Pi) fill, perform, carry out, consecrate as priest (252)

מָלֵא (adj) full, filled (61)

מְלֹא fullness, abundance (38)

מִלֻּאִים consecration, ordination (of a priest), setting (of stones) (15)

מלך

מָלַךְ (Q) to be(come) king or queen, reign, rule; (Hi) make someone king or queen, install someone as king or queen (350)

מֶלֶךְ king, ruler (2,530)

מַלְכָּה queen (35)

מַמְלָכָה kingdom, dominion, reign (117)

מַלְכוּת kingdom, dominion, royal power (91)

מְלוּכָה kingship, royalty (24)

מנה

מָנָה (Q) to count, number, reckon, assign, appoint (28)

מָנָה part, portion, share (12)

מעט

מָעַט (Q) to be(come) few or too small; (Hi) make small or few, diminish, reduce, collect or gather little (22)

מְעַט (adj) little, few (101)

מעל

מָעַל (Q) to be unfaithful, act unfaithfully or treacherously (36)

מַעַל unfaithfulness, infidelity (29)

מרה

מָרָה (Q) to be rebellious, obstinate or contentious; (Hi) behave rebelliously or obstinately (44)

מְרִי rebellion (23); 16x in Ezek

מרר

מָרַר (Q) to be bitter (of taste, experience or attitude), desperate; (Hi) embitter, cause bitterness or grief (16)

מַר (adj) bitter; (n) bitterness (38)

משח

מָשַׁח (Q) to smear (with a liquid, oil, or dye), anoint (with oil) (70)

מָשִׁיחַ (adj) anointed; (n) anointed one, Messiah (38)

מִשְׁחָה anointing (21)

משל

מָשַׁל (Q) to rule, reign, govern, have dominion (81)

מֶמְשָׁלָה rule, dominion, authority (17)

משל

מָשַׁל (Q) to use a proverb, to speak in parables or poetry; (Ni) be(come) like, similar, or the same as (17)

מָשָׁל proverb, wisdom saying (40)

נבא

נָבָא (Ni) to prophesy, be in a state of prophetic ecstasy; (Hith) speak or behave as a prophet (115)

נָבִיא prophet (317)

נבל

נָבֵל (Q) to fade, wither, decay, crumble away, wear out (20)

נְבֵלָה carcass, corpse (48)

107

נָגַן

נִגֵּן (Pi) to play a stringed instrument (15)

נְגִינָה music of a stringed instrument, song of mockery (14)

נָגַע

נָגַע (Q) to touch, strike, reach; (Hi) touch, reach, throw, arrive (150)

נֶגַע plague, affliction (78)

נָגַף

נָגַף (Q) to smite, strike, injure; (Ni) be smitten, struck (with) (49)

מַגֵּפָה plague, slaughter (26)

נָדַב

נָדַב (Q) to incite, instigate; (Hith) volunteer, make a voluntary decision, offer voluntarily, give a freewill offering (17)

נְדָבָה freewill offering, voluntary gift (26)

נָדִיב (adj) noble, willing, generous (26)

נָדַר

נָדַר (Q) to make (perform) a vow, keep (make) a promise (31)

נֶדֶר vow; also spelled נֵדֶר (60)

נוּחַ

נוּחַ (Q) to rest, settle down, repose; (Hi) cause to rest, secure rest, set, leave (behind or untouched) (140)

מְנוּחָה rest, resting place (21)

נוּף

נוּף (Hi) to move back and forth, wave, brandish, wield (34)

תְּנוּפָה wave offering, consecrated gift (30)

נזר

נָזַר (Ni) to devote, dedicate or consecrate oneself to (a deity), treat with awe, deal respectfully with; (Hi) restrain from, abstain from, live as a Nazirite (10)

נֵזֶר consecration, dedication, crown (25)

נָזִיר one who is devoted or consecrated, a Nazirite (16)

נחל

נָחַל (Q) to take (as a) possession, obtain (receive) property, give as an inheritance; (Hi) give as an inheritance (59)

נַחֲלָה inheritance, property, possession (222)

נכה

נָכָה (Hi) to strike, smite, beat, strike dead, destroy; (Hoph) be struck down dead, beaten (501)

מַכָּה wound, injury, defeat (48)

נכר

נָכַר (Hi) to recognize, know, investigate, be acquainted with, acknowledge (50)

נָכְרִי (adj) foreign, strange; (fs) נָכְרִיָּה (46)

נֵכָר foreigner, stranger (36)

נסך

נָסַךְ (Q) to pour out, pour (cast) a metal image or statue; (Hi) pour out libations, offer a drink offering (25)

נֵסֶךְ drink offering; also spelled נֶסֶךְ (60)

מַסֵּכָה molten (metal) image, idol (26)

נסע

נָסַע (Q) to pull (out or up), set out, start out, depart, journey (146)

מַסַּע breaking camp, setting out, journey (12)

נצב

נָצַב (Ni) to stand (firm), take one's stand, station oneself, be positioned; (Hi) station, set (up), place, establish (74)

מַצֵּבָה sacred stone, pillar (33)

נְצִיב pillar, post, military garrison (12)

מַצָּב military garrison, station (10)

נקה

נָקָה (Ni) to be free (of), without guilt, innocent, exempt from (punishment); (Pi) leave unpunished, regard as innocent (44)

נָקִי (adj) blameless, innocent (43)

נקם

נָקַם (Q) to avenge, take vengeance (on), take revenge; (Ni) avenge oneself, take revenge (35)

נְקָמָה vengeance, revenge (27)

נָקָם vengeance, revenge (17)

נשא

נָשָׂא (Q) to lift, carry, raise, bear (load or burden), take (away); (Ni) be carried, lifted up, exalted; (Pi) lift up, exalt; (Hith) lift oneself up, exalt oneself (659)

נָשִׂיא chief, leader, prince (130)

מַשָּׂא load, burden (44)

מַשָּׂא oracle, pronouncement (20)

מַשְׂאֵת something lifted up, gift, tribute (15)

נתן

נָתַן (Q) to give, put, set; (Ni) be given (2,014)

מַתָּנָה gift, present (17)

נתק

נָתַק (Q) to pull off, tear away; (Ni) be drawn out or away, torn apart; (Pi) tear apart, tear to pieces (27)

נֶתֶק skin disease, scab (14); all in Lev

סבב

סָבַב (Q) to turn (about), go around, surround; (Ni) turn; (Hi) cause to go around, lead around; (Polel) encompass with protection (163)

סָבִיב around, about; (substantive) surroundings (338)

סגר

סָגַר (Q) to shut (in), close; (Hi) deliver (up), hand over, surrender, give up (91)

מִסְגֶּרֶת rim, border, fortress, prison (18)

סלל

סָלַל (Q) to pile up, heap up, lift up, exalt, praise (12)

סֹלְלָה mound, siege ramp (11)

ספד

סָפַד (Q) to lament, wail, bewail, mourn for someone (30)

מִסְפֵּד wailing, mourning, funeral ceremony (16)

ספר

סָפַר (Q) to count; (Pi) count, recount, make known, proclaim, report, tell (107)

סֵפֶר book, scroll, document (191); סֵפֶר הַתּוֹרָה "the book of the law"

מִסְפָּר number (134)

סֹפֵר scribe, secretary (54)

סתר

סָתַר (Ni) to be hidden, hide oneself; (Hi) hide (82)

סֵתֶר hiding place, secret place, shelter (35)

מִסְתָּר secret place, hiding place (10)

עבד

עָבַד (Q) to work, serve, toil (289)

עֶבֶד slave, servant (803)

עֲבֹדָה work, labor, service, worship (145)

עבר

עָבַר   (Q) to pass over, pass through, pass by, cross; (Hi) cause to pass over, bring over, cause or allow to pass (through), cause to pass through fire, sacrifice (553)

עֵבֶר   beyond, other side, edge, bank (92)

עגל

עֵגֶל   calf, young bull (35)

עֶגְלָה   heifer, young cow (12)

עגל

עֲגָלָה   cart, wagon (25)

מַעְגָּל   path, wagon track (13)

עוד

עוּד   (Hi) to warn, admonish, witness, be a witness, testify (40)

עֵד   witness (69)

עֵדוּת   witness, testimony; (fp) עֵדֹת (61)

עוה

עָוָה   (Q) to do wrong; (Ni) be disturbed or irritated; (Hi) twist, pervert, do wrong (17)

עָוֹן   transgression, iniquity, guilt, punishment (of sin); (mp) עֲוֹנוֹת (233)

עוף

עוּף   (Q) to fly (27)

עוֹף   (coll) flying creatures, birds, insects (71)

עזז

עָזַז   (Q) to be strong, prevail (against), defy (11)

עֹז   strength, power, might; (with 3ms suff) עֻזּוֹ (76)

עַז   (adj) strong, mighty (23)

עֹז   refuge, protection (17)

עזר

עָזַר   (Q) to help, assist, come to the aid of (82)

עֶזְרָה   help, assistance, support (26)

עֵזֶר   help, assistance (17)

עלה

עָלָה (Q) to go up, ascend; (Ni) be taken up; (Hi) bring or lead up or out, offer up (sacrifice) (894)

עֹלָה whole burnt offering (sacrifice that is completely burned) (286)

מַעַל above, upward, on top of (140)

עֶלְיוֹן (adj) upper; (divine title) Most High (53)

מַעֲלָה ascent, step, stairs (49)

עֲלִיָּה upper room, roof chamber (20)

עלל

עָלַל (Poel) to deal or act severely with, treat violently, glean (19)

מַעֲלָל deed, act (42); 18x in Jeremiah

עֲלִילָה deed, action (24)

עמד

עָמַד (Q) to stand (up), take one's stand, stand still; (Hi) station, set up, appoint, designate (524)

עַמּוּד pillar, column, tent pole (112)

עמל

עָמַל (Q) to labor, toil, exert oneself (12)

עָמָל trouble, labor, toil (54)

עמק

עֵמֶק valley, plain (70)

עָמֹק (adj) deep, unfathomable, mysterious; (fs) עֲמֻקָּה (17)

ענה

עָנָה (Q) to be afflicted, humbled; (Pi) afflict, oppress, humiliate, violate (79); cf עָנָה (#152, #1467)

עָנִי (adj) poor, humble, afflicted (80)

עֳנִי poverty, affliction, misery (36)

עָנָו (adj) afflicted, oppressed, humble, meek (25)

עצם

עָצַם (Q) to be vast, mighty, powerful or numerous (17)

עָצוּם (adj) mighty, numerous (31)

עֶרֶב

עֶרֶב evening, sunset (134)

מַעֲרָב west, sunset (14)

עֶרֶה

עָרָה (Pi) to uncover, reveal, expose, lay bare, empty; (Hi) uncover, make naked, expose (15)

עֶרְוָה nakedness (54)

עָרוֹם (adj) naked (16)

עֵירֹם (adj) naked; (n) nakedness (10)

עֶרֶד

עָרַד (Q) to set in order, lay out, set in rows, arrange, stack (wood), draw up a battle formation (75)

עֵרֶד value, assessment (33)

מַעֲרָכָה row, battle line (19)

מַעֲרֶכֶת row (of bread), consecrated bread (10)

עֶרֶץ

עָרַץ (Q) to tremble, be terrified, in dread, startled, alarmed; (Hi) terrify, strike (inspire) with awe (15)

עָרִיץ (adj) ruthless, fierce, violent (20)

עֶשֶׂה

עָשָׂה (Q) to do, make; (Ni) be done, made (2,632)

מַעֲשֶׂה (ms) work, deed, act (235)

עֶשֶׂר

עָשַׂר (Q) to exact a tithe, take a tenth part of; (Pi) give, pay or receive a tenth, tithe (10)

עֶשֶׂר ten; (fs) עֲשָׂרָה; (mp) עֶשְׂרִים twenty, twentieth (492)

עֶשֶׂר ten; (fs) עֲשָׂרֵה; used in constructions to express numerals eleven to nineteen (337)

עָשׂוֹר ten, tenth (day) (16)

מַעֲשֵׂר tithe, tenth (32)

עֶשֶׁק

עָשַׁק (Q) to oppress, exploit, wrong (someone) (37)

עֹשֶׁק oppression, extortion (15)

עשר

עָשַׁר (Q) to be(come) rich; (Hi) make rich, gain riches (17)

עֹשֶׁר wealth, riches (37)

עָשִׁיר (adj) rich, wealthy (23)

פאר

פָּאַר (Pi) to glorify, exalt, beautify; (Hith) show or manifest one's glory, glorify oneself, be glorified, boast (13)

תִּפְאֶרֶת beauty, glory, splendor (49)

פחד

פָּחַד (Q) to tremble, shiver, be startled, in dread, in awe (25)

פַּחַד trembling, terror, dread (49)

פלא

פָּלָא (Ni) to be extraordinary, wonderful; (Hi) do something wonderful (71)

פֶּלֶא wonder, miracle, something extraordinary (13)

פלט

פָּלַט (Pi) to bring out, bring forth, bring to safety, save (27)

פְּלֵיטָה survivor, escape, deliverance (28)

פָּלִיט fugitive, survivor (19)

פלל

פָּלַל (Hith) to pray, make intercession (84)

תְּפִלָּה prayer (77)

פנה

פָּנָה (Q) to turn (toward, from, to the side, away) (134)

פָּנִים (cp) face, front; לִפְנֵי (prep לְ prefixed to cstr) before, in front of (2,126)

פְּנִימִי (adj) inner; (fs) פְּנִימִית (32)

פִּנָּה corner, cornerstone (30)

פְּנִימָה inside, within (14)

פסל

פֶּסֶל idol, carved image (31)

פָּסִיל idol, cultic statue (23)

115

פָּעַל

פָּעַל (Q) to do, make, perform (58)

פֹּעַל work, deed (36)

פְּעֻלָּה work, deed, reward, payment (14)

פָּקַד

פָּקַד (Q) to attend (to), pay attention to, take care of, miss (someone), number, appoint; (Ni) be missed, visited, appointed; (Hi) appoint, entrust (304)

פְּקֻדָּה appointment, service, watch, punishment (32)

פִּקּוּדִים precepts, directions, instructions (24); all in Pss, 21x in Ps 119

פָּקִיד leader, overseer, officer (13)

פָּרָה

פָּרָה (Q) to bear fruit, be fruitful (29)

פְּרִי fruit, offspring (119)

פָּרַח

פָּרַח (Q) to bud, sprout, bloom, shoot, break out, break open (34)

פֶּרַח blossom, bud, flower (17)

פָּרַס

פָּרַס (Q) to break; (Hi) have a divided hoof (14)

פַּרְסָה hoof (21)

פָּרַץ

פָּרַץ (Q) to break through (out or into), make a breach, burst open, spread out (46)

פֶּרֶץ breach, gap (19)

פָּשַׁע

פָּשַׁע (Q) to revolt, rebel (against), transgress, break with, break away from, behave as a criminal (41)

פֶּשַׁע transgression, rebellion (93)

פָּתָה

פָּתָה (Q) to be simple, inexperienced or gullible; (Pi) fool, deceive, persuade, seduce (27)

פֶּתִי naïve person, simpleton; (mp) פְּתָאיִם (17); 13x in Prov

פתח

פָּתַח (Q) to open (up); (Ni) be opened, loosened, set free; (Pi) let loose, loosen (136)

פֶּ֫תַח opening, entrance, doorway (164)

צבא

צָבָא (Q) to wage war, go to war, fight against (14)

צָבָא (cs) host, army, war, service; (cp) צְבָאוֹת (487); יְהוָה צְבָאוֹת "Yahweh of Hosts"

צדק

צָדַק (Q) to be in the right, have a just cause, be just (justified), be righteous; (Hi) justify, declare righteous, just or innocent (41)

צַדִּיק (adj) righteous, just, innocent (206)

צְדָקָה righteousness, righteous act, justice (159)

צֶ֫דֶק righteousness, equity (123)

צוד

צוּד (Q) to hunt (17)

צַ֫יִד game, hunting, hunter (14)

צֵידָה food, provisions (10)

צוה

צִוָּה (Pi) to command, give an order, charge; (Pu) be ordered, be told, receive a command (496)

מִצְוָה commandment; (fp) מִצְוֹת (184); מִצְוֹת יְהוָה "the commandments of Yahweh"

צום

צוּם (Q) to fast, abstain from food and drink (21)

צוֹם fast, (period of) fasting (26)

צמא

צָמֵא (Q) to thirst, be thirsty (10)

צָמָא thirst (17)

צמח

צָמַח (Q) to sprout, spring up, grow; (Hi) make grow or sprout (33)

צֶ֫מַח growth, sprout, branch (12)

צרע

צָרַע (Q) to be afflicted with a skin disease (usually leprosy); (Pu) be struck with a skin disease (20)

צָרַעַת leprosy, skin disease (35)

צרר

צָרַר (Q) to wrap (up), tie up, bind (transitive); be cramped, restricted, depressed (intransitive); (Hi) oppress, harass, afflict (47)

צָרָה distress, anxiety, trouble (70)

צַר (adj) narrow; (n) anxiety, distress (27)

מָצוֹר distress, siege, affliction (20)

צרר

צָרַר (Q) to be hostile (toward), treat with hostility, attack (26)

צַר adversary, enemy (72)

קבר

קָבַר (Q) to bury; (Ni) be buried (133)

קֶבֶר grave, burial site; (mp) קְבָרִים and קְבָרוֹת (67)

קְבוּרָה grave, burial (14)

קדם

קָדַם (Pi) to be in front, confront, meet, go before, walk at the head, do something early or for the first time (26)

קָדִים east, eastern, east wind (69)

קֶדֶם east, ancient times (61)

קֵדְמָה eastward, toward the east (26)

קַדְמֹנִי (adj) eastern, former, past (10)

קדש

קָדַשׁ (Q) to be holy, set apart or consecrated; (Ni) be honored or treated as holy; (Pi) set apart, consecrate or dedicate as holy; (Hi) consecrate, dedicate or declare as holy; (Hith) show or keep oneself holy (171)

קֹדֶשׁ holiness, something that is holy (470)

קָדוֹשׁ (adj) holy, set apart (117)

מִקְדָּשׁ sanctuary (75); 31x in Ezek

קָדֵשׁ cult or temple prostitute (11)

קהל

קָהַל (Ni) to assemble, meet together (intransitive); (Hi) assemble (transitive), summon (39)

קָהָל assembly, community, crowd (123)

קוה

קִוָּה (Pi) to wait (for), wait with eagerness, hope (47)

תִּקְוָה hope, expectation (32)

קום

קוּם (Q) to rise, arise, get up, stand (up); (Hi) set up, put up, cause to arise, establish (627)

מָקוֹם place, location; (mp) מְקֹמוֹת (401)

קוֹמָה height (46)

קָמָה standing grain (10)

קטר

קָטַר (Pi) to make a sacrifice go up in smoke, offer (a sacrifice) by burning; (Hi) cause a sacrifice to go up in smoke (115)

קְטֹרֶת incense, smoke (60)

קלל

קָלַל (Q) to be small, insignificant, of little account, swift; (Ni, Pi) declare cursed; (Hi) treat with contempt (82)

קְלָלָה curse (33)

קַל (adj) light, swift, agile (13)

קנא

    קָנָא   (Pi) to envy, be envious of, jealous of, zealous for (34)

    קִנְאָה jealousy, zeal (43)

קנה

    קָנָה   (Q) to get, acquire, buy (85)

    מִקְנֶה cattle, livestock, property (76)

    מִקְנָה purchase, acquisition (15)

    קִנְיָן property, possessions (10)

קסם

    קָסַם (Q) to practice divination, consult a spirit of the dead, predict (22)

    קֶסֶם divination, prediction (11)

קצף

    קָצַף (Q) to be(come) angry or furious (34)

    קֶצֶף wrath, anger (28)

קצץ

    קָצַץ (Q) to cut (chop) off, trim; (Pi) cut (chop) off, cut in pieces (14)

    קָצֶה (ms) end, border, outskirts (92)

    קֵץ end, border, limit (67)

קצר

    קָצַר (Q) to gather in, reap, harvest (36)

    קָצִיר harvest (49)

קרא

    קָרָא (Q) to call, summon, proclaim, read aloud, give a name to; (Ni) be called, summoned, proclaimed (739); cf קָרָא (#301)

    מִקְרָא summons, assembly (23); 20x in Exod–Num

קרב

קָרַב	(Q) to approach, draw near, come near; (Hi) bring (near), present, offer a sacrifice or offering (280)
קֶרֶב	inner part(s), organ(s), body; (prep) בְּקֶרֶב (155x) in the middle of, among (227)
קָרְבָּן	gift, offering (80)
קָרוֹב	(adj) near, close (75)
קָרֵב	approaching, drawing near (12)

קרה

קָרָה	(Q) to encounter, meet, befall, happen to (22)
מִקְרֶה	(ms) accident, chance, fate (10)

קשה

קָשָׁה	(Q) to be heavy, hard or difficult; (Hi) make hard, harden, make stubborn or obstinate (28)
קָשֶׁה	(adj) difficult, hard, severe; (fs) קָשָׁה (36)

קשר

קָשַׁר	(Q) to bind, be in league together, conspire (against) (44)
קֶשֶׁר	alliance, conspiracy, treason (16)

ראה

רָאָה	(Q) to see, perceive, understand; (Ni) appear; (Pu) be seen; (Hi) let or cause someone to see (something) (1,311)
מַרְאֶה	vision, sight, appearance (103)
מַרְאָה	appearance, vision (12)
רֹאֶה	seer (11)

ראש

רֹאשׁ	head, top, chief; (mp) רָאשִׁים (600)
רִאשׁוֹן	(adj) first, former; (fs) רִאשֹׁנָה; (mp) רִאשֹׁנִים (182)
רֵאשִׁית	beginning, first (51)
מְרַאֲשׁוֹת	(fp) at the head of, headrest (13)

Hebrew Words Arranged by Common Root

רבב

רָבַב (Q) to be(come) many, numerous, or great (23)

רַב (adj) great, many; (mp) רַבִּים (419)

רֹב multitude, abundance, greatness (150)

רַב chief, captain, ruler (30)

רְבָבָה ten thousand, great multitude, immense number (18)

רִבּוֹא (fs) ten thousand, countless number; also spelled רִבּוֹ (11)

רבה

רָבָה (Q) to be(come) numerous, great, increase; (Hi) make many, make great, multiply, increase (229)

אַרְבֶּה (ms) locust (24)

רבע

רָבַע (Q) to provide with four corners, make square (12)

אַרְבַּע four; (fs) אַרְבָּעָה; (mp) אַרְבָּעִים forty (455)

רְבִיעִי (adj) fourth; (fs) רְבִיעִית (55)

רגל

רִגֵּל (Pi) to spy (out), scout (26)

רֶגֶל (fs) foot (251)

רַגְלִי (adj) (one who goes) on foot, pedestrian, foot soldier (12)

רגע

רָגַע (Q) to crust over or become hard (of skin), stir up (sea); (Hi) give rest to, come to rest, make peace, linger (13)

רֶגַע moment, instant (22)

רוח

רָוַח (Q) to get relief; (Pu) be wide or spacious; (Hi) smell (14)

רוּחַ (cs) spirit, wind, breath; (cp) רוּחוֹת (378)

רֵיחַ smell, odor, scent (58)

רוֹם

רוּם (Q) to be high, exalted, rise, arise; (Hi) raise, lift up,
exalt, take away; (Hoph) be exalted; (Polel) exalt,
bring up, extol, raise (children) (197)

תְּרוּמָה offering, contribution, tribute (76)

מָרוֹם height, elevation, pride (54)

רוֹע

רוּעַ (Hi) to shout, cry (out), shout a war cry (alarm of
battle), sound a signal for war, cheer, shout in
triumph (44)

תְּרוּעָה shout, alarm, signal (36)

רחב

רָחַב (Q) to open wide; (Hi) make wide or large, extend
(26)

רֹחַב width, breadth, expanse (101)

רְחוֹב (fs) public square, street (43)

רָחָב (adj) wide, spacious (20)

רחם

רָחַם (Pi) to show love for, have compassion (for), take pity
on (47)

רַחֲמִים compassion, mercy (40)

רֶחֶם womb (26)

רַחוּם (adj) compassionate (13)

רחק

רָחַק (Q) to be(come) far or distant, keep far from; (Hi)
remove, put (keep) far away, keep at a distance (59)

רָחוֹק (adj) distant, remote, far away (84)

מֶרְחָק distance, distant place (18)

ריב

רִיב (Q) to strive, contend, quarrel, dispute, conduct a
legal case (72)

רִיב dispute, quarrel, lawsuit (62)

רִיק

    רִיק   (Hi) to empty out, pour out (19)

    רֵיקָם   empty-handed, without success (16)

    רֵיק   (adj) empty, vain (14)

    רִיק   emptiness, vanity (12)

רכב

    רָכַב   (Q) to ride, mount and ride; (Hi) cause or make to ride (78)

    רֶכֶב   chariot, (coll) chariots or chariot riders (120)

    מֶרְכָּבָה   chariot (44)

רמשׂ

    רָמַשׂ   (Q) to crawl, creep, swarm, teem (17)

    רֶמֶשׂ   creeping thing, animal that creeps upon the earth (17); 10x in Gen

רנן

    רָנַן   (Q) to call or cry aloud, shout with joy; (Pi) cry out (with joy), exult (53)

    רִנָּה   shout of joy or lament (33)

רעב

    רָעֵב   (Q) to be hungry, suffer famine (13)

    רָעָב   famine, hunger (101)

    רָעֵב   (adj) hungry (20)

רעה

    רָעָה   (Q) to pasture, tend (flocks), graze, shepherd, feed (167)

    מִרְעֶה   (ms) pasture, place of grazing (13)

    מַרְעִית   pasture, place of grazing (10)

רעע

    רָעַע   (Q) to be bad, evil, or displeasing; (Hi) do evil, do wickedly, do injury, harm, treat badly (98)

    רָעָה   evil, wickedness, calamity, disaster (354)

    רַע   (adj) bad, evil, wicked, worthless; also spelled רָע (312)

    רֹעַ   corruption, evil (19)

רעשׁ

   רָעַשׁ   (Q) to quake, shake (29)

   רַעַשׁ   earthquake, clatter, commotion (17)

רפא

   רָפָא   (Q) to heal; (Ni) be healed, become whole; (Pi) heal, make healthy (69)

   מַרְפֵּא   healing, cure, remedy (13)

רצה

   רָצָה   (Q) to be pleased with, favorable toward, well disposed toward, accept (with pleasure), become friends with (48)

   רָצוֹן   pleasure, acceptance, favor (56)

רשׁע

   רָשַׁע   (Hi) to condemn, declare or pronounce guilty (35)

   רָשָׁע   (adj) wicked, guilty (264)

   רֶשַׁע   evil, wickedness, offense, injustice, wrong (30)

   רִשְׁעָה   wickedness, guilt (15)

שׂבע

   שָׂבַע   (Q) to be satisfied, have one's fill (of), eat or drink one's fill; (Hi) satisfy (97)

   שָׂבֵעַ   (adj) satisfied, full (10)

שׂגב

   שָׂגַב   (Ni) to be high, exalted, inaccessible; (Pi) make high, make inaccessible, protect (20)

   מִשְׂגָּב   fortress, refuge, high point (17)

שׂושׂ

   שׂושׂ   (Q) to rejoice; also spelled שִׂישׂ (27)

   שָׂשׂוֹן   joy, exultation (22)

   מָשׂושׂ   joy, delight (16)

שׂחק

   שָׂחַק   (Q) to laugh, play; (Pi) play, entertain, dance, amuse (37)

   שְׂחוֹק   laughter, laughingstock, mockery (14)

שִׂיחַ

שִׂיחַ (Q) to consider, meditate, complain, lament, praise (20)

שִׂיחַ complaint, lament (14)

שֹׂכֶל

שָׂכַל (Hi) to understand, comprehend, have insight, make wise, have success (60)

שֵׂכֶל insight, understanding, success; also spelled שֶׂכֶל (16)

מַשְׂכִּיל undetermined technical term, perhaps indicating a song of wisdom or insight (14); all in psalm titles

שֹׂכֶר

שָׂכַר (Q) to hire (for wages) (20)

שָׂכָר wages, payment, reward (28)

שָׂכִיר (adj) hired worker; (n) day laborer (18)

שֹׂמַח

שָׂמַח (Q) to rejoice, be joyful, be glad; (Pi) cause to rejoice, gladden, make someone happy (156)

שִׂמְחָה joy, gladness (94)

שָׂמֵחַ (adj) joyful, glad, happy (21)

שֹׂנֵא

שָׂנֵא (Q) to hate; (Pi ptc) enemy (148)

שִׂנְאָה hatred, enmity, malice (17)

שֹׂרֹף

שָׂרַף (Q) to burn (completely), destroy; (Ni) be burned (117)

שְׂרֵפָה burning, fire (13)

שֹׁאַל

שָׁאַל (Q) to ask (of), inquire (of), request, demand (176)

שְׁאֵלָה request, petition (13)

שֹׁאַר

שָׁאַר (Ni) to remain, be left over, survive; (Hi) leave (someone or something) remaining (133)

שְׁאֵרִית remnant, remainder (66); 37x in Isa, Jer, Ezek

שְׁאָר remnant, remainder (26)

שׁבה

שָׁבָה   (Q) to take captive, deport (47)

שְׁבִי   captivity, captives (48)

שְׁבוּת   captivity, exile, imprisonment (29)

שְׁבִית   captivity (14)

שׁבע

שָׁבַע   (Ni) to swear (take) an oath; (Hi) cause to take an oath, plead with someone (186)

שְׁבוּעָה   oath; also spelled שְׁבֻעָה (30)

שׁבר

שָׁבַר   (Q) to break (up), break in pieces, smash, shatter; (Ni) be smashed, broken, shattered or destroyed; (Pi) shatter, smash, break (148)

שֶׁבֶר   break, fracture, collapse (44)

שׁבת

שָׁבַת   (Q) to stop, cease, rest; (Hi) put an end to, remove, put away (71)

שַׁבָּת   (cs) Sabbath, day or period of rest; (cp) שַׁבָּתוֹת (111)

שַׁבָּתוֹן   day of rest, Sabbath, feast (11)

שׁדד

שָׁדַד   (Q) to devastate, ruin, deal violently with, violently destroy; (Pu) be devastated (59)

שֹׁד   violence, destruction (25)

שׁוב

שׁוּב   (Q) to turn back, turn, return; (Hi) cause to return, bring back, restore; (Polel) bring back, restore (1,075)

מְשׁוּבָה   backsliding, falling away, apostasy (13)(13)

שׁוע

שָׁוַע   (Pi) to cry or call for help (21)

שַׁוְעָה   cry for help (11)

שׁחת

שָׁחַת   (Pi, Hi) to ruin, destroy, spoil, annihilate (152)

מַשְׁחִית   destroyer, destruction (10)

שׁיר

שִׁיר (Q) to sing (of); (Q and Polel ptc) singer (88)

שִׁיר song (78)

שִׁירָה song (13)

שׁכב

שָׁכַב (Q) to lie down, have sexual intercourse (with) (213)

מִשְׁכָּב bed, couch (46)

שׁכן

שָׁכַן (Q) to settle (down), abide, reside, dwell, inhabit; (Pi) abide, dwell (130)

מִשְׁכָּן dwelling place, tabernacle; (mp) מִשְׁכָּנוֹת (139)

שָׁכֵן neighbor, resident (19)

שׁכר

שָׁכַר (Q) to be(come) drunk; (Pi, Hi) make (someone) drunk (18)

שֵׁכָר intoxicating drink, beer (23)

שִׁכּוֹר (adj) drunk; (n) drunkard (13)

שׁלל

שָׁלַל (Q) to plunder, spoil, capture, rob (14)

שָׁלָל plunder, spoil (74)

שׁלם

שָׁלֵם (Q) to be complete, finished; (Pi) complete, finish, make whole, restore, reward; (Hi) bring to completion, consummate (116); cf שָׁלֵם (#1024)

שָׁלוֹם peace, welfare, wholeness (237)

שֶׁלֶם peace offering (87)

שָׁלֵם (adj) whole, complete, safe (28)

שׁמם

שָׁמֵם (Q) to be deserted, uninhabited; (Ni) be made uninhabited, desolate, deserted; (Hi) make deserted or desolated (92)

שְׁמָמָה desolation, waste, ruin (56)

שַׁמָּה desolation, horror (39)

שמע

שָׁמַע (Q) to hear, listen to, understand, obey; (Ni) be heard; (Hi) proclaim (1,165)

שְׁמוּעָה message, report, news (27)

שֵׁמַע report, news, rumor (17)

שמר

שָׁמַר (Q) to watch (over), guard, keep, observe, preserve, protect, take care of; (Ni) to be kept, protected, on one's guard (469)

מִשְׁמֶרֶת watch, guard, responsibility (78)

מִשְׁמָר prison, guard(ing), custody, watch (22)

שנה

שָׁנָה (Q) to change; (Pi) change, alter, pervert (15)

שָׁנָה year; (fp) שָׁנִים (878)

שען

שָׁעַן (Ni) to lean (on or against), support oneself on, depend on (22)

מִשְׁעֶנֶת staff, stick, support (11)

שפט

שָׁפַט (Q) to judge, make a judgment, decide (between), settle (a dispute or controversy); (Ni) go to court, plead, dispute (204)

מִשְׁפָּט judgment, decision, ordinance, law, custom (425)

שֶׁפֶט act of judgment, punishment (16)

שפל

שָׁפֵל (Q) to be(come) low, humble, humiliated; (Hi) bring down, overthrow, humiliate (30)

שְׁפֵלָה foothills, Shephelah (20)

שָׁפָל (adj) low, lowly, humble, deep (17)

שקה

שָׁקָה (Hi) to give drink (to), irrigate (62)

מַשְׁקֶה (ms) cupbearer, drink (19)

שׁקל

שָׁקַל (Q) to weigh (out) (23)

שֶׁקֶל shekel, measurement of weight (88)

מִשְׁקָל weight (49)

שׁרץ

שָׁרַץ (Q) to swarm, teem (with), be innumerable (14)

שֶׁרֶץ swarming things (15); 12x in Lev

שׁתה

שָׁתָה (Q) to drink (217)

מִשְׁתֶּה (ms) feast, banquet (46); 20x in Esth

תחת

תַּחַת (prep) under, below, instead of (510)

תַּחְתִּית (fs adj) lower; (fp) תַּחְתִּיּוֹת (19)

תַּחְתּוֹן (adj) lower, lowest (13)

תמם

תָּמַם (Q) to be(come) complete or finished, come to an end, cease, be consumed, burned out (64)

תָּמִים (adj) blameless, perfect, honest, devout (91)

תֹּם integrity, innocence, perfection; (with 3ms suff) תֻּמּוֹ (23)

תָּם (adj) blameless, complete, perfect; (mp) תַּמִּים (15)

תעב

תָּעַב (Pi) to abhor, loathe, commit an abomination (22)

תּוֹעֵבָה abomination, abhorrence, offensive thing (118)

130

Aramaic Words
Arranged by Frequency

The following list contains all Aramaic words, including proper nouns, that occur in the Aramaic portions of the Old Testament. Words are arranged by frequency—from the most to the least frequent. There are 705 words. In this list, for the sake of convenience and reference, each word is numbered sequentially. By way of convention, verbal roots are listed without vowels.

1	אָ	(definite article) the (also spelled הָ) (894)
2	וְ	(conj) and, and also, but, or, for, then, so (751)
3	לְ	(prep) to, for, as, near (386)
4	דִּי	(rel particle) that, which, who, what, of (347)
5	בְּ	(prep) in, through, by means of, with, from (227)
6	מֶלֶךְ	king (180)
7	מִן	(prep) from, out of; (temporal) since (125)
8	עַל	(prep) upon, about, over, above (114)
9	אֱלָהּ	God, a god; (p) אֱלָהִין (96)
10	כֹּל	all, every, whole (83)
11	לָא	(neg particle) no, not (82)
12	אמר	(Peal) to say, speak, tell (71)
13	הוה	(Peal) to be, happen, exist (71)
14	כְּ	(prep) like, as, corresponding to, about (63)
15	דְּנָה	(ms dmstr pron and adj) this (58)
16	אֱדַיִן	(adv) then (57)
17	מַלְכוּ	kingship, sovereignty, reign, kingdom, realm; (fs cstr) מַלְכוּת (57)
18	דָּנִיֵּאל	Daniel (52)
19	ידע	(Peal) to know, learn, understand; (Haphel) to make known, communicate (47)
20	קֳדָם	(prep) before, in front of, in the presence of (46)
21	בַּיִת	house, temple (44)
22	שְׁמַיִן	heaven, sky (38)
23	קום	(Peal) to rise, stand, endure; (Pael) to establish; (Haphel) to set up, found, appoint, establish; (Hophal) to be set up (36)
24	עַד	(prep) up to, even to, until, during, within (35)
25	פְּשַׁר	interpretation (32)

26	חֲזָה	(Peal) to see, perceive (31)
27	נְבוּכַדְנֶצַּר	Nebuchadnezzar (31)
28	טְעֵם	understanding, command, decree, advice, report (30)
29	עֲנָה	(Peal) to answer, begin talking (30)
30	קֳבֵל	for, because, consequently, although (29); כָּל־קֳבֵל דְּנָה therefore, thus, for this reason; כָּל־קֳבֵל דִּי because, just as, even though
31	יהב	(Peal) to give; (Hithpeel) to be given (28)
32	עבד	(Peal) to do, make; (Hithpeel) to be made, performed, turned (28)
33	אֱנָשׁ	man, mankind, person, (coll) people (27)
34	יְרוּשְׁלֵם	Jerusalem (26)
35	שִׂים	(Peal) to put, place, set, lay; (Hithpeel) to be put, turned into, given (26)
36	בָּבֶל	Babylon (25)
37	מִלָּה	word, matter, affair (24)
38	דְּהַב	gold (23)
39	רַב	(adj) great (23)
40	בנה	(Peal) to build; (Hithpeel) to be built (22)
41	חֵלֶם	dream (22)
42	עִם	(prep) with, together with (22)
43	שׁנה	(Peal) to be different, changed; (Pael) to change, violate an order; (Ithpaal) to be changed; (Haphel) to alter, violate (22)
44	אֲרַע	earth, land (also spelled אֲרַק) (21)
45	גְּבַר	man (21)
46	חֵיוָה	animal, beast (20)
47	עִלָּי	(adj) superior, highest (20)
48	עָלַם	eternity, forever (20)
49	פַּרְזֶל	iron (20)

50	אִיתַי	(particle of existence) there is, are (19)
51	בַּר	son; (mp cstr) בְּנֵי (19); cf בַּר (#134)
52	שׁכח	(Hithpeel) to be found; (Haphel) to get (18)
53	יַד	hand, paw; might, power (17)
54	נוּר	fire (17)
55	עלל	(Peal) to go in, enter; (Haphel) to bring in; (Hophal) to be brought (17)
56	צְלֵם	statue, image (17)
57	אֲנָה	(1cs pers pron) I (also spelled אֲנָא) (16)
58	אתה	(Peal) to come; (Haphel) to bring; (Hophal) to be brought (16)
59	הוּא	(3ms pers pron) he, it (16)
60	הֵן	(conj) if, whether (16)
61	יוֹם	day (16)
62	דָּֽרְיָוֶשׁ	Darius (15)
63	חוה	(Pael) to show, make known; (Haphel/Aphel) to make known, interpret (15)
64	נְהַר	stream, river (15)
65	עַם	people, nation (15)
66	אִלֵּךְ	(cp dmstr pron and adj) those (14)
67	אַנְתָּה	(2ms pers pron) you; Qere אַנְתְּ (14); cf אַנְתְּ (#438)
68	דָּת	law, command, decree (14)
69	חַד	one (14)
70	חַכִּים	(adj) wise, (n) wise man (14)
71	יכל	(Peal) to be able, prevail against, defeat (14)
72	מָה	(interrog pron) what?; לְמָה why?; כְּמָה how?; מָה דִי whatever (14)
73	מֵישַׁךְ	Meshak (14)
74	עֲבֵד נְגוֹ	Abed Nego (also spelled עֲבֵד נְגוֹא) (14)

75	עֲבַר	(prep) opposite, beyond (14)
76	קֶרֶן	horn (of animal or musical instrument) (14)
77	רֵאשׁ	head, top, chief (14)
78	שַׁדְרַךְ	Shadrak (14)
79	שׁלח	(Peal) to send; to stretch out (14)
80	שָׁלְטָן	dominion, powers (14)
81	גּוֹא	(prep) midst, middle (also spelled גֹּו) (13)
82	דור	(Peal) to live, dwell (13)
83	הֵיכַל	palace, temple (13)
84	כְּסַף	silver (13)
85	כְּעַן	(adv) now (13)
86	כַּשְׂדָּי	(gentilic n) Chaldean; (n) astrologer (13)
87	עִדָּן	time, moment (13)
88	קַדִּישׁ	(adj) holy (13)
89	שַׂגִּיא	(adj) great, much, many; (adv) very much (13)
90	בעא	(Peal) to seek, request; to be about to; (Pael) to call upon, beseech, search eagerly (12)
91	הִמּוֹן/הִמּוֹ	(3mp person pron) they, them; spelled הִמּוֹן in Dan and הִמּוֹ in Ezra (12)
92	חֵזוּ	vision, apparition (12)
93	כְּתָב	writing, inscription, document, instruction, rule (12)
94	נפל	(Peal) to fall (12)
95	נפק	(Peal) to go out; come forth, be issued; (Haphel) to take out (12)
96	סגד	(Peal) to pay homage, bow down in worship (12)
97	רמה	(Peal) to throw, place, impose; (Hithpeel) to be thrown (12)
98	שְׁאָר	rest, remains, remainder, remnant (12)
99	שֵׁם	name (12)

100	אָחֳרָן	(adj) other, another (11)
101	זְמָן	time, a fixed time, turn (11)
102	מְדִינָה	province, city (11)
103	קרא	(Peal) to call, shout, read; (Hithpeel) to be called (11)
104	רוּחַ	wind, spirit, mind (11)
105	תְּלָת	three (11)
106	אַרְיֵה	lion (10)
107	אַתּוּן	furnace (10)
108	גֹּב	pit, den (also spelled גּוֹב and גֵּב) (10)
109	דקק	(Peal) to be crushed into pieces; (Haphel) to crush (10)
110	יְהוּדִי	(gentilic n) Jew (10)
111	מַן	(interrog pron) who?; מַן דִּי whoever (10)
112	פֶּחָה	governor (10)
113	פלח	(Peal) to serve (10)
114	צבה	(Peal) to desire, wish for, like (10)
115	רְבִיעָי	(adj) fourth (10)
116	שַׁלִּיט	(adj) powerful, mighty (10)
117	אַב	father, ancestor (9)
118	אֲחַשְׁדַּרְפַּן	satrap (9)
119	גלה	(Peal) to reveal; (Haphel) to lead off into exile (9)
120	חֲסַף	moulded clay, pottery, earthenware (9)
121	נְחָשׁ	copper, bronze (9)
122	עדה	(Peal) to pass away, take away, revoke, touch (9)
123	קרב	(Peal) to approach; (Pael) to offer; (Haphel) to bring near, allow to enter (9)
124	קִרְיָה	village, town (9)
125	רַבְרְבָן	lord, noble (9)
126	רָז	secret, mystery (9)

136

127	שֵׁיזִב	(Shaphel) to rescue, save, deliver (9)
128	שמע	(Peal) to hear; (Hithpeel) to obey (9)
129	אֶבֶן	stone (8)
130	אֻמָּה	nation (8)
131	אַרְבַּע	four (8)
132	בהל	(Pael) to frighten, terrify; (Hithpeel) to hasten; (Hithpaal) to be frightened, terrified (8)
133	בֵּלְטְשַׁאצַּר	Belteshazzar (8)
134	בַּר	field, countryside (8); cf בַּר (#51)
135	חָכְמָה	wisdom (8)
136	יקד	(Peal) to burn (8)
137	יִשְׂרָאֵל	Israel (8)
138	יַתִּיר	(adj) extraordinary; (adv) exceedingly (8)
139	כָּהֵן	priest (8)
140	כּוֹרֶשׁ	Cyrus (8)
141	כלל	(Shaphel) to finish; (Hishtaphel) to be finished (8)
142	כֵּן	(adv) thus, so (8)
143	כתב	(Peal) to write (8)
144	מְאָה	hundred (8)
145	מטא	(Peal) to reach to, attain to, come upon, come over; to occur, happen (8)
146	נְבִיא	prophet (8)
147	סלק	(Peal) to go up, come up; (Haphel) to take up; (Hophal) to be lifted up (8)
148	עֲבֵד	servant, slave (8)
149	רְגַל	foot (8)
150	תוב	(Peal) to return, come back; ([H]aphel) to give back, bring back (8)
151	אבד	(Peal) to perish; (Haphel) to slay, destroy; (Hophal) to be destroyed (7)

152	אֲזַל	(Peal) to go, walk (7)
153	אֲכַל	(Peal) to feed on, to feed, to devastate (7)
154	אָסְפַּרְנָא	(adv) completely, exactly, diligently (7)
155	אֱסָר	prohibition, injunction (7)
156	אַרְתַּחְשַׁשְׂתְּא	Artaxerxes (7)
157	בֵּלְשַׁאצַּר	Belshazzar (7)
158	דָּךְ	(fs dmstr pron and adj) that (7)
159	הֲ	interrog particle (7)
160	הִיא	(3fs pers pron) she, it (7)
161	חַי	(adj) living, alive; (n) life (7)
162	חַיִל	strength, army (7)
163	יְהוּד	Judah, Judea (7)
164	יְקָר	dignity, honor (7)
165	כְּנָת	associate, colleague; (mp) כְּנָוָת (7)
166	לְבַב	heart (7)
167	לָהֵן	(conj) except; (adversative) but, yet (7); cf לָהֵן (#319)
168	לִשָּׁן	tongue, language (7)
169	מָאן	vessel (7)
170	מָדַי	(gentilic n) Media, the Medes (7)
171	נתן	(Peal) to give, pay (7)
172	קטל	(Peal) to kill; (Hithpeel) to be killed; (Pael) to kill; (Hithpaal) to be killed (7)
173	קָל	voice, sound (7)
174	רשם	(Peal) to write, inscribe (7)
175	שׁלט	(Peal) to rule over, to have power over, to make oneself master of; (Haphel) to make someone ruler (7)
176	שְׁנָה	year (7); cf שְׁנָה (#693)
177	תּוֹר	ox, bull (7)

178	אִילָן	tree (6)
179	אָשַׁף	enchanter, sorcerer (6)
180	בטל	(Peal) to cease, be discontinued; (Pael) to stop, bring to an end (6)
181	גזר	(Peal) to cut, divine; ([H]ithpeel) to be broken off, break away from (6)
182	גְּשֵׁם	body (6)
183	דָּא	(fs dmstr pron and adj) this (6)
184	דחל	(Peal) to fear; (Pael) to startle (6)
185	דֵּךְ	(ms dmstr pron and adj) that (6)
186	הַמְנִיךְ	chain (Kethiv הַמְונִךְ) (6)
187	זִיו	radiance, brightness, countenance (6)
188	חבל	(Pael) to hurt, inflict injury, destroy; (Hithpaal) to be destroyed, perish (6)
189	חיה	(Peal) to live; ([H]aphel) to let live, restore to life (6)
190	חֲמַר	wine (6)
191	מָרֵא	lord (6)
192	מִשְׁכַּב	bed (6)
193	נחת	(Peal) to come down; ([H]aphel) to deposit; (Hophal) to be deposed, deposited (6)
194	סָפַר	scribe (6)
195	עֲבִידָה	work, service, administration (6)
196	עֲשַׂר	ten (6)
197	פֻּם	entrance, opening, mouth (6)
198	פָּרַס	Persia, the Persians (6)
199	פִּתְגָם	decree, answer, word (6)
200	רבה	(Peal) to become great, grow up; become long; (Pael) to make great, make high (6)
201	רַעְיוֹן	thought (6)
202	שאל	(Peal) to ask, require (6)

203	שְׁבַע	seven (6)
204	שׁרה	(Peal) to loosen, dwell; (Pael) to begin, commence; (Hithpeel) to be loosened, shake, shudder (6)
205	אֲלוּ	(interjection) look! behold! (5)
206	אִלֵּין	(cp dmstr pron and adj) these (5)
207	אֲלַף	thousand (5)
208	אָע	wood, tree, beam (5)
209	אֲרוּ	(interjection) look! behold! (5)
210	אַרְיוֹךְ	Arioch (5)
211	אֲתַר	place, location (5)
212	בקר	(Pael) to seek, investigate; (Hithpaal) to be investigated (5)
213	בְּרַם	(conj) except what, yet, but, however (5)
214	דִּין	judgment, justice (5)
215	חַרְטֹם	magician (5)
216	טַל	dew (5)
217	יַצִּיב	(adj) certain, true, reliable, exact (5)
218	יתב	(Peal) to sit, be seated, dwell, reside; (Haphel) to allow to dwell (5)
219	כְּנֵמָא	(adv) thus, so (5)
220	לֵילִי	night (5)
221	מלל	(Pael) to speak (5)
222	מנה	(Peal) to count; (Pael) to install, appoint (5)
223	סְגַן	prefect, governor, official (5)
224	סוֹף	end (5)
225	סְפַר	book (5)
226	סְרַךְ	high official, administrator (5)
227	עַיִן	eye (5)
228	עֲשַׂב	plants, grass, herbage (5)

229	צְבַע	(Pael) to moisten, wet; (Hithpaal) to become moist, wet (5)
230	רְבוּ	greatness (5)
231	רוּם	height, highest point (5)
232	שָׂב	elder (5)
233	שׁבח	(Pael) to praise (5)
234	שׁבק	(Peal) to leave behind, leave alone; (Hithpeel) to be left, pass on to (5)
235	שָׁלוּ	negligence (5)
236	שֵׁן	tooth (5)
237	שָׁעָה	moment, a short time (5)
238	שׁתה	(Peal) to drink (5)
239	תְּחוֹת	(prep) under (5)
240	תַּקִּיף	(adj) strong, mighty (5)
241	תקף	(Peal) to be (become) strong; to grow hard, become arrogant; (Pael) to become strong, enforce (5)
242	אַל	(neg particle) no, not (4)
243	אַמָּה	cubit (4)
244	אֲנַחְנָא	(1cp pers pron) we (4)
245	אַף	(conj) also (4)
246	ברך	(Peal) to bless; (Pael) to bless, praise (4); cf בְּרַךְ (#498)
247	גָּלוּ	deportation, exile (4)
248	דָּר	generation (4)
249	הַדָּבַר	meaning uncertain; perhaps "high-ranking official" or "counsellor" (4)
250	זוּע	(Peal) to tremble, shake (4)
251	זְמָר	stringed music, musical instruments (4)
252	זַן	kind, sort (4)
253	חלף	(Peal) to pass over (4)

254	חֲנֻכָּה	dedication (4)
255	טרד	(Peal) to drive away (4)
256	כהל	(Peal) to be able, capable (4)
257	כְּעֶנֶת	(adv) now (4)
258	כפת	(Peal) to be bound; (Pael) to bind (4)
259	לֵוָי	(gentilic n) Levite (4)
260	מְדוֹר	abode, dwelling (4)
261	מחא	(Peal) to strike; (Pael) to strike; (Hithpeel) to be impaled (4)
262	מַנְדַּע	understanding (4)
263	מַשְׁרוֹקִי	pipe, musical instrument (4)
264	סוּמְפֹּנְיָה	pipe, bagpipe, double-barreled flute (4)
265	עֶלְיוֹן	(divine title) the Most High (4)
266	עֲנַף	bough, branch (4)
267	ערב	(Pael) to mix; (Hithpeel) to mingle (4)
268	פְּסַנְטֵרִין	stringed instrument, harp (4)
269	צלח	(Haphel) to cause someone to prosper, make progress, fare well (4)
270	צְפַּר	bird (4)
271	קַיתְרוֹס	musical instrument, zither (4)
272	קִיתְרוֹס	lyre; Qere קַתְרוֹס (4)
273	רום	(Peal) to rise up, be arrogant; (Polel) to praise; (Hithpolal) to rise up; (Haphel) to elevate, raise (4)
274	רְחוּם	Rehum (4)
275	שַׂבְּכָא	stringed musical instrument; trigon, harp (also spelled סַבְּכָא) (4)
276	שׁוּר	wall (4)
277	שְׁלָם	peace, welfare, health, greetings! (4)
278	שִׁמְשַׁי	Shimshai (4)

279	שְׁפַל	(Haphel) to humiliate, humble (4)
280	שִׁתִּין	sixty (4)
281	שְׁתַר בּוֹזְנַי	Shethar Bozenai (4)
282	תַּמָּה	(adv) there (4)
283	תְּרֵין	(ms) two (4)
284	תַּתְּנַי	Tatnai (4)
285	אִגְּרָה	letter (3)
286	אזה	(Peal) to set light to, heat up a furnace (3)
287	אַחַר	(prep) after (3)
288	אמן	(Haphel) to trust, (pass) be trusted (3)
289	אִמַּר	lamb (3)
290	אֵנֶב	fruit, fruit tree (3)
291	אִנּוּן	(3mp pers pron) they, (dmstr) those (3)
292	אֱסוּר	(s) fetter; (p) custody, imprisonment (3)
293	אֶצְבַּע	finger, toe (3)
294	אַרְגְּוָן	purple, purple garment (3)
295	אֹשׁ	foundation (3)
296	אָת	sign (3)
297	בָּאתַר	(prep) after, afterward, after this (3)
298	בֵּין	(prep) between (3)
299	בְּלוֹ	tax, tribute (3)
300	בְּעֵל	commander, owner, lord (3)
301	בְּשַׂר	flesh (human or animal); humanity (metaphorically) (3)
302	גְּנַז	treasure chambers, treasury (3)
303	גַּף	wing (3)
304	דִּכֵּן	(cs dmstr pron and adj) that (3)
305	דְּכַר	ram (3)
306	הדר	(Pael) to glorify (3)

307	הֲדַר	majesty (3)
308	הלך	(Pael) to walk (about); (Haphel) to walk (about) (3)
309	הֲלָךְ	field-tax, produce-tax (3)
310	חֲבָל	hurt, damage (3)
311	חֲבַר	friend, companion (3)
312	חֲלָק	share, portion (3)
313	טעם	(Pael) to feed, give to eat (3)
314	יבל	(Haphel) to bring (3)
315	יעט	(Peal) to advise, give counsel; (Ithpael) to take counsel together (3)
316	כנש	(Peal) to assemble; (Hithpeel) to gather together (3)
317	כָּרְסֵא	seat, throne (3)
318	לבש	(Peal) to be clothed; (Haphel) to clothe someone (3)
319	לָהֵן	(conj) therefore (3); cf לָהֵן (#167)
320	לְחֵנָה	concubine (3)
321	מְלַח	salt (3)
322	מְנֵא	Mene, reckon (3)
323	מַתְּנָה	gift (3)
324	נדב	(Hithpeel) to be agreeable, willing; to donate (3)
325	נְוָלוּ	dunghill (3)
326	נזק	(Peal) to come to grief; (Haphel) to damage, suffer harm (3)
327	נצל	(Haphel) to save (3)
328	נשא	(Peal) to take, carry away; (Hithpeel) to rise up against (3)
329	נִשְׁתְּוָן	letter (3)
330	עֶזְרָא	Ezra (3)
331	עִיר	watcher, angel (3)
332	עִלָּה	charge, complaint (3)

333	עֳפִי	foliage (3)
334	עִקַּר	stump (3)
335	עַתִּיק	(adj) ancient, old, aged (3)
336	פַּרְשֶׁגֶן	copy (3)
337	צַוַּאר	neck (3)
338	קבל	(Pael) to receive (3)
339	קַדְמָי	(adj) first (3)
340	קְטַר	joint, difficult task (3)
341	קְצָת	end, particle (3)
342	רִבּוֹ	(adj) a great quantity, myriad, ten thousand (3)
343	רגשׁ	(Haphel) to enter together, act in agreement (3)
344	שׂגא	(Peal) to become great, abound, increase (3)
345	שָׂכְלְתָנוּ	insight (3)
346	שְׂעַר	hair (3)
347	שֵׁגָל	wife (3)
348	שׁוה	(Peal) to be the same, made the same; (Pael) to make the same; (Hithpeel) to be made (3)
349	שׁחת	(Peal) to corrupt (3)
350	שׁלם	(Peal) to be finished; (Haphel) to make complete, deliver completely, pay out (3)
351	שׁפר	(Peal) to please, seem good (3)
352	שְׁרֵשׁ	root (3)
353	תְּלִיתָי	(adj) third (3)
354	תְּמַהּ	miracle, wonder (3)
355	אֲדַרְגָּזַר	counsellor (2)
356	אַזְדָּא	(adj) publicly announced, known, certain, definite, irrevocable (2)
357	אַח	brother (2)
358	אֵלֶּה	(cp dmstr pron and adj) these (2)

359	אֲנַף	face (2)
360	אֲפַרְסְכָי	official (2)
361	אֱרַח	way (2)
362	אַרְכָה	length of time, prolongation (2)
363	אַרְכְּוָי	inhabitant of Erech, Erechite (2)
364	אֶשַּׁרְן	structure, building complex, shrine (2)
365	אֶשְׁתַּדּוּר	rebellion, revolt (2)
366	בָּעוּ	petition, prayer (2)
367	בַּת	a liquid measure, a bath (2)
368	גַּב	back, side (2)
369	גְּבוּרָה	strength, might (2)
370	גִּזְבַּר	chief treasurer (2)
371	גדד	(Peal) to cut down (2)
372	גְּזֵרָה	decree, resolution (2)
373	גְּלָל	large stone, stone block (2)
374	דִּבְרָה	matter, cause; עַל־דִּבְרַת דִּי and עַד־דִּבְרַת דִּי "for the purpose of, so that" (2)
375	דִּין	(Peal) to make a judgment (2)
376	דִּכְרָן	record, memorandum (2)
377	דמה	(Peal) to resemble (2)
378	דֶּתֶא	grass (2)
379	דְּתָבַר	judge (2)
380	הַדָּם	limb, piece (2)
381	זְכַרְיָה	Zechariah (2)
382	זמן	(Hithpeel) to come to an understanding, agree, conspire (2)
383	חַגַּי	Haggai (2)
384	חֲזוֹת	appearance, sight (2)
385	חטא	(Pael) to sin, make a sin offering (2)

386	חֲטִי	sin (Kethiv חֲטִי; Qere חֲטָא) (2)
387	חֵמָא	fury (2)
388	חִנְטָה	wheat, grain of wheat (2)
389	חנן	(Peal) to show mercy; (Hithpaal) to implore (2)
390	חסן	(Haphel) to take possession of, occupy (2)
391	חֱסֵן	power, might (2)
392	חצף	([H]aphel) to be harsh, urgent (2)
393	טָב	(adj) good (2)
394	טוּר	rock, mountain (2)
395	טִין	clay, wet clay (2)
396	טְפַר	nail, claw (2)
397	ידה	(Haphel) to praise (2)
398	יַם	sea (2)
399	יַקִּיר	(adj) difficult, honorable (2)
400	יְרַח	month (2)
401	כְּתַל	wall (2)
402	לְבוּשׁ	garment (2)
403	מֵאמַר	word, command (2)
404	מִדָּה	contribution, tax (2)
405	מָזוֹן	nourishment, food (2)
406	מלא	(Peal) to fill; (Hithpeel) to be filled with (2)
407	מַלְאַךְ	angel, messenger (2)
408	מַלְכָּה	queen (2)
409	מִנְדָּה	see מִדָּה (2)
410	מִנְחָה	offering, grain-offering (2)
411	מָרָד	(adj) rebellious (2)
412	מְשַׁח	oil, anointing oil (2)
413	נְבִזְבָּה	gift, reward, present (2)
414	נִדְבָּךְ	row, layer (2)

147

415	נְהִירוּ	illumination (2)
416	נטל	(Peal) to lift up (2)
417	נִיחוֹחַ	offering, sacrifice (2)
418	נְכַס	property, goods, riches, treasury (2)
419	נִפְקָה	cost, expense, price (2)
420	נְשַׁר	eagle (2)
421	סוּף	(Peal) to be fulfilled; (Haphel) to put an end to something, annihilate (2)
422	סַרְבָּל	tunic, trousers, coat (2)
423	עִדּוֹא	Iddo (2)
424	עוֹף	bird (2)
425	עִזְקָה	signet-ring (2)
426	עקר	(Ithpeel) to be plucked out, uproot (2)
427	עָר	adversary, opponent (2)
428	פַּטִּישׁ	article of clothing; pants, trousers, coat, tunic (2)
429	פַּס	palm or back (2)
430	פְּרֵס	unit of size and weight; one-half of a mina, one-half of a shekel (2)
431	פַּרְסִי	(gentilic n) Persian, a Persian (2)
432	פשר	(Peal) to interpret; (Pael) to give an interpretation (2)
433	פתח	(Peal) to open (2)
434	פְּתָי	width, breath (2)
435	צַד	side; (prep) concerning, about (2)
436	צלה	(Pael) to pray (2)
437	קַדְמָה	(adv) formerly (2)
438	קְיָם	statute (2)
439	קַיָּם	(adj) enduring (2)
440	קְרָץ	charge, accusation (2)
441	קְשֹׁט	truth (2)

442	רֵו	appearance (2)
443	רְעוּ	will, decision (2)
444	רעע	(Peal) to crush; (Pael) to crush (2)
445	רפס	(Peal) to tread down, trample (2)
446	שׂנֵא	(Peal) to hate (2)
447	שְׁבִיב	flame (2)
448	שׁכן	(Peal) to dwell; to cause to dwell (2)
449	שִׁלְטֹן	ruler, official (2)
450	שָׁמְרַיִן	Samaria (2)
451	שַׁפִּיר	(adj) beautiful, fair (2)
452	שׁרשׁו	banishment, exile (Qere שְׁרֹשִׁי; Kethiv שְׁרֹשִׁי) (2)
453	שֵׁשְׁבַּצַּר	Sheshbazzar (2)
454	שֵׁת	six (2)
455	תְּדִיר	continually, constantly (2)
456	תְּלִיתָי	(adj) third (2)
457	תְּלָתִין	thirty (2)
458	תִּפְתָּי	magistrate, leader, official, police officer (2)
459	תְּקֵל	shekel, unit of measurement, weight (2)
460	תְּרַע	gate, door, opening (2)
461	אֲדָר	Adar, the name of the twelfth month (1)
462	אִדַּר	threshing floor (1)
463	אַדְרַזְדָּא	(adv) careful devotion, faithful in heart (1)
464	אֶדְרָע	arm, upper arm, force (1)
465	אֲחִידָה	puzzle, riddle (1)
466	אַחְמְתָא	Ecbatana, Achmetha (1)
467	אַחֲרִי	end, latter (1)
468	אָחֳרֵין	(adv) at last, finally (1)
460	אֵימְתָן	(adj) terrible (1)
470	אֵל	(cp dmstr pron and adj) these (1)

471	אִנִּין	(3fp pers pron) they; (dmstr) these (1)
472	אנס	(Peal) to oppress (1)
473	אַנְתְּ	(2ms pers pron) you (1); cf אַנְתָּה (#67)
474	אַנְתּוּן	(2mp pers pron) you (1)
475	אָסְנַפַּר	Osnappar or Ashurbanipal (1)
476	אֲפָרְסִי	official (1)
477	אֲפַרְסַתְכִי	ambassador, official (1)
478	אַפְּתֹם	revenue, income, treasury (1)
479	אֲרִיךְ	(adj) correct, appropriate, fitting (1)
480	אַרְכֻּבָּא	knee (1)
481	אַרְעִי	bottom (1)
482	אֲרַק	earth, land (also spelled אֲרַע) (1)
483	אֶשָּׁא	fire, offering made by fire (1)
484	בְּאִישׁ	(adj) bad, evil, wicked (1)
485	באשׁ	(Peal) to be bad, displeased, distressed (1)
486	בָּבְלִי	(gentilic n) Babylonian (1)
487	בדר	(Pael) to disperse, scatter fruit from a tree (1)
488	בְּהִילוּ	haste (1)
489	בִּינָה	discernment, understanding (1)
490	בִּירָה	fortress, capital (1)
491	בִּית	(Peal) to spend the night (1)
492	בָּל	mind, spirit, will (1)
493	בלא	(Pael) to wear out (1)
494	בִּנְיָן	building, construction work (1)
495	בנס	(Peal) to become angry, get enraged (1)
496	בִּקְעָה	valley, plain (1)
497	ברך	(Pael) to kneel (1); cf ברך (#246)
498	בֶּרֶךְ	knee (1)
499	גְּבַר	strong man (1)

500	גֵּוָה	pride (1)
501	גּוּחַ	(Aphel) to stir up (1)
502	גִּזְבָּר	treasurer (1)
503	גִּיר	plaster (1)
504	גַּלְגַּל	wheel (1)
505	גְּמַר	(Peal) to be complete, finished, perfect (1)
506	גֶּרֶם	bone (1)
507	דֹּב	bear (1)
508	דְּבַח	(Peal) to perform a sacrifice (1)
509	דְּבַח	animal sacrifice (1)
510	דְּבַק	(Peal) to cling to, stick together (1)
511	דּוּרָא	Dura (1)
512	דּוּשׁ	(Peal) to tread down, tread under (1)
513	דַּחֲוָה	uncertain meaning; frequently translated as "diversion" or "entertainment" (1)
514	דַּיָּן	judge (1)
515	דַּיָּנָא	judge (1)
516	דִּכְרוֹן	record, memorandum (1)
517	דְּלַק	(Peal) to burn (1)
518	דְּרַע	arm (1)
519	הָא	(interjection) look!, see! (1)
520	הֵא	even, just; הֵא־כְדִי just as, even as (1)
521	הַנְזָקָה	damage, injury (1)
522	הַרְהֹר	appearances, dream-fantasies (1)
523	הִתְנַדָּבוּ	gift, donation (1)
524	זְבַן	(Peal) to buy, gain (1)
525	זְהִיר	(adj) careful, cautious (1)
526	זוּד	(Haphel) to act presumptuously (with pride) (1)
527	זוּן	(Hithpeel) to live from, subsist on, feed (1)

528	זָכוּ	innocence (1)
529	זַמָּר	musician, singer (1)
530	זְעֵיר	(adj) small, little (1)
531	זעק	(Peal) to shriek, scream, cry out (1)
532	זקף	(Peal) to raise, impale (1)
533	זְרֻבָּבֶל	Zerubbabel (1)
534	זְרַע	seed, descendants (1)
535	חֲבוּלָה	hurtful act, crime (1)
536	חַבְרָה	female friend, female companion (1)
537	חֲדֵה	chest (1)
538	חֶדְוָה	joy (1)
539	חֲדַת	(adj) new (1)
540	חיט	(Peal or [H]aphel) to repair (1)
541	חִוָּר	(adj) white (1)
542	חֲנַנְיָה	Hananiah (1)
543	חַסִּיר	(adj) wanting, lacking, deficient (1)
544	חרב	(Hophal) to be laid waste (1)
545	חרך	(Hithpaal) to be singed, burned (1)
546	חֲרַץ	hip (1)
547	חשב	(Peal) to consider, respect, take for (1)
548	חֲשׁוֹךְ	darkness (1)
549	חשח	(Peal) to need, be in need of (1)
550	חַשְׁחָה	need (1)
551	חַשְׁחוּ	need (1)
552	חשל	(peal) to crush (1)
553	חתם	(peal) to seal (1)
554	טאב	(Peal) to be good (1)
555	טַבָּח	executioners, bodyguards (1)
556	טְוָת	(adv) fasting, hungrily (1)

557	טְלֵל	(Haphel) dwell, seek protection (1)
558	טַרְפְּלָי	official, Tarpelite (1)
559	יַבֶּשֶׁת	dry land (1)
560	יוֹצָדָק	Jozadak (1)
561	יטב	(Peal) to be pleasing, wished for (1)
562	יסף	(Hophal) to be added (1)
563	יצב	(Pael) to make certain, determine, ascertain (1)
564	יְקֵדָה	burning (1)
565	יַרְכָה	thigh (1)
566	יֵשׁוּעַ	Jeshua (1)
567	יָת	(accusative particle) not translated; definite direct object marker (1)
568	כִּדְבָה	lie, lying (1)
569	כָּה	(adv) here (1)
570	כַּוָּה	window (1)
571	כַּכַּר	talent; unit of measurement (1)
572	כֹּר	unit of measurement; *kor* (1)
573	כַּרְבְּלָה	hat, turban, head covering (1)
574	כרה	(Ithpeel) to be distressed (1)
575	כָּרוֹז	herald (1)
576	כרז	(Haphel) to make a proclamation (1)
577	לֵב	heart (1)
578	לְוָת	(prep) near, beside (1)
579	לְחֶם	bread, feast (1)
580	מֹאזְנֵא	balance, scale (1)
581	מְגִלָּה	scroll (1)
582	מגר	(Pael) to overthrow (1)
583	מַדְבַּח	altar (1)
584	מוֹת	death (1)

585	מַחְלְקָה	section, division (1)
586	מִישָׁאֵל	Mishael (1)
587	מלח	(Peal) to eat salt (1)
588	מְלַךְ	counsel (1)
589	מִנְיָן	number (1)
590	מַעֲבָד	work (1)
591	מְעֵה	belly (1)
592	מֵעַל	going in, going down (1)
593	מְרַד	rebellion (1)
594	מרט	(Peal) to pluck out (1)
595	מֹשֶׁה	Moses (1)
596	מִשְׁכַּן	dwelling place, abode (1)
597	מִשְׁתֵּא	drinking, banquet (1)
598	נבא	(Hithpeel) to act as a prophet, prophesy (1)
599	נְבוּאָה	prophecy, prophesying (1)
600	נֶבְרְשָׁה	candlestick (1)
601	נגד	(Peal) to flow, gush (1)
602	נֶגֶד	(prep) in the direction of, towards (1)
603	נְגַה	brightness (1)
604	נדד	(Peal) to flee (1)
605	נִדְנֶה	sheath, body (1)
606	נְהוֹר	light (1)
607	נְהִיר	light (1)
608	נוד	(Peal) to flee; shake, tremble (1)
609	נטר	(Peal) to keep (1)
610	נְמַר	leopard, panther (1)
611	נסח	(Hithpeel) to be pulled out (1)
612	נסך	(Pael) to offer up, pour out (1)
613	נְסַךְ	libation, drink offering (1)

614	נִצְבָּה	firmness, hardness (1)
615	נצח	(Hithpeel) to distinguish oneself, become distinguished (1)
616	נְקֵא	(adj) clean, pure (1)
617	נקשׁ	(Peal) to strike one another (1)
618	נְשִׁין	women, wives (1)
619	נִשְׁמָה	breath (1)
620	נְתִין	someone handed over, temple slave (1)
621	נתר	(Aphel) to shake off (1)
622	סבל	(Poel) to bear a load, be retained, determined (1)
623	סבר	(Peal) to intend (1)
624	סגר	(Peal) to shut, close (1)
625	סעד	(Pael) to aid, support (1)
626	סתר	(Pael) to hide, (pass) be hidden (1)
627	סתר	(Peal) to destroy, demolish (1)
628	עוֹד	(adv) still, while (1)
629	עֲוָיָה	iniquity (1)
630	עוּר	chaff (1)
631	עֵז	goat (1)
632	עֲזַרְיָה	Azariah (1)
633	עֵטָה	advice, counsel (1)
634	עֵלָּא	(prep) over, above (1)
635	עֲלָוָה	burnt offering (1)
636	עִלִּי	roof-chamber (1)
637	עֵלְמָי	(gentilic n) Elamite (1)
638	עֲלַע	rib (1)
639	עַמִּיק	(adj) deep, unfathomable (1)
640	עֲמַר	wool (1)
641	עֲנֵה	miserable, lowliness (1)

642	עֲנָן	cloud (1)
643	עֲנַשׁ	penalty, fine, confiscation of property (1)
644	עֲצִיב	(adj) troubled, sad (1)
645	עֲרָד	wild donkey, wild ass (1)
646	עֶרְוָה	nakedness, shame (1)
647	עֶשְׂרִין	twenty (1)
648	עֲשֵׁת	(Peal) to intend (1)
649	עֲתִיד	(adj) ready, prepared (1)
650	פֶּחָר	potter (1)
651	פְּלַג	(Peal) to divide (1)
652	פְּלַג	half (1)
653	פְּלֻגָּה	section, division (1)
654	פָּלְחָן	service, ritual observance (1)
655	פרס	(Peal) to divide (1)
656	פרק	(Peal) to remove, wipe away (1)
657	פרשׁ	(Pael) to separate (1)
658	צְבוּ	matter, concern (1)
659	צְדָא	truth (1)
660	צִדְקָה	righteousness, what is right (1)
661	צְפִיר	billy goat (1)
662	קַיִט	summer (1)
663	קנה	(Peal) to buy (1)
664	קצף	(Peal) to become furious (1)
665	קְצַף	fury, wrath, anger (1)
666	קצץ	(Pael) to cut off (1)
667	קְרָב	war, battle (1)
668	רגז	(Haphel) to anger, irritate (1)
669	רְגַז	anger, irritation (1)
670	רַחִיק	(adj) far, distant (1)

671	רַחֲמִין	compassion (1)
672	רחץ	(Hithpeel) to trust in (1)
673	רֵיחַ	smell (1)
674	רַעֲנַן	(adj) happy, fortunate (1)
675	שָׂהֲדוּתָא	witness, testimony (1)
676	שְׂטַר	side (1)
677	שׂכל	(Hithpaal) to consider, have regard for (1)
678	שְׁאֵלָה	request, question, sentence (1)
679	שְׁאַלְתִּיאֵל	Shealtiel (1)
680	שְׁבַט	tribe (1)
681	שבש	(Hithpeel) to become perplexed, be terrified, become anxious (1)
682	שׂדר	(Hithpaal) to strive (1)
683	שׁוּשַׁנְכִי	(gentilic n) resident of Susa (1)
684	שֵׁיצִיא	(Shaphel) to complete, finish (1)
685	שְׁלֵה	(adj) calm, at ease (1)
686	שְׁלֵוָה	prosperity (1)
687	שׁמד	(Haphel) to annihilate (1)
688	שׁמם	(Ithpolal) to be appalled (1)
689	שׁמש	(Pael) to serve (1)
690	שְׁמַשׁ	sun (1)
691	שְׁנָה	sleep (1); cf שְׁנָה (#176)
692	שׁפט	(Peal) to judge (1)
693	שְׁפַל	(adj) low, lowly (1)
694	שְׁפַרְפָּר	daybreak, dawn (1)
695	שָׁק	shin, leg (1)
696	תבר	(Peal) to break (1)
697	תוה	(Peal) to be amazed, frightened, horrified (1)
698	תְּלַג	snow (1)

699	תִּנְיָן	(adj) second (1)
700	תִּנְיָנוּת	(adv) second time, again (1)
701	תְּקַל	(Peal) to weigh (1)
702	תְּקַן	(Hophal) to be re-established (1)
703	תְּקֹף	strength (1)
704	תְּקָף	strength (1)
705	תָּרָע	gatekeeper (1)

Hebrew Homonymns
Listed Alphabetically

The following list contains Hebrew words that occur 10 times or more and are identical in spelling but differ in meaning and/or part of speech. We have selected 67 sets of identical forms with 137 total words. The most frequent of the identical forms is always listed first.

אוּלָם   porch; also spelled אֵילָם (61)

אוּלָם   but, however (19)

אוֹר   (cs) light, daylight, sunshine (120)

אוֹר   (Hi) to give light, shine, illuminate, light up (44)

אַיִל   ram, ruler; (adj) mighty (171)

אַיִל   pillar, doorpost (22); 21x in Ezek

אַיִן   (particle of nonexistence) is not, are not, nothing; most
often spelled אֵין (790)

אַיִן   wherefrom? whence? (17)

אֶלֶף   thousand; (md) אַלְפַּיִם two thousand (496)

אֶלֶף   clan, tribe, region (11)

אַף   nostril, nose; (metaphorically) anger; (md) אַפַּיִם (277)

אַף   (conj) also, indeed, even (133)

אֵת   (definite direct object marker) not translated; also spelled
אֶת־ with loss of accent or (with 3ms suff) אֹתוֹ (10,978)

אֵת   (prep) with, beside; also spelled אֶת־ with loss of accent or
(with 3ms suff) אִתּוֹ (890)

בַּד   carrying pole, gate bar (40)

בַּד   linen cloth (23)

בּוּז   (Q) to show contempt (for), despise (14)

בּוּז   contempt (11)

בָּעַר   (Q) to burn (up), consume; (Pi) kindle, burn (60)

בָּעַר   (Pi) to graze, sweep away, remove, get rid of, purge (27)

בַּת   daughter; (fp) בָּנוֹת (587)

בַּת   (ms) liquid measurement, bath; (mp) בַּתִּים (13)

גָּאַל (Q) to redeem, act as kinsman (perform the responsibilities of the next-of-kin), avenge (104)

גָּאַל (Ni, Pu) to be defiled, become impure; (Hith) defile oneself (11)

גּוּר (Q) to sojourn, dwell (stay) as a foreigner or alien (82)

גּוּר (Q) to be afraid, dread, stand in awe (10)

גַּל heap, pile; (mp) גַּלִּים (18)

גַּל wave (16)

דִּין (Q) to judge, minister or execute judgment, plead one's cause, contend with (24)

דִּין judgment, legal claim (19)

דָּמָה (Q) to be like, resemble; (Pi) liken, compare (30)

דָּמָה (Ni) to be destroyed, ruined (12)

הָלַל (Pi) to praise, sing hallelujah; (Pu) be praised, praiseworthy; (Hith) boast (146)

הָלַל (Q) to be infatuated, deluded; (Hithpolel) be mad, act like a madman (15)

הֵנָּה here (59)

הֵנָּה (3fp pers pron) they; (fp dmstr pron and adj) those (29)

הָרָה (Q) to conceive, be(come) pregnant (43)

הָרָה (fs adj) pregnant (15)

זָקֵן (Q) to be(come) old, grow old (26)

זָקֵן (adj) old; (n) elder, old man (180)

חָבַל (Q) to take, hold or seize (something) in pledge, exact a pledge from someone, bind by taking a pledge (13)

חָבַל (Q) to act corruptly or ruinously; (Pi) ruin, destroy (11)

161

חַיָּה   animal, beast, living thing (96)

חַיָּה   life; (with 3ms suff) חַיָּתוֹ (11)

חֹמֶר   mud, clay, mortar (17)

חֹמֶר   dry measurement, heap, pile, homer (13)

חָסֵר   (Q) to diminish, decrease, lack (22)

חָסֵר   (adj) lacking, wanting; (ms cstr) חֲסַר (17)

חָפֵץ   (Q) to delight in, take pleasure in, desire, be willing (74)

חָפֵץ   delighting (in), desiring (13)

חָפַר   (Q) to dig, track, search (for), scout out, spy out (23)

חָפַר   (Q) to be ashamed (17)

חָרֵב   (Q) to dry up (intransitive), lie in ruins; (Hi) cause to dry up, lay waste, make desolate (36)

חָרֵב   (adj) dry, desolate, wasted (10)

חָרַשׁ   (Q) to be silent, deaf; (Hi) be(come) silent, deaf, keep still (47)

חָרַשׁ   (Q) to plow, engrave, devise, plan (27)

טוֹב   (adj) good, pleasant (530)

טוֹב   (Q) to be good, pleasing, pleasant, joyful, well with (44)

טָמֵא   (Q) to be(come) unclean; (Ni) defile oneself; (Pi) defile, pronounce or declare unclean; (Hith) defile oneself, become unclean (162)

טָמֵא   (adj) unclean (88)

יָרֵא   (Q) to fear, be afraid, in awe of, reverence; (Ni) be feared, held in honor (317)

יָרֵא   (adj) fearful (63)

יָרָה (Hi) to instruct, teach (47)

יָרָה (Q, Hi) to throw, shoot, cast (lots) (28)

כָּבֵד (Q) to be heavy, weighty, honored; (Ni) be honored; (Pi) honor; (Hi) make heavy, dull or insensitive, harden (heart) (114)

כָּבֵד (adj) heavy, severe, important (41)

כָּבֵד (fs) liver (14)

כָּלָה (Q) to be complete, finished, at an end, accomplished, spent, exhausted, come to an end; (Pi) complete, finish, bring to an end (207)

כָּלָה complete destruction, annihilation (22)

כֵּן so, thus (741)

כֵּן (adj) honest, correct, right (24)

כֵּן base, stand; (with 3ms suff) כַּנּוֹ (11)

לָוָה (Q) to borrow; (Hi) lend to (14)

לָוָה (Ni) to join oneself to (12)

מוּל (prep) in front of, opposite (36)

מוּל (Q) to circumcise; (Ni) be circumcised (32)

מָלֵא (Q) to be full, fill (up); (Ni) be filled (with); (Pi) fill, perform, carry out, consecrate as priest (252)

מָלֵא (adj) full, filled (61)

מָנָה (Q) to count, number, reckon, assign, appoint (28)

מָנָה part, portion, share (12)

מַעַל above, upward, on top of (140)

מַעַל unfaithfulness, infidelity (29)

163

מַשָּׂא load, burden (44)

מַשָּׂא oracle, pronouncement (20)

מָשַׁל (Q) to rule, reign, govern, have dominion (81)

מָשַׁל (Q) to use a proverb, to speak in parables or poetry; (Ni) be(come) like, similar or the same as (17)

נֵבֶל stringed instrument, harp (28)

נֵבֶל jar, bottle (10)

עַד (prep) until, as far as (1,263)

עַד forever, eternal; spelled וְעַד with conjunction וְ (47)

עֹז strength, power, might; (with 3ms suff) עֻזּוֹ (76)

עֹז refuge, protection (17)

עָנָה (Q) to answer, respond, reply, testify; (Ni) be answered (316)

עָנָה (Q) to be afflicted, humbled; (Pi) afflict, oppress, humiliate, violate (79)

עָנָה (Q) to sing (16)

פָּרָה (Q) to bear fruit, be fruitful (29)

פָּרָה cow (26)

צָבָא (cs) host, army, war, service; (cp) צְבָאוֹת (487); יְהוָה צְבָאוֹת "Yahweh of Hosts;"

צָבָא (Q) to wage war, go to war, fight against (14)

צְבִי ornament, something beautiful, splendor (18)

צְבִי gazelle (12)

צוּר rock, boulder (73)

צוּר (Q) to tie up, bind, shut in, shut up, enclose, encircle, besiege (31)

164

צָפָה (Pi) to overlay, plate (with gold) (47)

צָפָה (Q) to keep watch, watch attentively, spy (37)

צַר adversary, enemy (72)

צַר (adj) narrow; (n) anxiety, distress (27)

צָרַר (Q) to wrap (up), tie up, bind (transitive); be cramped, restricted, depressed (intransitive); (Hi) oppress, harass, afflict (47)

צָרַר (Q) to be hostile (toward), treat with hostility, attack (26)

קָצַר (Q) to gather in, reap, harvest (36)

קָצַר (Q) to be(come) short, shortened, impatient (14)

קָרָא (Q) to call, summon, proclaim, read aloud, give a name to; (Ni) be called, summoned, proclaimed (739)

קָרָא (Q) to meet, encounter, happen; inf cstr with prep לְ (לִקְרַאת) toward, against, opposite (136)

רֹאשׁ head, top, chief; (mp) רָאשִׁים (600)

רֹאשׁ poisonous herb, venom (12)

רַב (adj) great, many; (mp) רַבִּים (419)

רַב chief, captain, ruler (30)

רִיב (Q) to strive, contend, quarrel, dispute, conduct a legal case (72)

רִיב dispute, quarrel, lawsuit (62)

רִיק (Hi) to empty out, pour out (19) and רִיק (#1601)

רִיק emptiness, vanity (12)

רָעֵב (adj) hungry (20)

רָעֵב (Q) to be hungry, suffer famine (13)

רָעָה evil, wickedness, calamity, disaster (354), רָעָה (#255), and
רֹע (#1310)

רָעָה (Q) to pasture, tend (flocks), graze, shepherd, feed (167)

שִׂיחַ (Q) to consider, meditate, complain, lament, praise (20)
שִׂיחַ complaint, lament (14)

שָׁבַר (Q) to break (up), break in pieces, smash, shatter; (Ni) be
smashed, broken, shattered or destroyed; (Pi) shatter,
smash, break (148)
שָׁבַר (Q) to buy grain (for food) (21)

שִׁיר (Q) to sing (of); (Q and Polel ptc) singer (88) and שִׁירָה
(#1675)
שִׁיר song (78) and שִׁירָה (#1675)

שָׁלֵם (Q) to be complete, finished; (Pi) complete, finish, make
whole, restore, reward; (Hi) bring to completion,
consummate (116)
שָׁלֵם (adj) whole, complete, safe (28)

שָׁנָה year; (fp) שָׁנִים (878)
שָׁנָה (Q) to change; (Pi) change, alter, pervert (15)

שֵׁשׁ six; (fs) שִׁשָּׁה; (fs cstr) שֵׁשֶׁת; (mp) שִׁשִּׁים sixty (274)
שֵׁשׁ linen (39); 33x in Exod

Nouns with Common Gender
Listed Alphabetically

In the Hebrew Old Testament, there are 43 common nouns with common gender with a total occurrence of approximately 5,700 times. 34 of these nouns occur 10 times or more.

אוֹר   light, daylight, sunshine (120)

אוֹת   sign, mark, pledge; (cp) אֹתוֹת (79)

אֲרוֹן   ark, chest, coffin (202); אֲרוֹן הַבְּרִית "the ark of the covenant"

אֹרַח   road, path, way (59)

אֵשׁ   fire (376)

גַּיְא   valley; also spelled גַּיְא (64)

גַּן   garden; (cp) גַּנִּים (41)

גֶּפֶן   vine, grapevine (55)

דֶּרֶךְ   way, road, journey (712)

זָקָן   beard (19)

חַלּוֹן   window; (cp) חַלּוֹנִים and חַלּוֹנוֹת (32)

חָצֵר   courtyard, village, settlement; (cp) חֲצֵרִים and חֲצֵרוֹת (192)

לָבִיא   lion, lioness (12)

לָשׁוֹן   tongue, language (117)

מָגֵן   shield; (cp) מָגִנִּים (60)

מַחֲנֶה   camp, army; (cp) מַחֲנוֹת and מַחֲנִים (215)

מְצִלְתַּיִם   (cd) cymbals (13)

מַקֵּל   rod, staff, branch; (cp) מַקְלוֹת (18)

סִיר   basin, pot, tub (29)

עֲבֹת   cord, rope; (cp) עֲבֹתִים and עֲבֹתֹת (19)

עַיִן   eye, spring (900)

עֵת   time, point of time; (cp) עִתִּים and עִתּוֹת (296)

פָּנִים   (cp) face, front; לִפְנֵי (prep לְ prefixed to cstr) before, in front of (2,126)

צֹאן   flock(s), flock of sheep and goats (274)

צָבָא   host, army, war, service; (cp) צְבָאוֹת (487); יְהוָה צְבָאוֹת "Yahweh of Hosts;" cf. צָבָא (#1589)

168

צִפּוֹר bird; (cp) צִפֳּרִים (40)

רוּחַ spirit, wind, breath; (cp) רוּחוֹת (378)

שְׁאוֹל underworld, Sheol (65)

שַׁבָּת Sabbath, period of rest; (cp) שַׁבָּתוֹת (111)

שֶׁמֶשׁ sun (134)

שֵׁן tooth, ivory (55)

תְּהוֹם primeval ocean, deep, depth (36)

תַּן jackal; (cp) תַּנִּים (15)

תַּנּוּר oven, firepot, furnace (15)

Endingless Feminine Singular Nouns
Listed Alphabetically

In the Hebrew Old Testament, there are some 1,500 feminine nouns with a total occurrence of approximately 28,000 times. There are 44 "endingless" feminine nouns that occur more than 10 times in the Hebrew Bible.

אֶבֶן   stone; (fp) אֲבָנִים (276)

אֹזֶן   ear; (fd cstr) אָזְנֵי (188)

אֵם   mother; (with 3ms suff) אִמּוֹ (220)

אֶצְבַּע   finger, toe (31)

אֶרֶץ   land, earth, ground (2,505)

אָתוֹן   female donkey (34)

בְּאֵר   well, pit, cistern (37)

בֶּטֶן   belly, stomach, womb (72)

בֶּרֶךְ   knee (26)

גֹּרֶן   threshing floor (37)

זְרוֹעַ   arm, forearm; (metaphorically) strength or power; (fp) זְרֹעוֹת (91)

חֶרֶב   sword (413)

יָד   hand; (metaphorically) power (1,627)

יָמִין   right hand, south (141)

יָרֵךְ   thigh, loin, side (34)

יָתֵד   tent peg, stake, pin (24)

כָּבֵד   liver (14)

כַּד   jar, pitcher; (fp) כַּדִּים (18)

כּוֹס   cup (31)

כִּכָּר   something round, talent (weight), valley; (fp) כִּכָּרִים (68)

כָּנָף   wing, edge, extremity (111)

כַּף   hand, palm, sole of the foot (195)

כָּתֵף   side, shoulder (67)

לְחִי   jaw, cheek, chin (21)

מְצָד   stronghold, fortress (12)

נַעַל   sandal, shoe (22)

נֶפֶשׁ   soul, life, person, neck, throat (757)

עֵז   goat, goat's hair; (fp) עִזִּים (74)

עִיר   city, town; (fp) עָרִים (1,088)

עֶצֶם   bone, skeleton (126)

עֶרֶשׂ   couch, bed (10)

פִּילֶגֶשׁ   concubine; (fp) פִּילַגְשִׁים (37)

פַּעַם   foot, pace, time; (fp) פְּעָמִים (118)

צֵלָע   rib, side (40)

צָפוֹן   north, northern (153)

צְפַרְדֵּעַ   frog; (fp) צְפַרְדְּעִים (13); 11x in Exod

קֶרֶן   horn (76)

רְבוֹא   ten thousand, countless number; also spelled רִבּוֹ (11)

רֶגֶל   foot (251)

רְחוֹב   public square, street (43)

שׁוֹק   thigh, leg (19)

תֵּבֵל   world (36)

תּוֹר   turtledove; (fp) תֹּרִים (14)

תֵּימָן   south; (with directional ה) תֵּימָנָה (24)

Segholate Nouns
Listed Alphabetically

The following list contains 194 two-syllable nouns that are accented on the penultima (next-to-last syllable).

אֵבֶל   mourning, funeral ceremony (24)

אֶבֶן   (fs) stone; (fp) אֲבָנִים (276)

אֶדֶן   base, pedestal (57)

אֹהֶל   tent (348)

אָוֶן   iniquity, wickedness, evildoer (81)

אֹזֶן   (fs) ear; (fd cstr) אָזְנֵי (188)

אֹכֶל   food (38)

אֶלֶף   thousand; (md) אַלְפַּיִם two thousand (496)

אֶלֶף   clan, tribe, region (11)

אֹמֶר   word, saying, speech (48)

אֶפֶס   end, nothing (43)

אֵפֶר   ashes, dust (22)

אֶרֶז   cedar (73)

אֹרַח   (cs) road, path, way (59)

אֹרֶךְ   length (95)

אֶרֶץ   (fs) land, earth, ground (2,505)

בֶּגֶד   clothes, garment, covering (216)

בֶּדֶק   damage, breach, crack (10)

בֹּהֶן   thumb, big toe (16)

בֶּטַח   security, safety (42)

בֶּטֶן   (fs) belly, stomach, womb (72)

בַּעַל   owner, master, husband, (divine title) Baal (161)

בֶּצַע   unjust gain or profit (23)

בֹּקֶר   morning (213)

בֶּרֶךְ   (fs) knee (26)

בֹּשֶׂם   spice, perfume (30)

בֹּשֶׁת   shame, disgrace (41)

גֶּבֶר   strong man, young man, hero (66)

גֹּדֶל   greatness, arrogance (13)

גֶּפֶן   (cs) vine, grapevine (55)

גֹּרֶן   (fs) threshing floor (37)

גֶּשֶׁם   rain, showers (35)

דֶּבֶר   plague, pestilence (46)

דֶּגֶל   division of a tribe, banner, standard (14); 13x in Num

דֶּלֶת   door (88)

דַּעַת   knowledge, understanding, ability (88)

דֶּרֶךְ   (cs) way, road, journey (712)

דֶּשֶׁא   grass, vegetation (14)

דֶּשֶׁן   fat, fat-soaked ashes (15)

הֶבֶל   vanity, futility, breath (73); 38x in Eccl

זֶבַח   sacrifice (162)

זֵכֶר   memory, remembrance (23)

זַעַם   anger, indignation, curse (22)

זֶרַע   seed, offspring, descendants (229)

חֶבֶל   rope, cord, field, region (48)

חֶדֶר   room, chamber (38)

חֹדֶשׁ   month, new moon (283)

חֵלֶב   fat; (metaphorically) best, choice part (92)

חֵלֶק   portion, share (66)

חֹמֶר   mud, clay, mortar (17)

חֹמֶר   dry measurement, heap, pile, homer (13)

חֶסֶד   loyalty, faithfulness, steadfast love, lovingkindness (249)

חֵפֶץ   delight, desire, pleasure, joy (38)

חֵקֶר   searching, something searched out (12)

175

חֶ֫רֶב   (fs) sword (413)

חֹ֫רֶב   dryness, drought, heat, waste (16)

חֵ֫רֶם   something set apart for destruction, devoted to destruction (29)

חֶ֫רֶשׂ   earthenware, potsherd (20)

חֹ֫שֶׁךְ   darkness (80)

חֹ֫שֶׁן   breastplate (of the high priest) (25); 23x in Exod

טֶ֫בַח   slaughtering, slaughter (12)

טַ֫עַם   taste, sense, discernment (13)

טֶ֫רֶף   prey, food (22)

יֶ֫לֶד   child, boy, youth (89)

יַ֫עַר   forest, woods, thicket (57)

יֶ֫קֶב   wine vat, winepress (16)

יֶ֫רַח   month (12)

יֶ֫שַׁע   salvation, deliverance, help; (with 1cs suff) יִשְׁעִי (36)

יֹ֫שֶׁר   uprightness, honesty, straightness (14)

יֶ֫תֶר   rest, remainder, excess (97)

כֶּ֫בֶשׂ   lamb, sheep (107)

כֶּ֫לֶא   prison, confinement (10)

כֶּ֫לֶב   dog, male temple prostitute (32)

כֶּ֫סֶף   silver, money (403)

כַּ֫עַס   anger, vexation (21)

כֹּ֫פֶר   ransom, bribe (13)

כֶּ֫רֶם   vineyard (94)

כֶּ֫שֶׂב   young ram, lamb (13)

לַ֫הַב   flame, blade (of a sword) (12)

לֶ֫חֶם   bread, food (340)

לַ֫חַץ   oppression, affliction (12)

מֶלַח salt (23)

מֶלֶךְ king, ruler (2,530)

מַעַל unfaithfulness, infidelity (29)

מֵצַח forehead, brow (13)

נֵבֶל stringed instrument, harp (28)

נֵבֶל jar, bottle (10)

נֶגֶב south, southward, Negev (29)

נֹגַה brightness, radiance (19)

נֶגַע plague, affliction (78)

נֵדֶר vow; also spelled נֶדֶר (60)

נֶזֶם earring, nose-ring (17)

נֵזֶר consecration, dedication, crown (25)

נַחַל stream, brook, wadi (137)

נֵסֶךְ drink offering; also spelled נֶסֶךְ (60)

נַעַל (fs) sandal, shoe (22)

נַעַר boy, youth, servant (240)

נֶפֶשׁ (fs) soul, life, person, neck, throat (757)

נֵצַח forever, everlasting (43)

נֶשֶׁךְ interest, usury (12)

נֶשֶׁף twilight, dusk (12)

נֶשֶׁר eagle, vulture (26)

נֵתַח piece of meat (13)

נֶתֶק skin disease, scab (14); all in Lev

סֶלַע rock, stone, cliff (59)

סֹלֶת flour (53)

סֵפֶר book, scroll, document (191); סֵפֶר הַתּוֹרָה "the book of the law"

סֶרֶן ruler, lord (21); 19x in Judg, 1 Sam

סֵתֶר   hiding place, secret place, shelter (35)

עֶבֶד   slave, servant (803)

עֵבֶר   beyond, other side, edge, bank (92)

עֵגֶל   calf, young bull (35)

עֵדֶר   flock, herd (38)

עָוֶל   iniquity, injustice, wrong (21)

עֵזֶר   help, assistance (17)

עֵמֶק   valley, plain (70)

עֶצֶם   (fs) bone, skeleton (126)

עֵקֶב   because, on account of; (n) result, wages (15)

עֶרֶב   evening, sunset (134)

עֵרֶךְ   value, assessment (33)

עֹרֶף   (back of) neck (33)

עֶרֶשׂ   (fs) couch, bed (10)

עֵשֶׂב   green plant, grass (33)

עֹשֶׁק   oppression, extortion (15)

עֹשֶׁר   wealth, riches (37)

פֶּגֶר   corpse, carcass (22)

פַּחַד   trembling, terror, dread (49)

פַּחַת   pit, ravine (10)

פֶּטֶר   firstborn (11)

פֶּלֶא   wonder, miracle, something extraordinary (13)

פֶּלֶג   water channel, canal (10)

פֶּסַח   Passover (49)

פֶּסֶל   idol, carved image (31)

פֹּעַל   work, deed (36)

פַּעַם   (fs) foot, pace, time; (fp) פְּעָמִים (118)

פֶּ֫רֶא wild donkey (10)

פֶּ֫רֶד mule (14)

פֶּ֫רַח blossom, bud, flower (17)

פֶּ֫רֶץ breach, gap (19)

פֶּ֫שַׁע transgression, rebellion (93)

פֶּ֫שֶׁת linen, flax; (fp) פִּשְׁתִּים (16)

פֶּ֫תַח opening, entrance, doorway (164)

צֶ֫דֶק righteousness, equity (123)

צֶ֫לֶם image, idol (15)

צֶ֫מֶד pair, team (15)

צֶ֫מַח growth, sprout, branch (12)

צֶ֫מֶר wool (16)

צַ֫עַד step, pace (14)

קֶ֫בֶר grave, burial site; (mp) קְבָרִים and קְבָרוֹת (67)

קֶ֫דֶם east, ancient times (61)

קֹ֫דֶשׁ holiness, something that is holy (470)

קֶ֫לַע curtain (16)

קֶ֫מַח flour (14)

קֶ֫סֶם divination, prediction (11)

קֶ֫צֶף wrath, anger (28)

קֶ֫רֶב inner part(s), organ(s), body; (prep) בְּקֶ֫רֶב in the middle of, among (227)

קֶ֫רֶן (fs) horn (76)

קֶ֫רֶס (curtain) hook, clasp (10); all in Exod

קֶ֫רֶשׁ board, plank (51); 48x in Exod

קֶ֫שֶׁר alliance, conspiracy, treason (16)

קֶ֫שֶׁת bow, weapon (76)

רֶ֫גֶל (fs) foot (251)

רֶגַע moment, instant (22

רֶחֶם womb (26)

רֶכֶב chariot, (coll) chariots or chariot riders (120)

רֹמַח spear, lance (15)

רֶמֶשׂ creeping thing, animal that creeps upon the earth (17); 10x in Gen

רַעַשׁ earthquake, clatter, commotion (17)

רֶשַׁע evil, wickedness, offense, injustice, wrong (30)

רֶשֶׁת net, trap (22)

שֶׂכֶל insight, understanding, success; also spelled שֵׂכֶל (16)

שֵׁבֶט rod, staff, scepter, tribe (190); שִׁבְטֵי יִשְׂרָאֵל "the tribes of Israel"

שֶׁבֶר break, fracture, collapse (44)

שֹׁהַם precious stone, carnelian (11)

שֹׁחַד bribe, gift (23)

שַׁחַק layer of dust, cloud of dust, cloud (21)

שַׁחַר dawn, daybreak (23)

שַׁחַת pit, grave (23)

שֶׁלֶג snow (20)

שֶׁלֶם peace offering (87)

שֶׁמֶן oil, fat (193)

שֵׁמַע report, news, rumor (17)

שֶׁמֶשׁ (cs) sun (134)

שַׁעַר gate (373)

שֶׁפֶט act of judgment, punishment (16)

שֶׁקֶל shekel, measurement of weight (88)

שֶׁקֶץ detestable thing, abomination (11)

שֶׁקֶר lie, deception, falsehood (113)

שֶׁרֶץ swarming things (15); 12x in Lev

שֹׁרֶשׁ root; (mp with 3ms suff) שָׁרָשָׁיו (33)

תֹּאַר form, shape, appearance (15)

תֶּבֶן straw, chaff (17)

תַּחַשׁ porpoise, dolphin, leather (14)

תַּעַר razor, knife, sheath (13)

Adjectives
Listed Alphabetically

In the Hebrew Old Testament, there are approximately 500 adjectives with a total occurrence of some 17,000 times. Excluding demonstrative adjectives and most numerals, there are 116 adjectives that occur more than 10 times.

אֶבְיוֹן poor, needy (61)

אַבִּיר mighty, strong, powerful (17)

אַדִּיר noble, majestic, mighty (27)

אַחֵר other, another; (fs) אַחֶרֶת (166)

אַחֲרוֹן last, behind, west (51)

אֵיתָן everflowing, constant, enduring; (mp) אֵתָנִים (14)

אָרֵךְ long, slow (15); 13x אֶרֶךְ־אַפַּיִם (lit) "long of nose;" (idiom) slow to anger or patient

בָּחִיר chosen, elect (13)

בְּלִיַּעַל useless, worthless; (n) worthlessness (27)

בָּצוּר fortified, inaccessible (26)

בָּרִיא fat, well fed (14)

גָּבֹהַּ high, exalted; (fs) גְּבֹהָה (41)

גִּבּוֹר mighty, valiant, heroic; (n) hero (160)

גָּדוֹל great, big, large (527)

דַּל poor, weak, needy (48)

דַּק thin, lean, skinny; (fp) דַּקּוֹת (14)

הָרָה (fs) pregnant (15)

זֵד proud, insolent, presumptuous (13)

זַךְ pure, clean (11)

זָקֵן old; (n) elder, old man (180)

זָר foreign, strange (70)

חָדָשׁ new, fresh (53)

חָזָק strong, mighty, hard (57)

חַטָּא sinful; (n) sinner (19)

חַי living, alive; (mp) חַיִּים (254)

חִיצוֹן outer, external (25)

חָכָם wise, skillful, experienced (138)

Adjectives

חָלָל   pierced, slain, defiled (94)

חָלָק   smooth, slippery, flattering (10)

חַנּוּן   gracious, merciful (13)

חָנֵף   godless, profane (13)

חָסִיד   godly, faithful, pious (34)

חָסֵר   lacking, wanting; (ms cstr) חֲסַר (17)

חָפֵץ   delighting (in), desiring (13); cf חָפֵץ (#471)

חָפְשִׁי   free, exempt (17)

חָרֵב   dry, desolate, wasted (10)

טָהוֹר   clean, pure (96)

טוֹב   good, pleasant (530)

טָמֵא   unclean (88)

יָחִיד   only (child), lonely, solitary (12)

יָלִיד   born (of); (n) son, slave (13)

יְמָנִית   (fs) right, southern; (ms) יְמָנִי (33)

יָפֶה   beautiful; (fs) יָפָה (42)

יָקָר   precious, valuable (36)

יָרֵא   fearful (63)

יָשָׁר   upright, just (119)

כָּבֵד   heavy, severe, important (41)

כַּבִּיר   mighty, strong, powerful (10)

כָּלִיל   entire, whole, complete (15)

כֵּן   honest, correct, right (24)

לָבָן   white (29)

מָלֵא   full, filled (61)

מְעַט   little, few (101)

מַר   bitter; (n) bitterness (38)

מָשִׁיחַ anointed; (n) anointed one, Messiah (38)

מָתוֹק sweet, pleasant (12)

נָאוֶה lovely, beautiful, desirable, suitable (10)

נָבָל foolish, good-for-nothing; (n) fool (18)

נָדִיב noble, willing, generous (26)

נָכְרִי foreign, strange; (fs) נָכְרִיָּה (46)

נָעִים pleasant, lovely, delightful (13)

נָקִי blameless, innocent (43)

עִוֵּר blind; (mp) עִוְרִים (26)

עַז strong, mighty (23)

עָיֵף tired, exhausted, weary (17)

עֵירֹם naked; (n) nakedness (10)

עֶלְיוֹן upper; (divine title) Most High (53)

עָמֹק deep, unfathomable, mysterious; (fs) עֲמֻקָה (17)

עָנָו afflicted, oppressed, humble, meek (25)

עָנִי poor, humble, afflicted (80)

עָצוּם mighty, numerous (31)

עָצֵל low, lazy; (n) sluggard (14); all in Prov

עָקָר barren, childless (12)

עִקֵּשׁ perverted, crooked, false (10)

עָרוּם crafty, cunning, clever, prudent (11)

עָרוֹם naked (16)

עָרִיץ ruthless, fierce, violent (20)

עָרֵל uncircumcised (35)

עָשִׁיר rich, wealthy (23)

פְּנִימִי inner; (fs) פְּנִימִית (32)

פִּסֵּחַ lame, crippled (14)

צַדִּיק righteous, just, innocent (206)

צָעִיר little, small, young (23)

צַר narrow; (n) anxiety, distress (27)

קָדוֹשׁ holy, set apart (117)

קַדְמֹנִי eastern, former, past (10)

קָטֹן small, young, insignificant; (fs) קְטַנָּה (74)

קָטָן small, young, insignificant, unimportant; (mp) קְטַנִּים (27)

קַל light, swift, agile (13)

קָרֵב approaching, drawing near (12)

קָרוֹב near, close (75)

קָשֶׁה difficult, hard, severe; (fs) קָשָׁה (36)

רִאשׁוֹן first, former; (fs) רִאשֹׁנָה ; (mp) רִאשֹׁנִים (182)

רַב great, many; (mp) רַבִּים (419)

רַגְלִי (one who goes) on foot, pedestrian, foot soldier (12)

רָחָב wide, spacious (20)

רַחוּם compassionate (13)

רָחוֹק distant, remote, far away (84)

רֵיק empty, vain (14)

רַךְ tender, frail, weak, soft (16)

רַע bad, evil, wicked, of little worth; also spelled רָע (312)

רָעֵב hungry (20)

רַעֲנָן green, fresh, luxuriant (19)

רָשָׁע wicked, guilty (264)

שָׂבֵעַ satisfied, full (10)

שָׂכִיר (adj) hired worker; (n) day laborer (18)

שָׂמֵחַ joyful, glad, happy (21)

שַׁאֲנָן at ease, secure, untroubled; (fp) שַׁאֲנַנּוֹת (10)

שִׁכּוֹר   drunk; (n) drunkard (13)

שָׁלֵם   whole, complete, safe (28)

שָׁמֵן   fat, rich (10)

שָׁפָל   low, lowly, humble, deep (17)

תַּחְתּוֹן   lower, lowest (13)

תַּחְתִּית   (fs) lower; (fp) תַּחְתִּיּוֹת (19)

תִּיכוֹן   middle, center (11)

תָּם   blameless, complete, perfect; (mp) תַּמִּים (15)

תָּמִים   blameless, perfect, honest, devout (91)

Prepositions
Listed Alphabetically

In the Hebrew Old Testament, there are approximately 50 prepositions with a total occurrence of approximately 57,000 times. There are 31 prepositions that occur more than 10 times.

אַחֲרֵי after, behind; also spelled אַחַר (718)

אֶל־ to, toward, into; (with 3ms suff) אֵלָיו (5,518)

אֵצֶל beside, near (62)

אֵת with, beside; also spelled אֶת־ with loss of accent or (with 3ms suff) אִתוֹ (890)

בְּ in, at, with, by, against (15,559)

בֵּין between (409)

בִּלְעֲדֵי apart from, except for, without (17)

בְּמוֹ in, at, with, by, against; alternate (poetic) form of prep בְּ (10)

בַּעֲבוּר on account of, in order that (49)

בְּעַד behind, through (104)

בְּקֶרֶב in the middle of, among (227)

בְּתוֹךְ in the midst (middle) of, inside (319); combination of בְּ and (n) תָּוֶךְ (middle, center); also מִתּוֹךְ and אֶל־תּוֹךְ

זוּלָה except, only (16)

יַעַן on account of, because; 33x with אֲשֶׁר (#9) as יַעַן אֲשֶׁר (100)

כְּ as, like, according to; (with 2ms suff) כָּמוֹךְ (3,053)

לְ to, toward, for (20,321)

לְמַעַן on account of, for the sake of (272)

לְעֻמַּת beside, alongside, corresponding to; combination of prep לְ and עֻמָּה (32)

לִפְנֵי before, in front of; combination of prep לְ and פָּנִים (2,126)

מוּל in front of, opposite (36)

מִן from, out of; also spelled מִ · (Nun assimilates as Daghesh Forte) when prefixed to another word (7,592)

מֵעַל above, upward, on top of (140)

נֶגֶד opposite, in front of (151)

189

נֹכַח   in front of, opposite (25)

סָבִיב   around, about; (substantive) surroundings (338)

עַד   until, as far as (1,263)

עַל   on, upon, on account of, according to (5,777)

עִם   with, together with; (with 3ms suff) עִמּוֹ (1,048)

עִמָּד   with (45)

תַּחַת   under, below, instead of (510)

All Verbs
Listed Alphabetically

In the Hebrew Old Testament, there are approximately 1,600 verbs with a total occurrence of some 73,000 times. 629 of these verbs occur more than 10 times.

אָבַד (Q) to perish, vanish, be(come) lost, go astray; (Pi) cause to perish, destroy; (Hi) exterminate (185)

אָבָה (Q) to be willing, consent, yield to, want something (54)

אָבַל (Q) to mourn, lament; (Hith) observe mourning rites (36)

אָדַם (Q) to be red; (Pu) be reddened, dyed red (10)

אָהַב (Q) to love (of human and divine love); (Pi ptc) lover (217)

אָוָה (Pi) to wish, desire, want; (Hith) crave, wish for, long for (30)

אוּץ (Q) to urge, press, be in a hurry, pressed (10)

אוֹר (Hi) to give light, shine, illuminate, light up (44)

אָזַן (Hi) to give ear to, listen (to), hear, heed (41)

אָזַר (Q) to gird (on), equip (16)

אָחַז (Q) to seize, grasp, take hold (of), hold fast (63)

אָחַר (Pi) to delay, detain, hesitate, linger (18)

אָכַל (Q) to eat, consume; (Ni) be eaten, consumed; (Hi) feed (820)

אָמַל (Pulal) to dry up, waste away, languish (15)

אָמַן (Ni) to be reliable, faithful, or trustworthy; (Hi) believe (in), trust, have trust in, put trust in (97)

אָמֵץ (Q) to be strong, be bold; (Pi) make firm, strengthen, harden someone's heart (41)

אָמַר (Q) to say; (Ni) be said, called; (Hi) declare, proclaim (5,316)

אָנַח (Ni) to sigh, groan (13)

אָנַף (Q) to be angry (14)

אָסַף (Q) to gather (in), take in, take away, destroy; (Ni) be gathered, taken away, assemble (200)

אָסַר (Q) to tie, bind, fetter, imprison (73)

אָפָה (Q) to bake (25)

אָרַב (Q) to ambush, lie in ambush, lie in wait (41)

אָרַג (Q) to weave; (Q ptc) weaver (13)

אָרַךְ (Hi) to make long, lengthen, extend (34)

אָרַר (Q) to curse (63)

אָרַשׂ (Pi) to betroth, be engaged; (Pu) be(come) betrothed or engaged (11)

אָשַׁם (Q) to be(come) guilty, commit an offense (35)

אָשַׁר (Pi) to call or consider blessed, fortunate, or happy; (Pu) be called blessed, fortunate, or happy (10)

אָתָה (Q) to come; (Hi) bring (21)

בָּאַשׁ (Q) to stink, have a bad smell; (Hi) make odious, become hated (18)

בָּגַד (Q) to act or deal treacherously, faithlessly, or deceitfully with (49)

בָּדַל (Ni) to separate oneself, withdraw; (Hi) divide, separate, set apart, make a distinction (between), single out (42)

בָּהַל (Ni) to be terrified, horrified, dismayed, disturbed, hasty, make haste; (Pi) terrify, make haste, act hastily (39)

בּוֹא (Q) to go in, enter, come to, come upon; (Hi) bring (in), come (in); (Hoph) be brought (2,592)

בּוּז (Q) to show contempt (for), despise (14)

בּוּס (Q) to tread down, trample under foot (12)

בּוֹשׁ (Q) to be ashamed; (Hi) put to shame (125)

בָּזָה (Q) to despise, regard with contempt (42)

בָּזַז (Q) to plunder, spoil (43)

בָּחַן (Q) to test, put to the test, try, examine (29)

בָּחַר (Q) to choose, test, examine (172)

בָּטַח (Q) to trust, rely upon (118)

בִּין (Q) to understand, perceive, consider, give heed to; (Ni) be discerning, have understanding; (Hi) understand, teach; (Hith) show oneself perceptive (171)

בָּכָה (Q) to weep (in grief or joy), weep (for) (114)

בָּלָה (Q) to be(come) worn out, used up, or exhausted (16)

בָּלַל (Q) to mix (up), confuse or confound (languages), mingle (44)

בָּלַע (Q, Pi) to swallow (up), engulf (42)

בָּנָה (Q) to build (up), rebuild, build (establish) a family; (Ni) be built, have a child (by or from) (377)

בָּעַל (Q) to rule over, be(come) lord or husband of, marry, own (take someone into possession as betrothed) (16)

בָּעַר (Q) to burn (up), consume; (Pi) kindle, burn (60)

בָּעַר (Pi) to graze, sweep away, remove, get rid of, purge (27)

בָּעַת (Pi) to terrify, frighten, startle (16)

בָּצַע (Q) to cut off, sever, break off (away), make profit (16)

בָּקַע (Q) to cleave, split, breach, break open; (Ni) be cleft, split (open); (Pi) split, rip open (51)

בָּקַשׁ (Pi) to seek, search for, look for, discover, demand, require; (Pu) be sought (225)

בָּרָא (Q) to create (only with God as subject); (Ni) be created (48)

בָּרַח (Q) to run away, flee, go or pass through (63)

בָּרַךְ (Q Pass ptc) blessed, praised, adored; (Pi) bless, praise (327)

בָּרַר (Q) to purify, purge, sort, choose, select (16)

בָּשַׂר (Pi) to bring good news, tell, announce (24)

בָּשַׁל (Q) to boil; (Pi) boil, cook, roast (28)

גָּאַל (Q) to redeem, act as kinsman (perform the responsibilities of the next-of-kin), avenge (104)

גָּאַל (Ni, Pu) to be defiled, become impure; (Hith) defile oneself (11)

גָּבַה (Q) to be high, tall, lofty, exalted, or haughty; (Hi) make high, exalt (34)

גָּבַר (Q) to be strong, mighty, superior, excel, achieve, accomplish, prevail (25)

גָּדַל (Q) to grow up, be(come) great, strong, wealthy, important; (Pi) bring up (children), make great, extol; (Hi) make great, magnify, do great things (117)

גָּדַע (Q) to cut off, cut down; (Ni) be cut off, cut down, cut into pieces; (Pi) cut down, cut to pieces (22)

גָּדַר (Q) to build a wall, block a road (10)

גָּוַע (Q) to die, expire, pass away, perish (24)

גּוּר (Q) to sojourn, dwell (stay) as a foreigner or alien (82)

גּוּר (Q) to be afraid, dread, stand in awe (10)

גָּזַז (Q) to shear, cut (15)

גָּזַל (Q) to tear off, tear away, seize, rob, take away by force (30)

גָּזַר (Q) to cut (in two, in pieces), divide, cut down, decide; (Ni) be cut off (from), decided (12)

גִּיל (Q) to shout with joy, rejoice (47)

גָּלָה (Q) to uncover, reveal, disclose; (Ni) uncover, reveal oneself, be revealed, exposed; (Pi) uncover, reveal, disclose; (Hi) take (carry away) into exile (187)

גָּלַח (Pi) to shave (23)

גָּלַל (Q) to roll (away) (18)

גָּמַל (Q) to complete, finish, wean, ripen, render; recompense, requite (37)

גָּנַב (Q) to steal, deceive (40)

גָּעַל (Q) to loathe, abhor, feel disgust (10)

גָּעַר (Q) to rebuke, reproach (14)

גָּעַשׁ (Q) to shake (10)

גָּרָה (Hith) to strive (against), oppose, battle (15)

גָּרַע (Q) to shave, trim (a beard), diminish, restrain, withdraw (21)

גָּרַשׁ (Q) to drive out, banish; (Pi) drive out (away) (45)

דָּבַק (Q) to cling, cleave to, stick to; (Hi) cause to cling, cleave or stick to, pursue closely (55)

דָּבַר (Q) to speak (rare in Q); (Pi) speak (1,136)

דּוּשׁ (Q) to tread on, trample down (out), thresh, exterminate, destroy; also spelled דִּישׁ (16)

דִּין (Q) to judge, minister or execute judgment, plead one's cause, contend with (24)

דָּכָא (Pi) to crush, beat to pieces (18)

דָּמָה (Q) to be like, resemble; (Pi) liken, compare (30)

דָּמָה (Ni) to be destroyed, ruined (12); cf דָּמָה (#965)

דָּמַם (Q) to be silent, still, motionless, (struck) dumb, keep quiet, stand still (19)

דָּקַק (Q) to crush, become fine through grinding; (Hi) crush fine, pulverize; (Hoph) be crushed fine (12)

דָּקַר (Q) to pierce (through), run through; (Pu) be pierced through (11)

דָּרַךְ (Q) to tread (often in the sense of pressing for wine or oil), march, draw a bow; (Hi) cause to tread, march or walk (63)

דָּרַשׁ (Q) to seek, inquire (of or about), investigate, require, demand (165)

דָּשֵׁן (Pi) to refresh, revive, clean away fat ashes; (Pu) be made fat (11)

הָגָה (Q) to utter a sound, growl, moan, groan, coo (of a dove), speak, proclaim (25)

הָדַף (Q) to thrust (away, out), push (away), drive away (out), shove (11)

הָיָה (Q) to be, become, happen, occur; (Ni) be done, brought about, come to pass, occur (3,576)

הָלַךְ (Q) to go, walk, (metaphorically) behave; (Pi) go, walk; (Hith) walk about, move to and fro (1,554)

הָלַל (Pi) to praise, sing hallelujah; (Pu) be praised, praiseworthy; (Hith) boast (146); cf הָלַל (#1501)

הָלַל (Q) to be infatuated, deluded; (Hithpolel) be mad, act like a madman (15); cf הָלַל (#282)

הָמָה (Q) to make (a) noise, make a sound, roar, growl, moan, groan, be boisterous (34)

הָמַם (Q) to make (a) noise, confuse, bring into motion and confusion (army), discomfit, disturb (13)

הָפַךְ (Q) to turn, overturn, overthrow, destroy; (Ni) be destroyed, turned into, changed (95)

הָרַג (Q) to kill, slay (167)

הָרָה (Q) to conceive, be(come) pregnant (43)

הָרַס (Q) to tear down, demolish, destroy, throw down, overthrow, break through; (Ni) be ruined (43)

זָבַח (Q) to slaughter (for sacrifice), sacrifice; (Pi) offer sacrifice, sacrifice (134)

זָהַר (Hi) to warn (about), admonish, caution (22)

זוּב (Q) to flow (away), suffer a discharge (42)

זִיד (Q) to act insolently; (Hi) boil or cook, become hot (with anger), behave arrogantly (10)

זָכַר (Q) to remember; (Ni) be remembered, thought of; (Hi) remind (235)

זָמַם (Q) to consider, think, ponder, devise, plan (evil), purpose (13)

זָמַר (Pi) to sing, praise, make music, play an instrument (45)

זָנָה (Q) to commit fornication, be a harlot (prostitute), be unfaithful (60)

זָנַח (Q) to reject, spurn (19)

זָעַם (Q) to curse, scold, denounce (12)

זָעַק (Q) to cry (out), call for help, summon (73)

זָקֵן (Q) to be(come) old, grow old (26)

זָרָה (Q) to scatter; (Pi) scatter, disperse, spread (38)

זָרַח (Q) to rise (sun), shine, come out, appear, break out (leprosy) (18)

זָרַע (Q) to sow, scatter seed (56)

זָרַק (Q) to toss, throw, scatter, sprinkle (34)

חָבָא (Ni) to hide (oneself), be hidden; (Hith) keep oneself hidden (34)

חָבַל (Q) to take, hold or seize (something) in pledge, exact a pledge from someone, bind by taking a pledge (13)

חָבַל (Q) to act corruptly or ruinously; (Pi) ruin, destroy (11)

חָבַק (Q) to embrace, fold the hands (in idleness); (Pi) embrace (13)

חָבַר (Q) to unite, ally oneself (with), join forces (28)

חָבַשׁ (Q) to saddle, bind or buckle on, bind up (wound), wrap, twist (rope), imprison (33)

חָגַג (Q) to stagger, reel, celebrate a pilgrimage festival (16)

חָגַר (Q) to gird, gird (oneself or someone), get ready (44)

חָדַל (Q) to cease, end, stop, refrain (from) (55)

חָדַשׁ (Pi) to make new, renew, restore (10)

חָוָה (Hishtaphel) to bow down, worship (173)

חוּל (Q) to go around, whirl (about), dance, writhe; also spelled חִיל (10)

חוּס (Q) to pity, look upon with compassion, spare (24)

חוּשׁ (Q) to hurry, make haste (18)

חָזָה (Q) to see, behold, perceive (55)

חָזַק (Q) to be(come) strong, have courage; (Pi) make strong, strengthen; (Hi) strengthen, seize, grasp, take hold of; (Hith) strengthen oneself, show oneself as strong or courageous (290)

חָטָא (Q) to miss (a goal or mark), sin, commit a sin; (Pi) make a sin offering; (Hi) cause to sin (240)

חָיָה (Q) to live, be alive, revive, restore to life; (Pi) preserve alive, let live, give life; (Hi) preserve, keep alive, revive, restore to life (283)

חִיל (Q) to writhe, travail, be in labor, tremble; also spelled חוּל (48)

חָכָה (Pi) to wait (for), tarry, long for, be patient (14)

חָכַם (Q) to be(come) wise, act wisely (28)

חָלָה (Q) to be(come) weak, tired, sick; (Ni) be exhausted; (Pi) appease, flatter (75)

חָלַל (Ni) to be defiled, profaned, defile oneself; (Pi) profane, pollute, defile; (Hi) let something be profaned (135)

חָלַם (Q) to dream (29)

חָלַף (Q) to pass on or away (quickly), pass by, vanish; (Hi) change, replace, substitute (26)

חָלַץ (Q) to draw out, take off, withdraw, be girded (ready for battle); (Pi) rescue, deliver (44)

חָלַק (Q) to divide, share (with or in), apportion, distribute; (Pi) divide (in pieces), apportion, scatter (55)

חָמַד (Q) to desire, take pleasure (delight) in, crave, covet (21)

חָמַל (Q) to have compassion (for), have pity (for), spare (41)

חָמַם (Q) to be(come) warm (23)

חָנָה (Q) to decline, camp, encamp, pitch camp, lay siege to (143)

חָנַן (Q) to be gracious to, show favor to, favor; (Hith) plead for grace, favor or compassion (77)

חָנֵף (Q) to be godless (of a priest or prophet), defiled (of land); (Hi) defile, pollute (11)

חָסָה (Q) to seek or take refuge (37)

חָסֵר (Q) to diminish, decrease, lack (22)

חָפָה (Q) to cover; (Pi) overlay (with) (12)

חָפַז (Q) to be in a hurry, hurry away (in alarm or fear), hasten in alarm; (Ni) run away in alarm (10)

חָפֵץ (Q) to delight in, take pleasure in, desire, be willing (74)

חָפַר (Q) to dig, track, search (for), scout out, spy out (23)

חָפֵר (Q) to be ashamed (17)

חָפַשׂ (Q) to search (out), examine; (Pi) search thoroughly, track down; (Hith) disguise oneself (23)

חָצַב (Q) to quarry, hew (out), dig, dress (stones) (16)

חָצָה (Q) to divide (into) (15)

חָקַק (Q) to hew out or carve out (a grave), inscribe, engrave, enact, decree (19)

חָקַר (Q) to explore, search, spy out (27)

חָרֵב (Q) to dry up (intransitive), lie in ruins; (Hi) cause to dry up, lay waste, make desolate (36)

חָרַד (Q) to tremble, do something with trembling, shudder, quake; (Hi) startle (39)

חָרָה (Q) to be(come) hot, burn with anger, become angry (93)

חָרַם (Hi) to devote to the ban, dedicate to destruction, exterminate (50)

חָרַף (Q) to taunt, reproach; (Pi) taunt, reproach, revile (38)

חָרַץ (Q) to decide, cut (10)

חָרַשׁ (Q) to be silent, deaf; (Hi) be(come) silent, deaf, keep still (47); cf חָרַשׁ (#1032)

חָרַשׁ (Q) to plow, engrave, devise, plan (27)

חָשַׂךְ (Q) to withhold, keep back, refrain, spare, save, restrain (28)

חָשַׂף (Q) to strip, strip off, bare, skim or scoop off (10)

חָשַׁב (Q) to think, consider, devise, plan, value, reckon; (Ni) be reckoned, accounted, considered (as); (Pi) think, consider, devise, plan (124)

חָשָׁה (Q) to be silent; (Hi) be silent, order (someone) to be silent, hesitate, delay (16)

חָשַׁךְ (Q) to be(come) dark, grow dim (eyes) (17)

חָשַׁק (Q) to be attached to, cling to, love (11)

חָתַם (Q) to seal (up), affix a seal (27)

חָתַן (Hith) to intermarry with, become related by marriage, become a son-in-law (11)

חָתַת (Q) to be shattered, dismayed, filled with terror (55)

טָבַח (Q) to slaughter, butcher, slay (11)

טָבַל (Q) to dip (something into) (16)

טָבַע (Q) to sink, penetrate; (Hoph) be sunk, settled, or planted (10)

טָהֵר (Q) to be clean (ceremonially), pure (morally); (Pi) cleanse, purify, pronounce clean; (Hith) purify or cleanse oneself (94)

טוֹב (Q) to be good, pleasing, pleasant, joyful, well with (44); cf טוֹב (#92) and יָטַב (#343)

טוּחַ (Q) to plaster (wall of a house), coat, overlay (11)

טוּל (Hi) to throw (far), cast, hurl; (Hoph) be thrown, hurled (14)

טָמֵא (Q) to be(come) unclean; (Ni) defile oneself; (Pi) defile, pronounce or declare unclean; (Hith) defile oneself, become unclean (162)

טָמַן (Q) to hide (31)

טָעַם (Q) to taste, eat, savor food (11)

טָרַף (Q) to tear (in pieces), rend (25)

יָאַל (Hi) to be intent on something, be determined, show willingness or undertake to do something (18)

יָבַל (Hi) to bring (as gift or tribute), lead; (Hoph) be brought, led (18)

יָבֵשׁ (Q) to dry up, be(come) dry, wither; (Hi) make dry (up), make wither (59)

יָגַע (Q) to toil, labor, struggle, grow or be weary (26)

יָדָה (Hi) to thank, praise, confess; (Hith) confess (111)

יָדַע (Q) to know, know sexually (have intercourse with); (Ni) be(come) known, reveal oneself; (Hi) make known, inform (956)

יָהַב (Q) to give, come (33)

201

יָחַל   (Pi, Hi) to wait (for), hope for (42)

יָחַשׁ   (Hith) to be registered or enrolled in a genealogical list; (Hith inf as noun) genealogy, registration (20)

יָטַב   (Q) to be well with, go well with, be pleasing (to); (Hi) make things go well for, do good to, deal well with, treat kindly (117)

יָכַח   (Hi) to reprove, rebuke, reproach, chasten, punish, decide, mediate, arbitrate (59)

יָכֹל   (Q) to be able, capable of, endure, prevail (193)

יָלַד   (Q) to bear (children), give birth, bring forth, beget; (Ni) be born; (Pi) help at birth, serve as midwife; (Pu) be born; (Hi) become the father of, beget (499)

יָלַל   (Hi) to howl, lament, wail (31)

יָנָה   (Q, Hi) to oppress, mistreat (19)

יָנַק   (Q) to suck; (Hi) suckle, nurse (33)

יָסַד   (Q) to found, establish, appoint, destine, allocate; (Pi) found, appoint, establish (41)

יָסַף   (Q) to add, continue (to do something again); (Hi) add, increase, do again and again (213)

יָסַר   (Pi) to teach, discipline, correct, chastise, rebuke (41)

יָעַד   (Q) to designate, appoint; (Ni) meet, gather or assemble by appointment (29)

יָעַל   (Hi) to profit, gain profit, benefit (23)

יָעַץ   (Q) to advise, counsel, plan, decide; (Ni) consult (take counsel) together (80)

יָצָא   (Q) to go or come out; (Hi) cause to go or come out, lead out, bring out (1,076)

יָצַב   (Hith) to take one's stand, stand firm, station oneself, present oneself before (48)

יָצַג   (Hi) to set, place, establish, take one's stand (17)

יָצַק   (Q) to pour, pour out (liquid), cast (metal), flow (into); (Hoph) be cast, poured out, emptied out (53)

יָצַר   (Q) to form, fashion, shape, create (63)

יָצַת (Q) to kindle, burn; (Hi) set on fire, set fire to (27)

יָקַץ (Q) to awake, wake up, become active (11)

יָקַר (Q) to be difficult, precious, prized, highly valued, esteemed, honored, costly or rare (11)

יָרֵא (Q) to fear, be afraid, be in awe of, reverence; (Ni) be feared, held in honor (317); cf יָרֵא (#539)

יָרַד (Q) to go down, descend; (Hi) bring down, lead down (382)

יָרָה (Hi) to instruct, teach (47)

יָרָה (Q, Hi) to throw, shoot, cast (lots) (28); cf יָרָה (#675)

יָרַשׁ (Q) to inherit, take possession of, dispossess, impoverish; (Hi) cause to possess or inherit, dispossess (232)

יָשַׁב (Q) to sit (down), dwell, inhabit; (Hi) cause to sit or dwell, settle (a city) (1,088)

יָשֵׁן (Q) to sleep, go to sleep, be asleep (16)

יָשַׁע (Ni) to be delivered, victorious, receive help; (Hi) help, save, deliver, rescue, come to the aid of (205)

יָשַׁר (Q) to be straight, upright or right, please (27)

יָתַר (Ni) to be left over, remain; (Hi) have (something) left over or remaining (106)

כָּבֵד (Q) to be heavy, weighty, honored; (Ni) be honored; (Pi) honor; (Hi) make heavy, dull or insensitive, harden (heart) (114); cf כָּבֵד (#773, #1563)

כָּבָה (Q) to go out, be quenched, extinguished; (Pi) put out, quench, extinguish (24)

כָּבַס (Pi) to clean, cleanse, wash away guilt (51)

כָּבַשׁ (Q) to subdue, subjugate, make subservient, bring into bondage, violate (rape) a woman; (Ni) be subdued, be subjugated (15)

כָּהַן (Pi) to perform the duties of a priest, minister as a priest (23)

כּוּל (Q) to comprehend; (Pilpel) contain, sustain, provide, support; (Hi) contain, hold (in), sustain, endure (38)

כּוּן (Ni) to be established, steadfast, ready, arranged, stand firm; (Hi) establish, set up, prepare, make ready, make firm; (Polel) set up, establish (219)

כָּזַב (Pi) to lie, deceive (16)

כָּחַד (Ni) to be hidden, effaced; (Pi) hide, conceal (32)

כָּחַשׁ (Pi) to deny, delude, deceive, lie, act deceptively, feign submission or obedience (22)

כָּלָא (Q) to shut up, restrain, withhold, keep back (17)

כָּלָה (Q) to be complete, finished, at an end, accomplished, spent, exhausted, come to an end; (Pi) complete, finish, bring to an end (207); cf כָּלָה (#1184)

כָּלַם (Ni) to be hurt, humiliated, ashamed, disgraced; (Hi) put to shame, humiliate, disgrace (38)

כָּנַס (Q) to gather, collect, amass; (Pi) gather, assemble (11)

כָּנַע (Ni) to be subdued, humbled, humble oneself; (Hi) humble or subdue someone (36)

כָּסָה (Q) to cover, conceal, hide; (Pi) cover (up), conceal, clothe (153)

כָּעַס (Q) to be angry, vexed; (Hi) vex, provoke, provoke (God) to anger (55)

כָּפַר (Pi) to cover (over), atone (for), make atonement (102)

כָּרָה (Q) to dig, excavate, hollow out (14)

כָּרַע (Q) to bow (down), kneel (down), fall to one's knees (36)

כָּרַת (Q) to cut, cut off, cut down; (idiom) to make a covenant (with בְּרִית); (Ni) be cut off (down); (Hi) cut off, destroy, exterminate (289)

כָּשַׁל (Q) to stumble, totter, stagger; (Ni) be caused to stumble, stumble (65)

כָּתַב (Q) to write (upon), register, record; (Ni) be written (225)

כָּתַת (Q) to beat, crush fine, hammer (into pieces); (Pi) beat, hammer, crush to pieces (17)

לָאָה (Q) to be(come) tired or weary; (Ni) tire (oneself) out, be tired of something; (Hi) make weary (19)

לָבַשׁ (Q) to put on a garment, clothe, be clothed; (Hi) clothe (112)

לָהַט (Q) to blaze, burn; (Pi) set ablaze, devour (with fire), scorch (10)

לָוָה (Q) to borrow; (Hi) lend to (14)

לָוָה (Ni) to join oneself to (12)

לוּן (Ni, Hi) to murmur (against), grumble (17)

לָחַם (Q, Ni) to fight, do battle with (rare in Q) (171)

לָחַץ (Q) to squeeze, crowd, press, oppress, torment (19)

לִין (Q) to remain overnight, spend the night (71)

לִיץ (Q) to boast (28)

לָכַד (Q) to take, capture, catch, seize; (Ni) be caught, captured (121)

לָמַד (Q) to learn; (Pi) teach (87)

לָעַג (Q, Hi) to mock, ridicule, deride (18)

לָקַח (Q) to take, grasp, capture, seize; (Ni) be captured, taken away (967)

לָקַט (Q) to gather (together), glean; (Pi) gather (up), collect (37)

מָאֵן (Pi) to refuse (41)

מָאַס (Q) to refuse, reject, despise (74)

מָדַד (Q) to measure, measure off (distance or expanse), measure out (grain) (52)

מָהַר (Pi) to hasten, hurry, go or come quickly (81)

מוּג (Q) to waver, melt; (Ni) wave, sway back and forth, undulate (17)

מוֹט (Q) to totter, shake, sway, stagger; (Ni) be made to stagger, stumble, or totter (39)

מוּל (Q) to circumcise; (Ni) be circumcised (32)

מוּר (Hi) to change, alter, exchange (14)

מוּשׁ (Q) to withdraw (from a place), cease from, leave off, depart (21)

מוּת (Q) to die; (Hi) kill, put to death; (Hoph) be killed (845)

מָחָה (Q) to wipe (out), destroy, annihilate (34)

מָחַץ (Q) to smash, shatter, beat to pieces, smite (14)

מָטַר (Hi) to cause rain to fall, send rain (17)

מָכַר (Q) to sell, hand over; (Ni) be sold, sell oneself (into slavery) (80)

מָלֵא (Q) to be full, fill (up); (Ni) be filled (with); (Pi) fill, perform, carry out, consecrate as priest (252)

מָלַט (Ni) to escape, flee to safety, slip away; (Pi) let someone escape, save someone, leave undisturbed (94)

מָלַךְ (Q) to be(come) king or queen, reign, rule; (Hi) make someone king or queen, install someone as king or queen (350)

מָנָה (Q) to count, number, reckon, assign, appoint (28)

מָנַע (Q) to withhold, hold back, retain, refuse, restrain (29)

מָסַס (Ni) to melt (away), dissolve, become weak (21)

מָעַט (Q) to be(come) few or too small; (Hi) make small or few, diminish, reduce, collect or gather little (22)

מָעַל (Q) to be unfaithful, act unfaithfully or treacherously (36)

מָצָא (Q) to find (out), reach, obtain, achieve; (Ni) be found (457)

מָקַק (Ni) to rot (away), fester (wounds), dwindle or waste away, decay, melt, dissolve (10)

מָרַד (Q) to rebel, revolt (25)

מָרָה (Q) to be rebellious, obstinate or contentious; (Hi) behave rebelliously or obstinately (44)

מָרַט (Q) to make smooth, bare, bald, polish, scour, pull out (hair), sharpen (sword); (Pu) be polished, smooth, bare (14)

מָרַר (Q) to be bitter (of taste, experience or attitude), desperate; (Hi) embitter, cause bitterness or grief (16)

מָשַׁח (Q) to smear (with a liquid, oil or dye), anoint (with oil) (70)

מָשַׁךְ (Q) to draw (out), pull, drag, prolong, stretch (36)

מָשַׁל (Q) to rule, reign, govern, have dominion (81)

מָשַׁל (Q) to use a proverb, to speak in parables or poetry; (Ni) be(come) like, similar or the same as (17)

מָשַׁשׁ (Q) to feel, touch; (Pi) feel (over, through), grope, search, rummage through (10)

נָאַף (Q) to commit adultery; (metaphorically) commit idolatry; (Pi) commit adultery (31)

נָאַץ (Q) to spurn, despise; (Pi) treat disrespectfully or with irreverence (24)

נָבָא (Ni) to prophesy, be in a state of prophetic ecstasy; (Hith) speak or behave as a prophet (115)

נָבַט (Hi) to look (at or out), gaze, behold (70)

נָבֵל (Q) to fade, wither, decay, crumble away, wear out (20)

נָבַע (Hi) to make (something) gush or bubble (forth), pour out or ferment (11)

נָגַד (Hi) to tell, announce, report, declare, inform; (Hoph) be told, announced, reported (371)

נָגַח (Q) to gore (ox as subject); (Pi) push, butt, thrust, knock down (11)

נָגַן (Pi) to play a stringed instrument (15)

נָגַע (Q) to touch, strike, reach; (Hi) touch, reach, throw, arrive (150)

נָגַף (Q) to smite, strike, injure; (Ni) be smitten, struck (with) (49)

נָגַר (Ni) to flow, gush forth, be poured (out), spilled, stretched out (hands); (Hi) pour (out, down) (10)

נָגַשׂ (Q) to oppress, force to work, be a slave driver or taskmaster, exact (contributions), collect (offerings) (23)

נָגַשׁ (Q) to draw near, approach; (Ni) draw near; (Hi) bring (near), offer (a sacrifice) (125)

נָדַב (Q) to incite, instigate; (Hith) volunteer, make a voluntary decision, offer voluntarily, give a freewill offering (17)

נָדַד (Q) to flee, wander (about), depart, move, flutter (wings) (28)

נָדַח (Ni) to be scattered, banished, driven away, thrust out; (Hi) scatter, drive away, disperse, thrust out (51)

נָדַר (Q) to make (perform) a vow, keep (make) a promise (31)

נָהַג (Q) to drive (flocks or herds), lead, guide; (Pi) lead or drive away (30)

נָהַל (Pi) to lead, guide, escort, provide (with food) (10)

נוּד (Q) to move to and fro, sway, wander, be(come) aimless, express grief or sympathy (by shaking the head) (25)

נוּחַ (Q) to rest, settle down, repose; (Hi) cause to rest, secure rest, set, leave (behind or untouched) (140)

נוּס (Q) to flee, escape (160)

נוּעַ (Q) to tremble, shake, totter, wave (of trees); (Hi) make unstable or unsteady, shake (up), disturb (42)

נוּף (Hi) to move back and forth, wave, brandish, wield (34)

נָזָה (Q) to spatter (blood); (Hi) sprinkle (24)

נָזַל (Q) to trickle, drip down, flow (16)

נָזַר (Ni) to devote, dedicate or consecrate oneself to (a deity), treat with awe, deal respectfully with; (Hi) restrain from, abstain from, live as a Nazirite (10)

נָחָה (Q) to lead; (Hi) lead, guide, conduct (39)

נָחַל (Q) to take (as a) possession, obtain (receive) property, give as an inheritance; (Hi) give as an inheritance (59)

נָחַם (Ni) to be sorry, regret, have compassion (on or for); (Pi) comfort, console (108)

נָחַשׁ (Pi) to practice divination, seek and give omens, observe signs, foretell, predict (11)

נָטָה (Q) to spread out, stretch out, extend, pitch (a tent), turn, bend; (Hi) turn, incline, stretch out, spread out (216)

נָטַע (Q) to plant (59)

נָטַף (Q) to drop, drip, secrete; (Hi) cause to drip, cause to flow (metaphorically, of prophetic speech) (18)

נָטַשׁ (Q) to leave, forsake, abandon, give up (something); (Ni) be forsaken (40)

נָכָה (Hi) to strike, smite, beat, strike dead, destroy; (Hoph) be struck down dead, beaten (501)

נָכַר (Hi) to recognize, know, investigate, be acquainted with, acknowledge (50)

נָסָה (Pi) to test, put someone to the test, tempt (36)

נָסַךְ (Q) to pour out, pour (cast) a metal image or statue; (Hi) pour out libations, offer a drink offering (25)

נָסַע (Q) to pull (out or up), set out, start out, depart, journey (146)

נָעַר (Q, Pi) to shake (out or off); (Ni) be shaken (out or off) (11)

נָפַח (Q) to breathe, blow, blow fire upon, set aflame, gasp, pant (12)

נָפַל (Q) to fall, fall upon; (Hi) cause to fall, bring to ruin (435)

נָפַץ (Q) to shatter, smash to pieces; (Pi) smash (19)

נָצַב (Ni) to stand (firm), take one's stand, station oneself, be positioned; (Hi) station, set (up), place, establish (74)

נָצַח (Pi) to supervise, oversee or inspect works and activities related to the temple; מְנַצֵּחַ (ptc) used as title (superscription) in 55 psalms (65)

נָצַל (Ni) to be rescued, delivered, saved; (Hi) tear from, take away, deliver from (213)

נָצַר (Q) to keep watch, watch over, guard, protect, preserve (63)

נָקַב (Q) to pierce, bore (through), stipulate, specify, designate, curse, slander (19)

נָקָה (Ni) to be free (of), without guilt, innocent, exempt from (punishment); (Pi) leave unpunished, regard as innocent (44)

נָקַם (Q) to avenge, take vengeance (on), take revenge; (Ni) avenge oneself, take revenge (35)

נָקַף (Hi) to surround, go around, encircle, encompass, enclose (17)

נָשָׂא (Q) to lift, carry, raise, bear (load or burden), take (away); (Ni) be carried, lifted up, exalted; (Pi) lift up, exalt; (Hith) lift oneself up, exalt oneself (659)

נָשַׂג (Hi) to reach, overtake (50)

נָשָׁא (Hi) to deceive, cheat, trick (14)

נָשָׁה (Q) to forget (18)

נָשַׁךְ (Q, Pi) to bite (11)

נָשַׁק (Q) to kiss (32)

נָתַךְ (Q) to gush forth, pour out; (Ni) gush forth, be poured (out or forth) (21)

נָתַן (Q) to give, put, place, set; (Ni) be given (2,014)

נָתַץ (Q) to tear down, pull down, break down, demolish (42)

נָתַק (Q) to pull off, tear away; (Ni) be drawn out or away, torn apart; (Pi) tear apart, tear to pieces (27)

נָתַשׁ (Q) to uproot, pull out, extract, pull up, remove, drive out (nations) (21)

סָבַב (Q) to turn (about), go around, surround; (Ni) turn; (Hi) cause to go around, lead around; (Polel) encompass with protection (163)

סָגַר (Q) to shut (in), close; (Hi) deliver (up), hand over, surrender, give up (91)

סוּג (Q) to backslide, be disloyal; (Ni) turn back, withdraw, become disloyal (24)

סוּךְ (Q) to grease (oneself) with oil, anoint (10)

סוּר (Q) to turn (aside), turn off, leave (off), desist; (Hi) remove, take away, get rid of (298)

סוּת (Hi) to incite (against), stir up, provoke, instigate, seduce, mislead, lead astray (18)

סָחַר (Q) to pass through (of shepherds), travel about (conducting business); (Q ptc) trader, merchant (21)

סָכַךְ (Q) to overshadow, cover (protectively), protect (16)

סָכַן (Q) to be of use or service; (Hi) be accustomed to, familiar (acquainted) with, in the habit of (13)

סָלַח (Q) to pardon, forgive; (Ni) be forgiven (47)

סָלַל (Q) to pile up, heap up, lift up, exalt, praise (12)

סָמַךְ (Q) to support, uphold, sustain, help, lean or lay (hand upon); (Ni) lean (on or against), support oneself (48)

סָעַד (Q) to support, sustain, strengthen (with food), uphold (12)

סָפַד (Q) to lament, wail, bewail, mourn for someone (30)

סָפָה (Q) to take, sweep, snatch or carry away; (Ni) be carried, swept or snatched away (19)

סָפַר (Q) to count; (Pi) count, recount, make known, proclaim, report, tell (107)

סָקַל (Q) to stone, put to death by stoning; (Ni) be stoned (to death) (22)

סָרַר (Q) to be stubborn or rebellious (17)

סָתַם (Q) to plug or stop up, shut up, close, hide, keep secret, disguise (13)

סָתַר (Ni) to be hidden, hide oneself; (Hi) hide (82)

עָבַד (Q) to work, serve, toil (289)

עָבַר (Q) to pass over, pass through, pass by, cross; (Hi) cause to pass over, bring over, cause or allow to pass (through), cause to pass through fire, sacrifice (553)

עוּד (Hi) to warn, admonish, witness, be a witness, testify (40)

עָוָה (Q) to do wrong; (Ni) be disturbed or irritated; (Hi) twist, pervert, do wrong (17)

עוּף (Q) to fly (27)

עוּר (Q) to be awake, stir up; (Hi) arouse, rouse, wake up, stir up; (Polel) arouse, disturb, awaken (80)

עָוַת (Q) to bend, make crooked, pervert (justice), falsify (balances), suppress (12)

עָזַב (Q) to leave, leave behind, forsake, abandon, set free (214)

עָזַז (Q) to be strong, prevail (against), defy (11)

עָזַר (Q) to help, assist, come to the aid of (82)

עָטָה (Q) to wrap, cover or envelop (oneself) with (13)

עָטַף (Q) to be(come) weak, feeble or faint; (Hith) feel weak or faint (11)

עָכַר (Q) to disturb, trouble, confuse, bring disaster (ruin); be stirred up, ruined, cut off (14)

עָלָה (Q) to go up, ascend; (Ni) be taken up; (Hi) bring or lead up or out, offer up (sacrifice) (894)

עָלַז (Q) to exult, triumph (17)

עָלַל (Poel) to deal or act severely with, treat violently, glean (19)

עָלַם (Ni) to be concealed, hidden; (Hi) conceal, hide, cover up; (Hith) hide oneself (28)

עָמַד (Q) to stand (up), take one's stand, stand still; (Hi) station, set up, appoint, designate (524)

עָמַל (Q) to labor, toil, exert oneself (12)

עָנַג (Hith) to pamper oneself, take delight (pleasure) in, refresh oneself (10)

עָנָה (Q) to answer, respond, reply, testify; (Ni) be answered (316)

עָנָה (Q) to be afflicted, humbled; (Pi) afflict, oppress, humiliate, violate (79); cf עָנָה (#152, #1467)

עָנָה (Q) to sing (16)

עָנַן (Poel) to practice soothsaying, conjure up (spirits), interpret signs (11)

עָצַב (Q) to hurt, pain, rebuke, grieve; (Ni) be pained for, in grieving for, worried, distressed (15)

עָצַם (Q) to be vast, mighty, powerful or numerous (17)

עָצַר (Q) to hold back, restrain, hinder, imprison; (Ni) be restrained, shut up, detained (46)

עָרַב (Q) to stand as surety for, pledge oneself (as surety for debts), be responsible for someone, conduct trade, barter (17)

עָרָה (Pi) to uncover, reveal, expose, lay bare, empty; (Hi) uncover, make naked, expose (15)

עָרַךּ (Q) to set in order, lay out, set in rows, arrange, stack (wood), draw up a battle formation (75)

עָרַץ (Q) to tremble, be terrified, in dread, startled, alarmed; (Hi) terrify, strike (inspire) with awe (15)

עָשָׂה (Q) to do, make; (Ni) be done, made (2,632)

עָשַׂר (Q) to exact a tithe, take a tenth part of; (Pi) give, pay or receive a tenth, tithe (10)

עָשַׁק (Q) to oppress, exploit, wrong (someone) (37)

עָשַׁר (Q) to be(come) rich; (Hi) make rich, gain riches (17)

עָתַר (Q) to pray, plead, entreat; (Ni) be entreated; (Hi) pray, plead (20)

פָּאַר (Pi) to glorify, exalt, beautify; (Hith) show or manifest one's glory, glorify oneself, be glorified, boast (13)

פָּגַע (Q) to meet, encounter, fall upon, attack, assail, reach (46)

פָּגַשׁ (Q) to meet, encounter, confront (14)

פָּדָה (Q) to ransom, redeem, buy out (60)

פּוּחַ (Hi) to testify (10)

פּוּץ (Q) to be spread, dispersed, scattered, overflow; (Ni) be scattered, dispersed; (Hi) scatter, disperse (65)

פָּזַר (Pi) to scatter, disperse (10)

פָּחַד (Q) to tremble, shiver, be startled, in dread, in awe (25)

פָּלָא (Ni) to be extraordinary, wonderful; (Hi) do something wonderful (71)

פָּלַט (Pi) to bring out, bring forth, bring to safety, save (27)

פָּלַל (Hith) to pray, make intercession (84)

פָּנָה (Q) to turn (toward, from, to the side, away) (134)

פָּעַל (Q) to do, make, perform (58)

פָּצָה (Q) to open (the mouth), speak (15)

פָּקַד (Q) to attend (to), pay attention to, take care of, miss (someone), number, appoint; (Ni) be missed, visited, appointed; (Hi) appoint, entrust (304)

פָּקַח (Q) to open (the) eyes (21)

פָּרַד (Ni) to divide, separate (intransitive), be scattered, separated (26)

פָּרָה (Q) to bear fruit, be fruitful (29)

פָּרַח (Q) to bud, sprout, bloom, shoot, break out, break open (34)

פָּרַס (Q) to break; (Hi) have a divided hoof (14)

פָּרַע (Q) to let go, loose or free, let the hair of the head hang loose, allow to run wild, leave unattended (16)

פָּרַץ (Q) to break through (out or into), make a breach, burst open, spread out (46)

פָּרַק (Q) to tear away, pull away, rescue; (Pi) pull or tear off; (Hith) pull or tear off from oneself, be pulled or torn off (10)

פָּרַר (Hi) to break (out), destroy, put an end to, make ineffectual (47)

פָּרַשׂ (Q) to spread out (as with hands in prayer), stretch (out or over) (67)

פָּשָׂה (Q) to spread (the symptoms of disease) (22)

פָּשַׁט (Q) to take off (clothes), strip off, rush out, make a raid; (Hi) take off (clothes or armor), strip off (skin), flay (43)

פָּשַׁע (Q) to revolt, rebel (against), transgress, break with, break away from, behave as a criminal (41)

פָּתַח (Q) to open (up); (Ni) be opened, loosened, set free; (Pi) let loose, loosen (136)

צָבָא (Q) to wage war, go to war, fight against (14)

214

צָדַק (Q) to be in the right, have a just cause, be just (justified), be righteous; (Hi) justify, declare righteous, just or innocent (41)

צוּד (Q) to hunt (17)

צָוָה (Pi) to command, give an order, charge; (Pu) be ordered, be told, receive a command (496)

צוּם (Q) to fast, abstain from food and drink (21)

צוּק (Hi) to oppress, press hard, harass, constrain (12)

צוּר (Q) to tie up, bind, shut in, shut up, enclose, encircle, besiege (31)

צָחַק (Q) to laugh; (Pi) joke (with), play (with), amuse oneself, fondle (13)

צָלַח (Q) to succeed, prosper, be successful; (Hi) be successful, succeed, cause to succeed or prosper (65)

צָמֵא (Q) to thirst, be thirsty (10)

צָמַח (Q) to sprout, spring up, grow; (Hi) make grow or sprout (33)

צָמַת (Hi) to silence, exterminate, annihilate (15)

צָעַק (Q) to shout, cry (out), call for help; (Ni) be called together, summoned (55)

צָפָה (Pi) to overlay, plate (with gold) (47)

צָפָה (Q) to keep watch, watch attentively, spy (37)

צָפַן (Q) to hide, store (up), treasure (up), keep (34)

צָרַע (Q) to be afflicted with a skin disease (usually leprosy); (Pu) be struck with a skin disease (20)

צָרַף (Q) to smelt (metal), refine (by smelting), test (34)

צָרַר (Q) to wrap (up), tie up, bind (transitive); be cramped, restricted, depressed (intransitive); (Hi) oppress, harass, afflict (47)

צָרַר (Q) to be hostile (toward), treat with hostility, attack (26)

קָבַב (Q) to curse (14)

קָבַל (Pi) to take, receive, accept (14)

קָבַץ (Q) to collect, gather, assemble; (Ni) be gathered, assembled; (Pi) gather together, assemble (127)

קָבַר (Q) to bury; (Ni) be buried (133)

קָדַד (Q) to bow down, kneel down (15)

קָדַם (Pi) to be in front, confront, meet, go before, walk at the head, do something early or for the first time (26)

קָדַר (Q) to be(come) dark, dirty, untidy, dressed in the clothes of mourning (17)

קָדַשׁ (Q) to be holy, set apart or consecrated; (Ni) be honored or treated as holy; (Pi) set apart, consecrate or dedicate as holy; (Hi) consecrate, dedicate or declare as holy; (Hith) show or keep oneself holy (171)

קָהַל (Ni) to assemble, meet together (intransitive); (Hi) assemble (transitive), summon (39)

קָוָה (Pi) to wait (for), wait with eagerness, hope (47)

קוּם (Q) to rise, arise, get up, stand (up); (Hi) set up, put up, cause to arise, establish (627)

קָטַר (Pi) to make a sacrifice go up in smoke, offer (a sacrifice) by burning; (Hi) cause a sacrifice to go up in smoke (115)

קִיץ (Hi) to awake, wake up (22)

קָלַל (Q) to be small, insignificant, of little account, swift; (Ni, Pi) declare cursed; (Hi) treat with contempt (82)

קָנָא (Pi) to envy, be envious of, jealous of, zealous for (34)

קָנָה (Q) to get, acquire, buy (85)

קָסַם (Q) to practice divination, consult a spirit of the dead, predict (22)

קָצַף (Q) to be(come) angry or furious (34)

קָצַץ (Q) to cut (chop) off, trim; (Pi) cut (chop) off, cut in pieces (14)

קָצַר (Q) to gather in, reap, harvest (36)

קָצַר (Q) to be(come) short, shortened, impatient (14); cf קָצַר (#855)

קָרָא (Q) to call, summon, proclaim, read aloud, give a name to; (Ni) be called, summoned, proclaimed (739); cf קָרָא (#301)

קָרָא (Q) to meet, encounter, happen; inf cstr with prep לְ (לִקְרַאת) toward, against, opposite (136); cf קָרָא (#70) and קָרָה (#1198)

קָרַב (Q) to approach, draw near, come near; (Hi) bring (near), present, offer a sacrifice or offering (280)

קָרָה (Q) to encounter, meet, befall, happen to (22)

קָרַע (Q) to tear, rend, cut up, tear away (63)

קָשַׁב (Hi) to give (pay) attention, listen carefully or attentively (46)

קָשָׁה (Q) to be heavy, hard or difficult; (Hi) make hard, harden, make stubborn or obstinate (28)

קָשַׁר (Q) to bind, be in league together, conspire (against) (44)

רָאָה (Q) to see, perceive, understand; (Ni) appear; (Pu) be seen; (Hi) let or cause someone to see (something) (1,311)

רָבַב (Q) to be(come) many, numerous or great (23)

רָבָה (Q) to be(come) numerous, great, increase; (Hi) make many, make great, multiply, increase (229)

רָבַע (Q) to provide with four corners, make square (12)

רָבַץ (Q) to lie down, crouch (of animals), rest, stretch out (30)

רָגַז (Q) to shake, quake, tremble, be agitated, perturbed, excited, upset (41)

רָגַל (Pi) to spy (out), scout (26)

רָגַם (Q) to stone, kill by stoning (16)

רָגַע (Q) to crust over or become hard (of skin), stir up (sea); (Hi) give rest to, come to rest, make peace, linger (13)

רָדָה (Q) to rule (over), have dominion over, govern (with the nuance of oppression), tread (in) the winepress (22)

רָדַף (Q) to pursue, follow after, chase, persecute (144)

רָוָה (Q) to drink one's fill; (Pi, Hi) drink abundantly, water thoroughly, drench, saturate (14)

217

רָוַח (Q) to get relief; (Pu) be wide or spacious; (Hi) smell (14)

רוּם (Q) to be high, be exalted, rise, arise; (Hi) raise, lift up, exalt, take away; (Hoph) be exalted; (Polel) exalt, bring up, extol, raise (children) (197)

רוּעַ (Hi) to shout, cry (out), shout a war cry (alarm of battle), sound a signal for war, cheer, shout in triumph (44)

רוּץ (Q) to run (104)

רוּשׁ (Q) to be poor (24)

רָחַב (Q) to open wide; (Hi) make wide or large, extend (26)

רָחַם (Pi) to show love for, have compassion (for), take pity on (47)

רָחַץ (Q) to wash (with water), wash (off or away), bathe, bathe oneself (72)

רָחַק (Q) to be(come) far or distant, keep far from; (Hi) remove, put (keep) far away, keep at a distance (59)

רִיב (Q) to strive, contend, quarrel, dispute, conduct a legal case (72)

רִיק (Hi) to empty out, pour out (19) and רֵיק (#1601)

רָכַב (Q) to ride, mount and ride; (Hi) cause or make to ride (78)

רָכַל (Q ptc) to go about as a trader (tradesman), merchant (17)

רָמַס (Q) to trample (down), tread (potter's clay or grapes), crush to pieces (19)

רָמַשׂ (Q) to crawl, creep, swarm, teem (17)

רָנַן (Q) to call or cry aloud, shout with joy; (Pi) cry out (with joy), exult (53)

רָעֵב (Q) to be hungry, suffer famine (13)

רָעָה (Q) to pasture, tend (flocks), graze, shepherd, feed (167)

רָעַם (Q) to rage, roar (sea), thunder, storm; (Hi) thunder, storm (11)

רָעַע (Q) to be bad, evil or displeasing; (Hi) do evil, do wickedly, do injury, harm, treat badly (98)

רָעַשׁ (Q) to quake, shake (29)

רָפָא (Q) to heal; (Ni) be healed, become whole; (Pi) heal, make healthy (69)

רָפָה (Q) to sink, drop, relax, grow slack; (Hi) abandon, forsake, desert, leave (someone) alone (46)

רָצָה (Q) to be pleased with, favorable toward, well disposed toward, accept (with pleasure), become friends with (48)

רָצַח (Q) to kill, murder, slay (47)

רָצַץ (Q) to crush, oppress, mistreat (19)

רָקַע (Q) to stamp (down or out), trample, spread out; (Pi) beat out, hammer out (11)

רָשַׁע (Hi) to condemn, declare or pronounce guilty (35)

שָׂבַע (Q) to be satisfied, have one's fill (of), eat or drink one's fill; (Hi) satisfy (97)

שָׂגַב (Ni) to be high, exalted, inaccessible; (Pi) make high, make inaccessible, protect (20)

שׂוּשׂ (Q) to rejoice; also spelled שִׂישׂ (27)

שָׂחַק (Q) to laugh, play; (Pi) play, entertain, dance, amuse (37)

שִׂיחַ (Q) to consider, meditate, complain, lament, praise (20)

שִׂים (Q) to set (up), put, place, set in place, establish; also spelled שׂוּם (588)

שָׂכַל (Hi) to understand, comprehend, have insight, make wise, have success (60)

שָׂכַר (Q) to hire (for wages) (20)

שָׂמַח (Q) to rejoice, be joyful, glad; (Pi) cause to rejoice, gladden, make someone happy (156)

שָׂנֵא (Q) to hate; (Pi ptc) enemy (148)

שָׂרַף (Q) to burn (completely), destroy; (Ni) be burned (117)

שָׁאַב (Q) to draw water (19)

שָׁאַג (Q) to roar (21)

שָׁאַל (Q) to ask (of), inquire (of), request, demand (176)

שָׁאַף (Q) to gasp, pant (for or after), long for (14)

שָׁאַר (Ni) to remain, be left over, survive; (Hi) leave (someone or something) remaining (133)

שָׁבָה (Q) to take captive, deport (47)

שָׁבַע (Ni) to swear (take) an oath; (Hi) cause to take an oath, plead with someone (186)

שָׁבַר (Q) to break (up), break in pieces, smash, shatter; (Ni) be smashed, broken, shattered or destroyed; (Pi) shatter, smash, break (148)

שָׁבַר (Q) to buy grain (for food) (21)

שָׁבַת (Q) to stop, cease, rest; (Hi) put an end to, remove, put away (71)

שָׁגָה (Q) to stray (of sheep), go astray (morally), err, do or go wrong (unintentionally), stagger, reel (21)

שָׁדַד (Q) to devastate, ruin, deal violently with, violently destroy; (Pu) be devastated (59)

שׁוּב (Q) to turn back, turn, return; (Hi) cause to return, bring back, restore; (Polel) bring back, restore (1,075)

שָׁוָה (Q) to be(come) like or similar to, be the equal of, resemble; (Pi) make like, make level (16)

שׁוּט (Q) to roam (around), go (rove) about, row (across water); (Polel) roam about (around) (13)

שָׁוַע (Pi) to cry or call for help (21)

שׁוּר (Q) to behold, regard (15)

שָׁזַר (Hoph ptc) twisted; always spelled מָשְׁזָר (21); all in Exod 26–39

שָׁחַח (Q) to cower, crouch, bow down (18)

שָׁחַט (Q) to slaughter (animals for sacrifice) (81)

שָׁחַר (Pi) to seek eagerly for, look diligently for, be intent on (12)

שָׁחַת (Pi, Hi) to ruin, destroy, spoil, annihilate (152)

שָׁטַף (Q) to flood (over), overflow, rinse, wash (away) (31)

שִׁיר (Q) to sing (of); (Q and Polel ptc) singer (88) and שִׁירָה (#1675)

שִׁית (Q) to set, put, place, set one's mind to (86)

שָׁכַב (Q) to lie down, have sexual intercourse (with) (213)

שָׁכַח (Q) to forget; (Ni) be forgotten (102)

שָׁכֹל (Q) to become childless; (Pi) make someone childless, deprive of children, cause a miscarriage (24)

שָׁכֵם (Hi) to get up early, rise early, do (something) early (65)

שָׁכַן (Q) to settle (down), abide, reside, dwell, inhabit; (Pi) abide, dwell (130)

שָׁכַר (Q) to be(come) drunk; (Pi, Hi) make (someone) drunk (18)

שָׁלַח (Q) to send, stretch out; (Pi) send, stretch out, send away, expel, let go free; (Pu) be sent away (off) (847)

שָׁלַךְ (Hi) to send, throw, cast; (Hoph) be thrown, cast (125)

שָׁלַל (Q) to plunder, spoil, capture, rob (14)

שָׁלֵם (Q) to be complete, finished; (Pi) complete, finish, make whole, restore, reward; (Hi) bring to completion, consummate (116); cf שָׁלֵם (#1024)

שָׁלַף (Q) to draw out (sword), pull out, take out (25)

שָׁמַד (Ni) to be exterminated, destroyed or annihilated; (Hi) exterminate, annihilate, destroy (90)

שָׁמַט (Q) to let loose, let fall, let drop, release, abandon, leave fallow (10)

שָׁמֵם (Q) to be deserted, uninhabited; (Ni) be made uninhabited, desolate, deserted; (Hi) make deserted or desolated (92)

שָׁמַע (Q) to hear, listen to, understand, obey; (Ni) be heard; (Hi) proclaim (1,165)

שָׁמַר (Q) to watch (over), guard, keep, observe, preserve, protect, take care of; (Ni) to be kept, protected, on one's guard (469)

שָׁנָה (Q) to change; (Pi) change, alter, pervert (15)

שָׂסָה (Q) to plunder, spoil (11)

שָׁעָה (Q) to gaze at, look at, look (regard) with favor, be concerned about (13)

שָׁעַן (Ni) to lean (on or against), support oneself on, depend on (22)

שָׁפַט (Q) to judge, make a judgment, decide (between), settle (a dispute or controversy); (Ni) go to court, plead, dispute (204)

שָׁפַךְ (Q) to pour (out), spill, shed (blood) (117)

שָׁפֵל (Q) to be(come) low, humble, humiliated; (Hi) bring down, overthrow, humiliate (30)

שָׁקַד (Q) to (keep) watch, be wakeful, vigilant, concerned about, watch over (12)

שָׁקָה (Hi) to give drink (to), irrigate (62)

שָׁקַט (Q) to be quiet, peaceful, at peace, at rest; (Hi) give (keep) peace (42)

שָׁקַל (Q) to weigh (out) (23)

שָׁקַף (Ni) to look down on (from above); (Hi) look down from above (22)

שָׁרַץ (Q) to swarm, teem (with), be innumerable (14)

שָׁרַק (Q) to hiss, whistle (12)

שָׁרַת (Pi) to minister, serve (98)

שָׁתָה (Q) to drink (217)

שָׁתַל (Q) to plant, transplant (10)

תּוּר (Q) to spy out, reconnoiter, explore, investigate (24)

תָּכַן (Q) to examine, consider, weigh; (Ni) be examined (18)

תָּלָה (Q) to hang (up) (29)

תָּמַךְ (Q) to grasp, take hold of, hold, support (21)

תָּמַם (Q) to be(come) complete or finished, come to an end, cease, be consumed, burned out (64)

תָּעַב (Pi) to abhor, loathe, commit an abomination (22)

תָּעָה (Q) to err, wander (about), stagger, go astray (animal); (Hi) lead astray, cause to err (51)

תָּפַשׂ (Q) to take hold of, seize, capture, grasp; (Ni) be seized, caught, captured, conquered (65)

תָּקַע (Q) to drive or thrust (weapon into a person), pitch (tent), blow (trumpet), clap one's hands (70)

Weak Verbs: I-נ
Listed Alphabetically

In the Hebrew Old Testament, there are 137 I-נ verbal roots with a total occurrence of 7,103 times. 64 of these verbs occur more than 10 times.

נָאַף (Q) to commit adultery; (metaphorically) commit idolatry; (Pi) commit adultery (31)

נָאַץ (Q) to spurn, despise; (Pi) treat disrespectfully or with irreverence (24)

נָבָא (Ni) to prophesy, be in a state of prophetic ecstasy; (Hith) speak or behave as a prophet (115)

נָבַט (Hi) to look (at or out), gaze, behold (70)

נָבֵל (Q) to fade, wither, decay, crumble away, wear out (20)

נָבַע (Hi) to make (something) gush or bubble (forth), pour out or ferment (11)

נָגַד (Hi) to tell, announce, report, declare, inform; (Hoph) be told, announced, reported (371)

נָגַח (Q) to gore (ox as subject); (Pi) push, butt, thrust, knock down (11)

נָגַן (Pi) to play a stringed instrument (15)

נָגַע (Q) to touch, strike, reach; (Hi) touch, reach, throw, arrive (150)

נָגַף (Q) to smite, strike, injure; (Ni) be smitten, struck (with) (49)

נָגַר (Ni) to flow, gush forth, be poured (out), spilled, stretched out (hands); (Hi) pour (out, down) (10)

נָגַשׂ (Q) to oppress, force to work, be a slave driver or taskmaster, exact (contributions), collect (offerings) (23)

נָגַשׁ (Q) to draw near, approach; (Ni) draw near; (Hi) bring (near), offer (a sacrifice) (125)

נָדַב (Q) to incite, instigate; (Hith) volunteer, make a voluntary decision, offer voluntarily, give a freewill offering (17)

נָדַד (Q) to flee, wander (about), depart, move, flutter (wings) (28)

נָדַח (Ni) to be scattered, banished, driven away, thrust out; (Hi) scatter, drive away, disperse, thrust out (51)

נָדַר (Q) to make (perform) a vow, keep (make) a promise (31)

נָהַג (Q) to drive (flocks or herds), lead, guide; (Pi) lead or drive away (30)

נָהַל (Pi) to lead, guide, escort, provide (with food) (10)

נָזָה (Q) to spatter (blood); (Hi) sprinkle (24)

נָזַל (Q) to trickle, drip down, flow (16)

נָזַר (Ni) to devote, dedicate or consecrate oneself to (a deity), treat with awe, deal respectfully with; (Hi) restrain from, abstain from, live as a Nazirite (10)

נָחָה (Q) to lead; (Hi) lead, guide, conduct (39)

נָחַל (Q) to take (as a) possession, obtain (receive) property, give as an inheritance; (Hi) give as an inheritance (59)

נָחַם (Ni) to be sorry, regret, have compassion (on or for); (Pi) comfort, console (108)

נָחַשׁ (Pi) to practice divination, seek and give omens, observe signs, foretell, predict (11)

נָטָה (Q) to spread out, stretch out, extend, pitch (a tent), turn, bend; (Hi) turn, incline, stretch out, spread out (216)

נָטַע (Q) to plant (59)

נָטַף (Q) to drop, drip, secrete; (Hi) cause to drip, cause to flow (metaphorically, of prophetic speech) (18)

נָטַשׁ (Q) to leave, forsake, abandon, give up (something); (Ni) be forsaken (40)

נָכָה (Hi) to strike, smite, beat, strike dead, destroy; (Hoph) be struck down dead, beaten (501)

נָכַר (Hi) to recognize, know, investigate, be acquainted with, acknowledge (50)

נָסָה (Pi) to test, put someone to the test, tempt (36)

נָסַךְ (Q) to pour out, pour (cast) a metal image or statue; (Hi) pour out libations, offer a drink offering (25)

נָסַע (Q) to pull (out or up), set out, start out, depart, journey (146)

נָעַר (Q, Pi) to shake (out or off); (Ni) be shaken (out or off) (11)

נָפַח (Q) to breathe, blow, blow fire upon, set aflame, gasp, pant (12)

נָפַל (Q) to fall, fall upon; (Hi) cause to fall, bring to ruin (435)

נָפַץ (Q) to shatter, smash to pieces; (Pi) smash (19)

נָצַב (Ni) to stand (firm), take one's stand, station oneself, be positioned; (Hi) station, set (up), place, establish (74)

נָצַח (Pi) to supervise, oversee or inspect works and activities related to the temple; מְנַצֵּחַ (ptc) used as title (superscription) in 55 psalms (65)

נָצַל (Ni) to be rescued, delivered, saved; (Hi) tear from, take away, deliver from (213)

נָצַר (Q) to keep watch, watch over, guard, protect, preserve (63)

נָקַב (Q) to pierce, bore (through), stipulate, specify, designate, curse, slander (19)

נָקָה (Ni) to be free (of), without guilt, innocent, exempt from (punishment); (Pi) leave unpunished, regard as innocent (44)

נָקַם (Q) to avenge, take vengeance (on), take revenge; (Ni) avenge oneself, take revenge (35)

נָקַף (Hi) to surround, go around, encircle, encompass, enclose (17)

נָשָׂא (Q) to lift, carry, raise, bear (load or burden), take (away); (Ni) be carried, lifted up, exalted; (Pi) lift up, exalt; (Hith) lift oneself up, exalt oneself (659)

נָשַׂג (Hi) to reach, overtake (50)

נָשָׁא (Hi) to deceive, cheat, trick (14)

נָשָׁה (Q) to forget (18)

נָשַׁךְ (Q, Pi) to bite (11)

נָשַׁק (Q) to kiss (32)

נָתַךְ (Q) to gush forth, pour out; (Ni) gush forth, be poured (out or forth) (21)

נָתַן (Q) to give, put, place, set; (Ni) be given (2,014)

נָתַץ (Q) to tear down, pull down, break down, demolish (42)

נָתַק (Q) to pull off, tear away; (Ni) be drawn out or away, torn apart; (Pi) tear apart, tear to pieces (27)

נָתַשׁ (Q) to uproot, pull out, extract, pull up, remove, drive out (nations) (21)

Weak Verbs: I-י
Listed Alphabetically

In the Hebrew Old Testament, there are 84 I-י verbal roots with a total occurrence of 6,554 times. 40 of these verbs occur more than 10 times.

יָאַל (Hi) to be intent on something, be determined, show willingness or undertake to do something (18)

יָבַל (Hi) to bring (as gift or tribute), lead; (Hoph) be brought, led (18)

יָבֵשׁ (Q) to dry up, be(come) dry, wither; (Hi) make dry (up), make wither (59)

יָגַע (Q) to toil, labor, struggle, grow or be weary (26)

יָדָה (Hi) to thank, praise, confess; (Hith) confess (111)

יָדַע (Q) to know, know sexually (have intercourse with); (Ni) be(come) known, reveal oneself; (Hi) make known, inform (956)

יָהַב (Q) to give, come (33)

יָחַל (Pi, Hi) to wait (for), hope for (42)

יָחַשׂ (Hith) to be registered or enrolled in a genealogical list; (Hith inf as noun) genealogy, registration (20)

יָטַב (Q) to be well with, go well with, be pleasing (to); (Hi) make things go well for, do good to, deal well with, treat kindly (117)

יָכַח (Hi) to reprove, rebuke, reproach, chasten, punish, decide, mediate, arbitrate (59)

יָכֹל (Q) to be able, capable of, endure, prevail (193)

יָלַד (Q) to bear (children), give birth, bring forth, beget; (Ni) be born; (Pi) help at birth, serve as midwife; (Pu) be born; (Hi) become the father of, beget (499)

יָלַל (Hi) to howl, lament, wail (31)

יָנָה (Q, Hi) to oppress, mistreat (19)

יָנַק (Q) to suck; (Hi) suckle, nurse (33)

יָסַד (Q) to found, establish, appoint, destine, allocate; (Pi) found, appoint, establish (41)

יָסַף (Q) to add, continue (to do something again); (Hi) add, increase, do again and again (213)

יָסַר (Pi) to teach, discipline, correct, chastise, rebuke (41)

‏יָעַד‎ (Q) to designate, appoint; (Ni) meet, gather or assemble by appointment (29)

‏יָעַל‎ (Hi) to profit, gain profit, benefit (23)

‏יָעַץ‎ (Q) to advise, counsel, plan, decide; (Ni) consult (take counsel) together (80)

‏יָצָא‎ (Q) to go or come out; (Hi) cause to go or come out, lead out, bring out (1,076)

‏יָצַב‎ (Hith) to take one's stand, stand firm, station oneself, present oneself before (48)

‏יָצַג‎ (Hi) to set, place, establish, take one's stand (17)

‏יָצַק‎ (Q) to pour, pour out (liquid), cast (metal), flow (into); (Hoph) be cast, poured out, emptied out (53)

‏יָצַר‎ (Q) to form, fashion, shape, create (63)

‏יָצַת‎ (Q) to kindle, burn; (Hi) set on fire, set fire to (27)

‏יָקַץ‎ (Q) to awake, wake up, become active (11)

‏יָקַר‎ (Q) to be difficult, precious, prized, highly valued, esteemed, honored, costly, or rare (11)

‏יָרֵא‎ (Q) to fear, be afraid, be in awe of, reverence; (Ni) be feared, held in honor (317); cf ‏יָרֵא‎ (#539)

‏יָרַד‎ (Q) to go down, descend; (Hi) bring down, lead down (382)

‏יָרָה‎ (Q, Hi) to throw, shoot, cast (lots) (28); cf ‏יָרָה‎ (#675)

‏יָרָה‎ (Hi) to instruct, teach (47)

‏יָרַשׁ‎ (Q) to inherit, take possession of, dispossess, impoverish; (Hi) cause to possess or inherit, dispossess (232)

‏יָשַׁב‎ (Q) to sit (down), dwell, inhabit; (Hi) cause to sit or dwell, settle (a city) (1,088)

‏יָשֵׁן‎ (Q) to sleep, go to sleep, be asleep (16)

‏יָשַׁע‎ (Ni) to be delivered, victorious, receive help; (Hi) help, save, deliver, rescue, come to the aid of (205)

‏יָשַׁר‎ (Q) to be straight, upright or right, please (27)

‏יָתַר‎ (Ni) to be left over, remain; (Hi) have (something) left over or remaining (106)

Weak Verbs: I-Guttural
Listed Alphabetically

In the Hebrew Old Testament, there are 312 verbal roots of this type with a total occurrence of 14,719 times. 116 of these verbs occur more than 10 times.

אָבַד (Q) to perish, vanish, be(come) lost, go astray; (Pi) cause to perish, destroy; (Hi) exterminate (185)

אָבַל (Q) to mourn, lament; (Hith) observe mourning rites (36)

אָדַם (Q) to be red; (Pu) be reddened, dyed red (10)

אָהַב (Q) to love (of human and divine love); (Pi ptc) lover (217)

אוּץ (Q) to urge, press, be in a hurry, be pressed (10)

אוֹר (Hi) to give light, shine, illuminate, light up (44)

אָזַן (Hi) to give ear to, listen (to), hear, heed (41)

אָזַר (Q) to gird (on), equip (16)

אָחַז (Q) to seize, grasp, take hold (of), hold fast (63)

אָחַר (Pi) to delay, detain, hesitate, linger (18)

אָכַל (Q) to eat, consume; (Ni) be eaten, consumed; (Hi) feed (820)

אָמַל (Pulal) to dry up, waste away, languish (15)

אָמַן (Ni) to be reliable, faithful or trustworthy; (Hi) believe (in), trust, have trust in, put trust in (97)

אָמֵץ (Q) to be strong, be bold; (Pi) make firm, strengthen, harden someone's heart (41)

אָמַר (Q) to say; (Ni) be said, called; (Hi) declare, proclaim (5,316)

אָנַח (Ni) to sigh, groan (13)

אָנַף (Q) to be angry (14)

אָסַף (Q) to gather (in), take in, take away, destroy; (Ni) be gathered, taken away, assemble (200)

אָסַר (Q) to tie, bind, fetter, imprison (73)

אָרַב (Q) to ambush, lie in ambush, lie in wait (41)

אָרַג (Q) to weave; (Q ptc) weaver (13)

אָרַךְ (Hi) to make long, lengthen, extend (34)

אָרַר (Q) to curse (63)

אָרַשׂ (Pi) to betroth, be engaged; (Pu) be(come) betrothed or engaged (11)

אָשֵׁם (Q) to be(come) guilty, commit an offense (35)

אָשַׁר (Pi) to call or consider blessed, fortunate or happy; (Pu) be called blessed, fortunate or happy (10)

הָדַף (Q) to thrust (away, out), push (away), drive away (out), shove (11)

הָלַךְ (Q) to go, walk, (metaphorically) behave; (Pi) go, walk; (Hith) walk about, move to and fro (1,554)

הָלַל (Pi) to praise, sing hallelujah; (Pu) be praised, praiseworthy; (Hith) boast (146); cf הָלַל (#1501)

הָלַל (Q) to be infatuated, deluded; (Hithpolel) be mad, act like a madman (15); cf הָלַל (#282)

הָמַם (Q) to make (a) noise, confuse, bring into motion and confusion (army), discomfit, disturb (13)

הָפַךְ (Q) to turn, overturn, overthrow, destroy; (Ni) be destroyed, turned into, changed (95)

הָרַג (Q) to kill, slay (167)

הָרַס (Q) to tear down, demolish, destroy, throw down, overthrow, break through; (Ni) be ruined (43)

חָבָא (Ni) to hide (oneself), be hidden; (Hith) keep oneself hidden (34)

חָבַל (Q) to take, hold or seize (something) in pledge, exact a pledge from someone, bind by taking a pledge (13)

חָבַל (Q) to act corruptly or ruinously; (Pi) ruin, destroy (11)

חָבַק (Q) to embrace, fold the hands (in idleness); (Pi) embrace (13)

חָבַר (Q) to unite, ally oneself (with), join forces (28)

חָבַשׁ (Q) to saddle, bind or buckle on, bind up (wound), wrap, twist (rope), imprison (33)

חָגַג (Q) to stagger, reel, celebrate a pilgrimage festival (16)

חָגַר (Q) to gird, gird (oneself or someone), get ready (44)

חָדַל (Q) to cease, end, stop, refrain (from) (55)

חָדַשׁ (Pi) to make new, renew, restore (10)

חוּל (Q) to go around, whirl (about), dance, writhe; also spelled חִיל (10)

חוּס (Q) to pity, look upon with compassion, spare (24)

חוּשׁ (Q) to hurry, make haste (18)

חָזַק (Q) to be(come) strong, have courage; (Pi) make strong, strengthen; (Hi) strengthen, seize, grasp, take hold of; (Hith) strengthen oneself, show oneself as strong or courageous (290)

חָטָא (Q) to miss (a goal or mark), sin, commit a sin; (Pi) make a sin offering; (Hi) cause to sin (240)

חִיל (Q) to writhe, travail, be in labor, tremble; also spelled חוּל (48)

חָכַם (Q) to be(come) wise, act wisely (28)

חָלַל (Ni) to be defiled, profaned, defile oneself; (Pi) profane, pollute, defile; (Hi) let something be profaned (135)

חָלַם (Q) to dream (29)

חָלַף (Q) to pass on or away (quickly), pass by, vanish; (Hi) change, replace, substitute (26)

חָלַץ (Q) to draw out, take off, withdraw, be girded (ready for battle); (Pi) rescue, deliver (44)

חָלַק (Q) to divide, share (with or in), apportion, distribute; (Pi) divide (in pieces), apportion, scatter (55)

חָמַד (Q) to desire, take pleasure (delight) in, crave, covet (21)

חָמַל (Q) to have compassion (for), have pity (for), spare (41)

חָמַם (Q) to be(come) warm (23)

חָנַן (Q) to be gracious to, show favor to, favor; (Hith) plead for grace, favor, or compassion (77)

חָנַף (Q) to be godless (of a priest or prophet), defiled (of land); (Hi) defile, pollute (11)

חָסֵר (Q) to diminish, decrease, lack (22)

חָפַז (Q) to be in a hurry, hurry away (in alarm or fear), hasten in alarm; (Ni) run away in alarm (10)

חָפֵץ (Q) to delight in, take pleasure in, desire, be willing (74)

חָפַר (Q) to dig, track, search (for), scout out, spy out (23)

חָפֵר (Q) to be ashamed (17)

חָפַשׂ (Q) to search (out), examine; (Pi) search thoroughly, track down; (Hith) disguise oneself (23)

חָצַב (Q) to quarry, hew (out), dig, dress (stones) (16)

חָקַק (Q) to hew out or carve out (a grave), inscribe, engrave, enact, decree (19)

חָקַר (Q) to explore, search, spy out (27)

חָרֵב (Q) to dry up (intransitive), lie in ruins; (Hi) cause to dry up, lay waste, make desolate (36)

חָרַד (Q) to tremble, do something with trembling, shudder, quake; (Hi) startle (39)

חָרַם (Hi) to devote to the ban, dedicate to destruction, exterminate (50)

חָרַף (Q) to taunt, reproach; (Pi) taunt, reproach, revile (38)

חָרַץ (Q) to decide, cut (10)

חָרַשׁ (Q) to be silent, deaf; (Hi) be(come) silent, deaf, keep still (47); cf חָרַשׁ (#1032)

חָרַשׁ (Q) to plow, engrave, devise, plan (27)

חָשַׂךְ (Q) to withhold, keep back, refrain, spare, save, restrain (28)

חָשַׂף (Q) to strip, strip off, bare, skim or scoop off (10)

חָשַׁב (Q) to think, consider, devise, plan, value, reckon; (Ni) be reckoned, accounted, considered (as); (Pi) think, consider, devise, plan (124)

חָשַׁךְ (Q) to be(come) dark, grow dim (eyes) (17)

חָשַׁק (Q) to be attached to, cling to, love (11)

חָתַם (Q) to seal (up), affix a seal (27)

חָתַן (Hith) to intermarry with, become related by marriage, become a son-in-law (11)

236

חָתַת (Q) to be shattered, dismayed, filled with terror (55)

עָבַד (Q) to work, serve, toil (289)

עָבַר (Q) to pass over, pass through, pass by, cross; (Hi) cause to pass over, bring over, cause or allow to pass (through), cause to pass through fire, sacrifice (553)

עוּד (Hi) to warn, admonish, witness, be a witness, testify (40)

עוּף (Q) to fly (27)

עוּר (Q) to be awake, stir up; (Hi) arouse, rouse, wake up, stir up; (Polel) arouse, disturb, awaken (80)

עָוַת (Q) to bend, make crooked, pervert (justice), falsify (balances), suppress (12)

עָזַב (Q) to leave, leave behind, forsake, abandon, set free (214)

עָזַז (Q) to be strong, prevail (against), defy (11)

עָזַר (Q) to help, assist, come to the aid of (82)

עָטַף (Q) to be(come) weak, feeble or faint; (Hith) feel weak or faint (11)

עָכַר (Q) to disturb, trouble, confuse, bring disaster (ruin); be stirred up, ruined, cut off (14)

עָלַז (Q) to exult, triumph (17)

עָלַל (Polel) to deal or act severely with, treat violently, glean (19)

עָלַם (Ni) to be concealed, hidden; (Hi) conceal, hide, cover up; (Hith) hide oneself (28)

עָמַד (Q) to stand (up), take one's stand, stand still; (Hi) station, set up, appoint, designate (524)

עָמַל (Q) to labor, toil, exert oneself (12)

עָנַג (Hith) to pamper oneself, take delight (pleasure) in, refresh oneself (10)

עָנַן (Polel) to practice soothsaying, conjure up (spirits), interpret signs (11)

עָצַב (Q) to hurt, pain, rebuke, grieve; (Ni) be pained for, in grieving for, worried, distressed (15)

עָצֵם (Q) to be vast, mighty, powerful, or numerous (17)

עָצַר (Q) to hold back, restrain, hinder, imprison; (Ni) be restrained, shut up, detained (46)

עָרַב (Q) to stand as surety for, pledge oneself (as surety for debts), be responsible for someone, conduct trade, barter (17)

עָרַךְ (Q) to set in order, lay out, set in rows, arrange, stack (wood), draw up a battle formation (75)

עָרַץ (Q) to tremble, be terrified, in dread, startled, alarmed; (Hi) terrify, strike (inspire) with awe (15)

עָשַׂר (Q) to exact a tithe, take a tenth part of; (Pi) give, pay or receive a tenth, tithe (10)

עָשַׁק (Q) to oppress, exploit, wrong (someone) (37)

עָשַׁר (Q) to be(come) rich; (Hi) make rich, gain riches (17)

עָתַר (Q) to pray, plead, entreat; (Ni) be entreated; (Hi) pray, plead (20)

Weak Verbs: I-Guttural and III-ה
Listed Alphabetically

In the Hebrew Old Testament, there are 84 verbal roots of this type with a total occurrence of 8,787 times. 27 of these verbs occur more than 10 times.

אָבָה (Q) to be willing, consent, yield to, want something (54)

אָוָה (Pi) to wish, desire, want; (Hith) crave, wish for, long for (30)

אָפָה (Q) to bake (25)

אָתָה (Q) to come; (Hi) bring (21)

הָגָה (Q) to utter a sound, growl, moan, groan, coo (of a dove), speak, proclaim (25)

הָיָה (Q) to be, become, happen, occur; (Ni) be done, brought about, come to pass, occur (3,576)

הָמָה (Q) to make (a) noise, make a sound, roar, growl, moan, groan, be boisterous (34)

הָרָה (Q) to conceive, be(come) pregnant (43)

חָוָה (Hishtaphel) to bow down, worship (173)

חָזָה (Q) to see, behold, perceive (55)

חָיָה (Q) to live, be alive, revive, restore to life; (Pi) preserve alive, let live, give life; (Hi) preserve, keep alive, revive, restore to life (283)

חָכָה (Pi) to wait (for), tarry, long for, be patient (14)

חָלָה (Q) to be(come) weak, tired, sick; (Ni) be exhausted; (Pi) appease, flatter (75)

חָנָה (Q) to decline, camp, encamp, pitch camp, lay siege to (143)

חָסָה (Q) to seek or take refuge (37)

חָפָה (Q) to cover; (Pi) overlay (with) (12)

חָצָה (Q) to divide (into) (15)

חָרָה (Q) to be(come) hot, burn with anger, become angry (93)

חָשָׁה (Q) to be silent; (Hi) be silent, order (someone) to be silent, hesitate, delay (16)

עָוָה (Q) to do wrong; (Ni) be disturbed or irritated; (Hi) twist, pervert, do wrong (17)

עָטָה (Q) to wrap, cover or envelop (oneself) with (13)

עָלָה (Q) to go up, ascend; (Ni) be taken up; (Hi) bring or lead up or out, offer up (sacrifice) (894)

עָנָה (Q) to answer, respond, reply, testify; (Ni) be answered (316)

עָנָה (Q) to be afflicted, humbled; (Pi) afflict, oppress, humiliate, violate (79); cf עָנָה (#152, #1467)

עָנָה (Q) to sing (16)

עָרָה (Pi) to uncover, reveal, expose, lay bare, empty; (Hi) uncover, make naked, expose (15)

עָשָׂה (Q) to do, make; (Ni) be done, made (2,632)

Weak Verbs: II-Guttural
Listed Alphabetically

In the Hebrew Old Testament, there are 415 II-Guttural verbal roots with a total occurrence of 10,965 times. 154 of these verbs occur more than 10 times.

אָהַב (Q) to love (of human and divine love); (Pi ptc) lover (217)

אָחַז (Q) to seize, grasp, take hold (of), hold fast (63)

אָחַר (Pi) to delay, detain, hesitate, linger (18)

אָרַב (Q) to ambush, lie in ambush, lie in wait (41)

אָרַג (Q) to weave; (Q ptc) weaver (13)

אָרַךְ (Hi) to make long, lengthen, extend (34)

אָרַר (Q) to curse (63)

אָרַשׂ (Pi) to betroth, be engaged; (Pu) be(come) betrothed or engaged (11)

בָּאַשׁ (Q) to stink, have a bad smell; (Hi) make odious, become hated (18)

בָּהַל (Ni) to be terrified, horrified, dismayed, disturbed, hasty, make haste; (Pi) terrify, make haste, act hastily (39)

בָּחַן (Q) to test, put to the test, try, examine (29)

בָּחַר (Q) to choose, test, examine (172)

בָּעַל (Q) to rule over, be(come) lord or husband of, marry, own (take someone into possession as betrothed) (16)

בָּעַר (Q) to burn (up), consume; (Pi) kindle, burn (60)

בָּעַר (Pi) to graze, sweep away, remove, get rid of, purge (27)

בָּעַת (Pi) to terrify, frighten, startle (16)

בָּרָא (Q) to create (only with God as subject); (Ni) be created (48)

בָּרַח (Q) to run away, flee, go or pass through (63)

בָּרַךְ (Q Pass ptc) blessed, praised, adored; (Pi) bless, praise (327)

בָּרַר (Q) to purify, purge, sort, choose, select (16)

גָּאַל (Q) to redeem, act as kinsman (perform the responsibilities of the next-of-kin), avenge (104)

גָּאַל (Ni, Pu) to be defiled, become impure; (Hith) defile oneself (11)

גָּעַל (Q) to loathe, abhor, feel disgust (10)

גָּעַר (Q) to rebuke, reproach (14)

גָּעַשׁ (Q) to shake (10)

גָּרָה (Hith) to strive (against), oppose, battle (15)

גָּרַע (Q) to shave, trim (a beard), diminish, restrain, withdraw (21)

גָּרַשׁ (Q) to drive out, banish; (Pi) drive out (away) (45)

דָּרַךְ (Q) to tread (often in the sense of pressing for wine or oil), march, draw a bow; (Hi) cause to tread, march or walk (63)

דָּרַשׁ (Q) to seek, inquire (of or about), investigate, require, demand (165)

הָרַג (Q) to kill, slay (167)

הָרָה (Q) to conceive, be(come) pregnant (43)

הָרַס (Q) to tear down, demolish, destroy, throw down, overthrow, break through; (Ni) be ruined (43)

זָהַר (Hi) to warn (about), admonish, caution (22)

זָעַם (Q) to curse, scold, denounce (12)

זָעַק (Q) to cry (out), call for help, summon (73)

זָרָה (Q) to scatter; (Pi) scatter, disperse, spread (38)

זָרַח (Q) to rise (sun), shine, come out, appear, break out (leprosy) (18)

זָרַע (Q) to sow, scatter seed (56)

זָרַק (Q) to toss, throw, scatter, sprinkle (34)

חָרֵב (Q) to dry up (intransitive), lie in ruins; (Hi) cause to dry up, lay waste, make desolate (36)

חָרַד (Q) to tremble, do something with trembling, shudder, quake; (Hi) startle (39)

חָרָה (Q) to be(come) hot, burn with anger, become angry (93)

חָרַם (Hi) to devote to the ban, dedicate to destruction, exterminate (50)

חָרַף (Q) to taunt, reproach; (Pi) taunt, reproach, revile (38)

חָרַץ (Q) to decide, cut (10)

חָרַשׁ (Q) to be silent, deaf; (Hi) be(come) silent, deaf, keep still (47); cf חָרֵשׁ (#1032)

חָרַשׁ (Q) to plow, engrave, devise, plan (27)

טָהֵר (Q) to be clean (ceremonially), pure (morally); (Pi) cleanse, purify, pronounce clean; (Hith) purify or cleanse oneself (94)

טָעַם (Q) to taste, eat, savor food (11)

טָרַף (Q) to tear (in pieces), rend (25)

יָאַל (Hi) to be intent on something, be determined, show willingness or undertake to do something (18)

יָהַב (Q) to give, come (33)

יָחַל (Pi, Hi) to wait (for), hope for (42)

יָחַשׂ (Hith) to be registered or enrolled in a genealogical list; (Hith inf as noun) genealogy, registration (20)

יָעַד (Q) to designate, appoint; (Ni) meet, gather or assemble by appointment (29)

יָעַל (Hi) to profit, gain profit, benefit (23)

יָעַץ (Q) to advise, counsel, plan, decide; (Ni) consult (take counsel) together (80)

יָרֵא (Q) to fear, be afraid, be in awe of, reverence; (Ni) be feared, held in honor (317); cf יָרֵא (#539)

יָרַד (Q) to go down, descend; (Hi) bring down, lead down (382)

יָרָה (Q, Hi) to throw, shoot, cast (lots) (28); cf יָרָה (#675)

יָרָה (Hi) to instruct, teach (47)

יָרַשׁ (Q) to inherit, take possession of, dispossess, impoverish; (Hi) cause to possess or inherit, dispossess (232)

כָּהַן (Pi) to perform the duties of a priest, minister as a priest (23)

כָּחַד (Ni) to be hidden, effaced; (Pi) hide, conceal (32)

245

כָּחַשׁ (Pi) to deny, delude, deceive, lie, act deceptively, feign submission or obedience (22)

כָּעַס (Q) to be angry, vexed; (Hi) vex, provoke, provoke (God) to anger (55)

כָּרָה (Q) to dig, excavate, hollow out (14)

כָּרַע (Q) to bow (down), kneel (down), fall to one's knees (36)

כָּרַת (Q) to cut, cut off, cut down; (idiom) to make a covenant (with בְּרִית); (Ni) be cut off (down); (Hi) cut off, destroy, exterminate (289)

לָאָה (Q) to be(come) tired or weary; (Ni) tire (oneself) out, be tired of something; (Hi) make weary (19)

לָהַט (Q) to blaze, burn; (Pi) set ablaze, devour (with fire), scorch (10)

לָחַם (Q, Ni) to fight, do battle with (rare in Q) (171)

לָחַץ (Q) to squeeze, crowd, press, oppress, torment (19)

לָעַג (Q, Hi) to mock, ridicule, deride (18)

מָאֵן (Pi) to refuse (41)

מָאַס (Q) to refuse, reject, despise (74)

מָהַר (Pi) to hasten, hurry, go or come quickly (81)

מָחָה (Q) to wipe (out), destroy, annihilate (34)

מָחַץ (Q) to smash, shatter, beat to pieces, smite (14)

מָעַט (Q) to be(come) few or too small; (Hi) make small or few, diminish, reduce, collect or gather little (22)

מָעַל (Q) to be unfaithful, act unfaithfully or treacherously (36)

מָרַד (Q) to rebel, revolt (25)

מָרָה (Q) to be rebellious, obstinate or contentious; (Hi) behave rebelliously or obstinately (44)

מָרַט (Q) to make smooth, bare, bald, polish, scour, pull out (hair), sharpen (sword); (Pu) be polished, smooth, bare (14)

מָרַר (Q) to be bitter (of taste, experience or attitude), desperate; (Hi) embitter, cause bitterness or grief (16)

נָאַף (Q) to commit adultery; (metaphorically) commit idolatry; (Pi) commit adultery (31)

נָאַץ (Q) to spurn, despise; (Pi) treat disrespectfully or with irreverence (24)

נָהַג (Q) to drive (flocks or herds), lead, guide; (Pi) lead or drive away (30)

נָהַל (Pi) to lead, guide, escort, provide (with food) (10)

נָחָה (Q) to lead; (Hi) lead, guide, conduct (39)

נָחַל (Q) to take (as a) possession, obtain (receive) property, give as an inheritance; (Hi) give as an inheritance (59)

נָחַם (Ni) to be sorry, regret, have compassion (on or for); (Pi) comfort, console (108)

נָחַשׁ (Pi) to practice divination, seek and give omens, observe signs, foretell, predict (11)

נָעַר (Q, Pi) to shake (out or off); (Ni) be shaken (out or off) (11)

סָחַר (Q) to pass through (of shepherds), travel about (conducting business); (Q ptc) trader, merchant (21)

סָעַד (Q) to support, sustain, strengthen (with food), uphold (12)

סָרַר (Q) to be stubborn or rebellious (17)

עָרַב (Q) to stand as surety for, pledge oneself (as surety for debts), be responsible for someone, conduct trade, barter (17)

עָרָה (Pi) to uncover, reveal, expose, lay bare, empty; (Hi) uncover, make naked, expose (15)

עָרַךְ (Q) to set in order, lay out, set in rows, arrange, stack (wood), draw up a battle formation (75)

עָרַץ (Q) to tremble, be terrified, be in dread, be startled, be alarmed; (Hi) terrify, strike (inspire) with awe (15)

פָּאַר (Pi) to glorify, exalt, beautify; (Hith) show or manifest one's glory, glorify oneself, be glorified, boast (13)

פָּחַד (Q) to tremble, shiver, be startled, in dread, in awe (25)

247

פָּעַל (Q) to do, make, perform (58)

פָּרַד (Ni) to divide, separate (intransitive), be scattered, separated (26)

פָּרָה (Q) to bear fruit, be fruitful (29)

פָּרַח (Q) to bud, sprout, bloom, shoot, break out, break open (34)

פָּרַס (Q) to break; (Hi) have a divided hoof (14)

פָּרַע (Q) to let go, loose or free, let the hair of the head hang loose, allow to run wild, leave unattended (16)

פָּרַץ (Q) to break through (out or into), make a breach, burst open, spread out (46)

פָּרַק (Q) to tear away, pull away, rescue; (Pi) pull or tear off; (Hith) pull or tear off from oneself, be pulled or torn off (10)

פָּרַר (Hi) to break (out), destroy, put an end to, make ineffectual (47)

פָּרַשׂ (Q) to spread out (as with hands in prayer), stretch (out or over) (67)

צָחַק (Q) to laugh; (Pi) joke (with), play (with), amuse oneself, fondle (13)

צָעַק (Q) to shout, cry (out), call for help; (Ni) be called together, summoned (55)

צָרַע (Q) to be afflicted with a skin disease (usually leprosy); (Pu) be struck with a skin disease (20)

צָרַף (Q) to smelt (metal), refine (by smelting), test (34)

צָרַר (Q) to wrap (up), tie up, bind (transitive); be cramped, restricted, depressed (intransitive); (Hi) oppress, harass, afflict (47)

צָרַר (Q) to be hostile (toward), treat with hostility, attack (26)

קָהַל (Ni) to assemble, meet together (intransitive); (Hi) assemble (transitive), summon (39)

קָרָא (Q) to call, summon, proclaim, read aloud, give a name to; (Ni) be called, summoned, proclaimed (739); cf קָרָה (#301)

קָרָא (Q) to meet, encounter, happen; inf cstr with prep לְ (לִקְרַאת) toward, against, opposite (136); cf קָרָא (#70) and קָרָה (#1198)

קָרַב (Q) to approach, draw near, come near; (Hi) bring (near), present, offer a sacrifice or offering (280)

קָרָה (Q) to encounter, meet, befall, happen to (22)

קָרַע (Q) to tear, rend, cut up, tear away (63)

רָאָה (Q) to see, perceive, understand; (Ni) appear; (Pu) be seen; (Hi) let or cause someone to see (something) (1,311)

רָחַב (Q) to open wide; (Hi) make wide or large, extend (26)

רָחַם (Pi) to show love for, have compassion (for), take pity on (47)

רָחַץ (Q) to wash (with water), wash (off or away), bathe, bathe oneself (72)

רָחַק (Q) to be(come) far or distant, keep far from; (Hi) remove, put (keep) far away, keep at a distance (59)

רָעֵב (Q) to be hungry, suffer famine (13)

רָעָה (Q) to pasture, tend (flocks), graze, shepherd, feed (167)

רָעַם (Q) to rage, roar (sea), thunder, storm; (Hi) thunder, storm (11)

רָעַע (Q) to be bad, evil or displeasing; (Hi) do evil, do wickedly, do injury, harm, treat badly (98)

רָעַשׁ (Q) to quake, shake (29)

שָׂחַק (Q) to laugh, play; (Pi) play, entertain, dance, amuse (37)

שָׂרַף (Q) to burn (completely), destroy; (Ni) be burned (117)

שָׁאַב (Q) to draw water (19)

שָׁאַג (Q) to roar (21)

שָׁאַל (Q) to ask (of), inquire (of), request, demand (176)

שָׁאַף (Q) to gasp, pant (for or after), long for (14)

שָׁאַר (Ni) to remain, be left over, survive; (Hi) leave (someone or something) remaining (133)

שָׁחַח (Q) to cower, crouch, bow down (18)

שָׁחַט (Q) to slaughter (animals for sacrifice) (81)

שָׁחַר (Pi) to seek eagerly for, look diligently for, be intent on (12)

שָׁחַת (Pi, Hi) to ruin, destroy, spoil, annihilate (152)

שָׁעָה (Q) to gaze at, look at, look (regard) with favor, be concerned about (13)

שָׁעַן (Ni) to lean (on or against), support oneself on, depend on (22)

שָׁרַץ (Q) to swarm, teem (with), be innumerable (14)

שָׁרַק (Q) to hiss, whistle (12)

שָׁרַת (Pi) to minister, serve (98)

תָּעַב (Pi) to abhor, loathe, commit an abomination (22)

תָּעָה (Q) to err, wander (about), stagger, go astray (animal); (Hi) lead astray, cause to err (51)

Weak Verbs: III-ה
Listed Alphabetically

In the Hebrew Old Testament, there are 235 III-ה verbal roots with a total occurrence of 15,081 times. 89 of these verbs occur more than 10 times.

אָבָה (Q) to be willing, consent, yield to, want something (54)

אָוָה (Pi) to wish, desire, want; (Hith) crave, wish for, long for (30)

אָפָה (Q) to bake (25)

אָתָה (Q) to come; (Hi) bring (21)

בָּזָה (Q) to despise, regard with contempt (42)

בָּכָה (Q) to weep (in grief or joy), weep (for) (114)

בָּלָה (Q) to be(come) worn out, used up or exhausted (16)

בָּנָה (Q) to build (up), rebuild, build (establish) a family; (Ni) be built, have a child (by or from) (377)

גָּלָה (Q) to uncover, reveal, disclose; (Ni) uncover, reveal oneself, be revealed, exposed; (Pi) uncover, reveal, disclose; (Hi) take (carry away) into exile (187)

גָּרָה (Hith) to strive (against), oppose, battle (15)

דָּמָה (Q) to be like, resemble; (Pi) liken, compare (30)

דָּמָה (Ni) to be destroyed, ruined (12); cf דָּמָה (#965)

הָגָה (Q) to utter a sound, growl, moan, groan, coo (of a dove), speak, proclaim (25)

הָיָה (Q) to be, become, happen, occur; (Ni) be done, brought about, come to pass, occur (3,576)

הָמָה (Q) to make (a) noise, make a sound, roar, growl, moan, groan, be boisterous (34)

הָרָה (Q) to conceive, be(come) pregnant (43)

זָנָה (Q) to commit fornication, be a harlot (prostitute), be unfaithful (60)

זָרָה (Q) to scatter; (Pi) scatter, disperse, spread (38)

חָוָה (Hishtaphel) to bow down, worship (173)

חָזָה (Q) to see, behold, perceive (55)

חָיָה (Q) to live, be alive, revive, restore to life; (Pi) preserve alive, let live, give life; (Hi) preserve, keep alive, revive, restore to life (283)

חָכָה (Pi) to wait (for), tarry, long for, be patient (14)

חָלָה (Q) to be(come) weak, tired, sick; (Ni) be exhausted; (Pi) appease, flatter (75)

חָנָה (Q) to decline, camp, encamp, pitch camp, lay siege to (143)

חָסָה (Q) to seek or take refuge (37)

חָפָה (Q) to cover; (Pi) overlay (with) (12)

חָצָה (Q) to divide (into) (15)

חָרָה (Q) to be(come) hot, burn with anger, become angry (93)

חָשָׁה (Q) to be silent; (Hi) be silent, order (someone) to be silent, hesitate, delay (16)

יָדָה (Hi) to thank, praise, confess; (Hith) confess (111)

יָנָה (Q, Hi) to oppress, mistreat (19)

יָרָה (Q, Hi) to throw, shoot, cast (lots) (28); cf יָרָה (#675)

יָרָה (Hi) to instruct, teach (47)

כָּבָה (Q) to go out, be quenched, extinguished; (Pi) put out, quench, extinguish (24)

כָּלָה (Q) to be complete, finished, at an end, accomplished, spent, exhausted, come to an end; (Pi) complete, finish, bring to an end (207); cf כָּלָה (#1184)

כָּסָה (Q) to cover, conceal, hide; (Pi) cover (up), conceal, clothe (153)

כָּרָה (Q) to dig, excavate, hollow out (14)

לָאָה (Q) to be(come) tired or weary; (Ni) tire (oneself) out, be tired of something; (Hi) make weary (19)

לָוָה (Q) to borrow; (Hi) lend to (14)

לָוָה (Ni) to join oneself to (12)

מָחָה (Q) to wipe (out), destroy, annihilate (34)

מָנָה (Q) to count, number, reckon, assign, appoint (28)

מָרָה (Q) to be rebellious, obstinate or contentious; (Hi) behave rebelliously or obstinately (44)

נָזָה (Q) to spatter (blood); (Hi) sprinkle (24)

נָחָה (Q) to lead; (Hi) lead, guide, conduct (39)

נָטָה (Q) to spread out, stretch out, extend, pitch (a tent), turn, bend; (Hi) turn, incline, stretch out, spread out (216)

נָכָה (Hi) to strike, smite, beat, strike dead, destroy; (Hoph) be struck down dead, beaten (501)

נָסָה (Pi) to test, put someone to the test, tempt (36)

נָקָה (Ni) to be free (of), without guilt, innocent, exempt from (punishment); (Pi) leave unpunished, regard as innocent (44)

נָשָׁה (Q) to forget (18)

סָפָה (Q) to take, sweep, snatch or carry away; (Ni) be carried, swept or snatched away (19)

עָוָה (Q) to do wrong; (Ni) be disturbed or irritated; (Hi) twist, pervert, do wrong (17)

עָטָה (Q) to wrap, cover or envelop (oneself) with (13)

עָלָה (Q) to go up, ascend; (Ni) be taken up; (Hi) bring or lead up or out, offer up (sacrifice) (894)

עָנָה (Q) to answer, respond, reply, testify; (Ni) be answered (316)

עָנָה (Q) to be afflicted, humbled; (Pi) afflict, oppress, humiliate, violate (79); cf עָנָה (#152, #1467)

עָנָה (Q) to sing (16)

עָרָה (Pi) to uncover, reveal, expose, lay bare, empty; (Hi) uncover, make naked, expose (15)

עָשָׂה (Q) to do, make; (Ni) be done, made (2,632)

פָּדָה (Q) to ransom, redeem, buy out (60)

פָּנָה (Q) to turn (toward, from, to the side, away) (134)

פָּצָה (Q) to open (the mouth), speak (15)

פָּרָה (Q) to bear fruit, be fruitful (29)

פָּשָׂה (Q) to spread (the symptoms of disease) (22)

פָּתָה (Q) to be simple, inexperienced, or gullible; (Pi) fool, deceive, persuade, seduce (27)

צִוָּה (Pi) to command, give an order, charge; (Pu) be ordered, be told, receive a command (496)

צָפָה (Q) to keep watch, watch attentively, spy (37)

צִפָּה (Pi) to overlay, plate (with gold) (47)

קִוָּה (Pi) to wait (for), wait with eagerness, hope (47)

קָנָה (Q) to get, acquire, buy (85)

קָרָה (Q) to encounter, meet, befall, happen to (22)

קָשָׁה (Q) to be heavy, hard, or difficult; (Hi) make hard, harden, make stubborn or obstinate (28)

רָאָה (Q) to see, perceive, understand; (Ni) appear; (Pu) be seen; (Hi) let or cause someone to see (something) (1,311)

רָבָה (Q) to be(come) numerous, great, increase; (Hi) make many, make great, multiply, increase (229)

רָדָה (Q) to rule (over), have dominion over, govern (with the nuance of oppression), tread (in) the winepress (22)

רָוָה (Q) to drink one's fill; (Pi, Hi) drink abundantly, water thoroughly, drench, saturate (14)

רָעָה (Q) to pasture, tend (flocks), graze, shepherd, feed (167)

רָפָה (Q) to sink, drop, relax, grow slack; (Hi) abandon, forsake, desert, leave (someone) alone (46)

רָצָה (Q) to be pleased with, favorable toward, well disposed toward, accept (with pleasure), become friends with (48)

שָׁבָה (Q) to take captive, deport (47)

שָׁגָה (Q) to stray (of sheep), go astray (morally), err, do or go wrong (unintentionally), stagger, reel (21)

שָׁוָה (Q) to be(come) like or similar to, be the equal of, resemble; (Pi) make like, make level (16)

שָׁנָה (Q) to change; (Pi) change, alter, pervert (15)

שָׁסָה (Q) to plunder, spoil (11)

שָׁעָה (Q) to gaze at, look at, look (regard) with favor, be concerned about (13)

שָׁקָה (Hi) to give drink (to), irrigate (62)

שָׁתָה (Q) to drink (217)

תָּלָה (Q) to hang (up) (29)

תָּעָה (Q) to err, wander (about), stagger, go astray (animal); (Hi) lead astray, cause to err (51)

Weak Verbs: III-ה/ע
Listed Alphabetically

In the Hebrew Old Testament, there are 144 III-ה/ע verbal roots with a total occurrence of 7,207 times. 60 of these verbs occur more than 10 times.

אָנַח (Ni) to sigh, groan (13)

בָּטַח (Q) to trust, rely upon (118)

בָּלַע (Q, Pi) to swallow (up), engulf (42)

בָּצַע (Q) to cut off, sever, break off (away), make profit (16)

בָּקַע (Q) to cleave, split, breach, break open; (Ni) be cleft, split (open); (Pi) split, rip open (51)

בָּרַח (Q) to run away, flee, go or pass through (63)

גָּדַע (Q) to cut off, cut down; (Ni) be cut off, cut down, cut into pieces; (Pi) cut down, cut to pieces (22)

גָּוַע (Q) to die, expire, pass away, perish (24)

גִּלַּח (Pi) to shave (23)

גָּרַע (Q) to shave, trim (a beard), diminish, restrain, withdraw (21)

זָבַח (Q) to slaughter (for sacrifice), sacrifice; (Pi) offer sacrifice, sacrifice (134)

זָנַח (Q) to reject, spurn (19)

זָרַח (Q) to rise (sun), shine, come out, appear, break out (leprosy) (18)

זָרַע (Q) to sow, scatter seed (56)

טָבַח (Q) to slaughter, butcher, slay (11)

טָבַע (Q) to sink, penetrate; (Hoph) be sunk, settled, or planted (10)

יָגַע (Q) to toil, labor, struggle, grow or be weary (26)

יָדַע (Q) to know, know sexually (have intercourse with); (Ni) be(come) known, reveal oneself; (Hi) make known, inform (956)

יָכַח (Hi) to reprove, rebuke, reproach, chasten, punish, decide, mediate, arbitrate (59)

יָשַׁע (Ni) to be delivered, victorious, receive help; (Hi) help, save, deliver, rescue, come to the aid of (205)

כָּנַע (Ni) to be subdued, humbled, humble oneself; (Hi) humble or subdue someone (36)

258

כָּרַע (Q) to bow (down), kneel (down), fall to one's knees (36)

לָקַח (Q) to take, grasp, capture, seize; (Ni) be captured, taken away (967)

מָנַע (Q) to withhold, hold back, retain, refuse, restrain (29)

מָשַׁח (Q) to smear (with a liquid, oil, or dye), anoint (with oil) (70)

נָבַע (Hi) to make (something) gush or bubble (forth), pour out or ferment (11)

נָגַח (Q) to gore (ox as subject); (Pi) push, butt, thrust, knock down (11)

נָגַע (Q) to touch, strike, reach; (Hi) touch, reach, throw, arrive (150)

נָדַח (Ni) to be scattered, banished, driven away, thrust out; (Hi) scatter, drive away, disperse, thrust out (51)

נָטַע (Q) to plant (59)

נָסַע (Q) to pull (out or up), set out, start out, depart, journey (146)

נָפַח (Q) to breathe, blow, blow fire upon, set aflame, gasp, pant (12)

נָצַח (Pi) to supervise, oversee or inspect works and activities related to the temple; מְנַצֵּחַ (ptc) used as title (superscription) in 55 psalms (65)

סָלַח (Q) to pardon, forgive; (Ni) be forgiven (47)

פָּגַע (Q) to meet, encounter, fall upon, attack, assail, reach (46)

פָּרַח (Q) to bud, sprout, bloom, shoot, break out, break open (34)

פָּרַע (Q) to let go, loose or free, let the hair of the head hang loose, allow to run wild, leave unattended (16)

פָּשַׁע (Q) to revolt, rebel (against), transgress, break with, break away from, behave as a criminal (41)

פָּתַח (Q) to open (up); (Ni) be opened, loosened, set free; (Pi) let loose, loosen (136)

צָלַח (Q) to succeed, prosper, be successful; (Hi) be successful, succeed, cause to succeed or prosper (65)

צָמַח (Q) to sprout, spring up, grow; (Hi) make grow or sprout (33)

צָרַע (Q) to be afflicted with a skin disease (usually leprosy); (Pu) be struck with a skin disease (20)

קָרַע (Q) to tear, rend, cut up, tear away (63)

רָבַע (Q) to provide with four corners, make square (12)

רָגַע (Q) to crust over or become hard (of skin), stir up (sea); (Hi) give rest to, come to rest, make peace, linger (13)

רָוַח (Q) to get relief; (Pu) be wide or spacious; (Hi) smell (14)

רָעַע (Q) to be bad, evil or displeasing; (Hi) do evil, do wickedly, do injury, harm, treat badly (98)

רָצַח (Q) to kill, murder, slay (47)

רָקַע (Q) to stamp (down or out), trample, spread out; (Pi) beat out, hammer out (11)

רָשַׁע (Hi) to condemn, declare or pronounce guilty (35)

שָׂבַע (Q) to be satisfied, have one's fill (of), eat or drink one's fill; (Hi) satisfy (97)

שָׂמַח (Q) to rejoice, be joyful, glad; (Pi) cause to rejoice, gladden, make someone happy (156)

שָׁבַע (Ni) to swear (take) an oath; (Hi) cause to take an oath, plead with someone (186)

שָׁוַע (Pi) to cry or call for help (21)

שָׁחַח (Q) to cower, crouch, bow down (18)

שָׁכַח (Q) to forget; (Ni) be forgotten (102)

שָׁלַח (Q) to send, stretch out; (Pi) send, stretch out, send away, expel; (Pu) be sent away (off) (847)

שָׁמַע (Q) to hear, listen to, understand, obey; (Ni) be heard; (Hi) proclaim (1,165)

תָּקַע (Q) to drive or thrust (weapon into a person), pitch (tent), blow (trumpet), clap one's hands (70)

Weak Verbs: III-א
Listed Alphabetically

In the Hebrew Old Testament, there are 49 III-א verbal roots with a total occurrence of 4,696 times. 21 of these verbs occur more than 10 times.

בָּרָא (Q) to create (only with God as subject); (Ni) be created (48)

דָּכָא (Pi) to crush, beat to pieces (18)

חָבָא (Ni) to hide (oneself), be hidden; (Hith) keep oneself hidden (34)

חָטָא (Q) to miss (a goal or mark), sin, commit a sin; (Pi) make a sin offering; (Hi) cause to sin (240)

טָמֵא (Q) to be(come) unclean; (Ni) defile oneself; (Pi) defile, pronounce or declare unclean; (Hith) defile oneself, become unclean (162)

יָצָא (Q) to go or come out; (Hi) cause to go or come out, lead out, bring out (1,076)

יָרֵא (Q) to fear, be afraid, be in awe of, reverence; (Ni) be feared, held in honor (317); cf יָרֵא (#539)

כָּלָא (Q) to shut up, restrain, withhold, keep back (17)

מָלֵא (Q) to be full, fill (up); (Ni) be filled (with); (Pi) fill, perform, carry out, consecrate as priest (252)

מָצָא (Q) to find (out), reach, obtain, achieve; (Ni) be found (457)

נָבָא (Ni) to prophesy, be in a state of prophetic ecstasy; (Hith) speak or behave as a prophet (115)

נָשָׂא (Q) to lift, carry, raise, bear (load or burden), take (away); (Ni) be carried, lifted up, exalted; (Pi) lift up, exalt; (Hith) lift oneself up, exalt oneself (659)

נָשָׁא (Hi) to deceive, cheat, trick (14)

פָּלָא (Ni) to be extraordinary, wonderful; (Hi) do something wonderful (71)

צָבָא (Q) to wage war, go to war, fight against (14)

צָמֵא (Q) to thirst, be thirsty (10)

קָנָא (Pi) to envy, be envious of, jealous of, zealous for (34)

קָרָא (Q) to call, summon, proclaim, read aloud, give a name to; (Ni) be called, summoned, proclaimed (739); cf קָרָה (#301)

קָרָא (Q) to meet, encounter, happen; inf cstr with prep לְ
(לִקְרַאת) toward, against, opposite (136); cf קָרָא (#70)
and קָרָה (#1198)

רָפָא (Q) to heal; (Ni) be healed, become whole; (Pi) heal,
make healthy (69)

שָׂנֵא (Q) to hate; (Pi ptc) enemy (148)

Weak Verbs: Biconsonantal
Listed Alphabetically

In the Hebrew Old Testament, there are approximately 180 Biconsonantal verbal roots with a total occurrence of approximately 9,000 times. 67 of these verbs occur more than 10 times.

אוּץ (Q) to urge, press, be in a hurry, pressed (10)

אוֹר (Hi) to give light, shine, illuminate, light up (44)

בּוֹא (Q) to go in, enter, come to, come upon; (Hi) bring (in), come (in); (Hoph) be brought (2,592)

בּוּז (Q) to show contempt (for), despise (14)

בּוּס (Q) to tread down, trample under foot (12)

בּוֹשׁ (Q) to be ashamed; (Hi) put to shame (125)

בִּין (Q) to understand, perceive, consider, give heed to; (Ni) be discerning, have understanding; (Hi) understand, teach; (Hith) show oneself perceptive (171)

גּוּר (Q) to sojourn, dwell (stay) as a foreigner or alien (82)

גּוּר (Q) to be afraid, dread, stand in awe (10)

גִּיל (Q) to shout with joy, rejoice (47)

דּוּשׁ (Q) to tread on, trample down (out), thresh, exterminate, destroy; also spelled דִּישׁ (16)

דִּין (Q) to judge, minister or execute judgment, plead one's cause, contend with (24)

זוּב (Q) to flow (away), suffer a discharge (42)

זִיד (Q) to act insolently; (Hi) boil or cook, become hot (with anger), behave arrogantly (10)

חוּל (Q) to go around, whirl (about), dance, writhe; also spelled חִיל (10)

חוּס (Q) to pity, look upon with compassion, spare (24)

חוּשׁ (Q) to hurry, make haste (18)

חִיל (Q) to writhe, travail, be in labor, tremble; also spelled חוּל (48)

טוֹב (Q) to be good, pleasing, pleasant, joyful, well with (44); cf טוֹב (#92) and יָטַב (#343)

טוּחַ (Q) to plaster (wall of a house), coat, overlay (11)

טוּל (Hi) to throw (far), cast, hurl; (Hoph) be thrown, hurled (14)

כּוּל (Q) to comprehend; (Pilpel) contain, sustain, provide, support; (Hi) contain, hold (in), sustain, endure (38)

כּוּן (Ni) to be established, steadfast, ready, arranged, stand firm; (Hi) establish, set up, prepare, make ready, make firm; (Polel) set up, establish (219)

לוּן (Ni, Hi) to murmur (against), grumble (17)

לִין (Q) to remain overnight, spend the night (71)

לִיץ (Q) to boast (28)

מוּג (Q) to waver, melt; (Ni) wave, sway back and forth, undulate (17)

מוֹט (Q) to totter, shake, sway, stagger; (Ni) be made to stagger, stumble, or totter (39)

מוּל (Q) to circumcise; (Ni) be circumcised (32)

מוּר (Hi) to change, alter, exchange (14)

מוּשׁ (Q) to withdraw (from a place), cease from, leave off, depart (21)

מוּת (Q) to die; (Hi) kill, put to death; (Hoph) be killed (845)

נוּד (Q) to move to and fro, sway, wander, be(come) aimless, express grief or sympathy (by shaking the head) (25)

נוּחַ (Q) to rest, settle down, repose; (Hi) cause to rest, secure rest, set, leave (behind or untouched) (140)

נוּס (Q) to flee, escape (160)

נוּעַ (Q) to tremble, shake, totter, wave (of trees); (Hi) make unstable or unsteady, shake (up), disturb (42)

נוּף (Hi) to move back and forth, wave, brandish, wield (34)

סוּג (Q) to backslide, be disloyal; (Ni) turn back, withdraw, become disloyal (24)

סוּךְ (Q) to grease (oneself) with oil, anoint (10)

סוּר (Q) to turn (aside), turn off, leave (off), desist; (Hi) remove, take away, get rid of (298)

סוּת (Hi) to incite (against), stir up, provoke, instigate, seduce, mislead, lead astray (18)

עוּד (Hi) to warn, admonish, witness, be a witness, testify (40)

עוּף (Q) to fly (27)

עוּר (Q) to be awake, stir up; (Hi) arouse, rouse, wake up, stir up; (Polel) arouse, disturb, awaken (80)

פּוּחַ (Hi) to testify (10)

פּוּץ (Q) to be spread, dispersed, scattered, overflow; (Ni) be scattered, dispersed; (Hi) scatter, disperse (65)

צוּד (Q) to hunt (17)

צוּם (Q) to fast, abstain from food and drink (21)

צוּק (Hi) to oppress, press hard, harass, constrain (12)

צוּר (Q) to tie up, bind, shut in, shut up, enclose, encircle, besiege (31)

קוּם (Q) to rise, arise, get up, stand (up); (Hi) set up, put up, cause to arise, establish (627)

קיץ (Hi) to awake, wake up (22)

רוּם (Q) to be high, exalted, rise, arise; (Hi) raise, lift up, exalt, take away; (Hoph) be exalted; (Polel) exalt, bring up, extol, raise (children) (197)

רוּעַ (Hi) to shout, cry (out), shout a war cry (alarm of battle), sound a signal for war, cheer, shout in triumph (44)

רוּץ (Q) to run (104)

רוּשׁ (Q) to be poor (24)

רִיב (Q) to strive, contend, quarrel, dispute, conduct a legal case (72)

רִיק (Hi) to empty out, pour out (19) and רִיק (#1601)

שׂוּשׂ (Q) to rejoice; also spelled שִׂישׂ (27)

שִׂיחַ (Q) to consider, meditate, complain, lament, praise (20)

שִׂים (Q) to set (up), put, place, set in place, establish; also spelled שׂוּם (588)

שׁוּב (Q) to turn back, turn, return; (Hi) cause to return, bring back, restore; (Polel) bring back, restore (1,075)

שׁוּט (Q) to roam (around), go (rove) about, row (across water); (Polel) roam about (around) (13)

שׁוּר (Q) to behold, regard (15)

שִׁיר (Q) to sing (of); (Q and Polel ptc) singer (88) and שִׁירָה (#1675)

שִׁית (Q) to set, put, place, set one's mind to (86)

תּוּר (Q) to spy out, reconnoiter, explore, investigate (24)263

Weak Verbs: Geminate
Listed Alphabetically

In the Hebrew Old Testament, there are 174 Geminate verbal roots with a total occurrence of 2,316 times. 50 of these verbs occur more than 10 times.

אָרַר (Q) to curse (63)

בָּזַז (Q) to plunder, spoil (43)

בָּלַל (Q) to mix (up), confuse or confound (languages), mingle (44)

בָּרַר (Q) to purify, purge, sort, choose, select (16)

גָּזַז (Q) to shear, cut (15)

גָּלַל (Q) to roll (away) (18)

דָּמַם (Q) to be silent, still, motionless, (struck) dumb, keep quiet, stand still (19)

דָּקַק (Q) to crush, become fine through grinding; (Hi) crush fine, pulverize; (Hoph) be crushed fine (12)

הָלַל (Pi) to praise, sing hallelujah; (Pu) be praised, praiseworthy; (Hith) boast (146); cf הָלַל (#1501)

הָלַל (Q) to be infatuated, deluded; (Hithpolel) be mad, act like a madman (15); cf הָלַל (#282)

הָמַם (Q) to make (a) noise, confuse, bring into motion and confusion (army), discomfit, disturb (13)

זָמַם (Q) to consider, think, ponder, devise, plan (evil), purpose (13)

חָגַג (Q) to stagger, reel, celebrate a pilgrimage festival (16)

חָלַל (Ni) to be defiled, profaned, defile oneself; (Pi) profane, pollute, defile; (Hi) let something be profaned (135)

חָמַם (Q) to be(come) warm (23)

חָנַן (Q) to be gracious to, show favor to, favor; (Hith) plead for grace, favor, or compassion (77)

חָקַק (Q) to hew out or carve out (a grave), inscribe, engrave, enact, decree (19)

חָתַת (Q) to be shattered, dismayed, filled with terror (55)

יָלַל (Hi) to howl, lament, wail (31)

כָּתַת (Q) to beat, crush fine, hammer (into pieces); (Pi) beat, hammer, crush to pieces (17)

מָדַד (Q) to measure, measure off (distance or expanse), measure out (grain) (52)

מָסַס (Ni) to melt (away), dissolve, become weak (21)

מָקַק (Ni) to rot (away), fester (wounds), dwindle or waste away, decay, melt, dissolve (10)

מָרַר (Q) to be bitter (of taste, experience or attitude), desperate; (Hi) embitter, cause bitterness or grief (16)

מָשַׁשׁ (Q) to feel, touch; (Pi) feel (over, through), grope, search, rummage through (10)

נָדַד (Q) to flee, wander (about), depart, move, flutter (wings) (28)

סָבַב (Q) to turn (about), go around, surround; (Ni) turn; (Hi) cause to go around, lead around; (Polel) encompass with protection (163)

סָכַךְ (Q) to overshadow, cover (protectively), protect (16)

סָלַל (Q) to pile up, heap up, lift up, exalt, praise (12)

סָרַר (Q) to be stubborn or rebellious (17)

עָזַז (Q) to be strong, prevail (against), defy (11)

עָלַל (Polel) to deal or act severely with, treat violently, glean (19)

עָנַן (Polel) to practice soothsaying, conjure up (spirits), interpret signs (11)

פָּלַל (Hith) to pray, make intercession (84)

פָּרַר (Hi) to break (out), destroy, put an end to, make ineffectual (47)

צָרַר (Q) to wrap (up), tie up, bind (transitive); be cramped, restricted, depressed (intransitive); (Hi) oppress, harass, afflict (47)

צָרַר (Q) to be hostile (toward), treat with hostility, attack (26)

קָבַב (Q) to curse (14)

קָדַד (Q) to bow down, kneel down (15)

קָלַל (Q) to be small, insignificant, of little account, swift; (Ni, Pi) declare cursed; (Hi) treat with contempt (82)

271

קָצַץ (Q) to cut (chop) off, trim; (Pi) cut (chop) off, cut in pieces (14)

רָבַב (Q) to be(come) many, numerous or great (23)

רָנַן (Q) to call or cry aloud, shout with joy; (Pi) cry out (with joy), exult (53)

רָעַע (Q) to be bad, evil or displeasing; (Hi) do evil, do wickedly, do injury, harm, treat badly (98)

רָצַץ (Q) to crush, oppress, mistreat (19)

שָׁדַד (Q) to devastate, ruin, deal violently with, violently destroy; (Pu) be devastated (59)

שָׁחַח (Q) to cower, crouch, bow down (18)

שָׁלַל (Q) to plunder, spoil, capture, rob (14)

שָׁמֵם (Q) to be deserted, uninhabited; (Ni) be made uninhabited, desolate, deserted; (Hi) make deserted or desolated (92)

תָּמַם (Q) to be(come) complete or finished, come to an end, cease, be consumed, burned out (64)

Index of Hebrew Words

The following index contains an alphabetical listing of the Hebrew words found throughout this volume. This index does not include inflected forms listed within entries. Identical words are distinguished by their entry numbers in the frequency lists.

אָב	34
אָבַד	13, 192, 233
אָבָה	30, 192, 240, 252
אֶבְיוֹן	27, 183
אַבִּיר	61, 183
אֵבֶל	51, 86, 174
אָבֵל	77
אֶבֶל	40, 86, 192, 233
אֶבֶן	10, 171, 174
אִגֶּרֶת	80
אָדוֹן	4
אֵדוֹת	77
אַדִּיר	48, 86, 183
אָדָם	80, 192, 233
אָדָם	6
אֲדָמָה	11
אֶדֶן	28, 174
אַדֶּרֶת	75, 86
אָהַב	11, 86, 192, 233, 243
אַהֲבָה	43, 86
אָהָה	67
אֹהֶל	8, 174
אוֹ	8
אוֹב	64
אָוָה	45, 86, 192, 240, 252
אוֹי	51
אֱוִיל	48
אוּלַי	34
אוּלָם	(#552) 27, 160
אוּלָם	(#1273) 58, 160
אוֶּלֶת	50
אָוֶן	22, 174
אוֹן	64
אוֹפָן	41

אוּץ	80, 192, 233, 265
אוֹצָר	23
אוֹר	(#332) 17, 86, 160, 168
אוֹר	(#707) 34, 86, 160, 192, 233, 265
אוֹת	23, 168
אָז	15
אֵזוֹב	81
אֵזוֹר	69, 86
אֹזֶן	13, 86, 171, 174
אָזַן	36, 86, 192, 233
אָזַר	64, 86, 192, 233
אֶזְרָח	61
אָח	5
אֶחָד	4
אָחוֹר	36
אָחוֹת	17
אָחַז	26, 86, 192, 233, 243
אֲחֻזָּה	26, 86
אָחַר	60, 86, 192, 233, 243
אַחַר	5, 86, 189
אַחֵר	14, 86, 183
אַחֲרוֹן	30, 86, 183
אַחֲרֵי	5, 86, 189
אַחֲרִית	27, 86
אִי	42
אִי	40
אֹיֵב	9
אֵיד	51
אַיֵּה	52
אֵיךְ	27
אֵיכָה	61
אַיִל	77

אַיִל	(#247) 13, 160
אַיִל	(#1173) 54, 160
אַיָּלָה	77
אֵילָם	27
אֵימָה	61
אַיִן	(#60) 4, 160
אַיִן	(#1361) 61, 160
אֵיפָה	37
אֵיפֹה	81
אִישׁ	3
אֵיתָן	69, 183
אַךְ	14
אָכַל	4, 87, 192, 233
אֹכֶל	38, 87, 174
אָכְלָה	60, 87
אָכֵן	61
אַל	5
אֶל	2, 189
אֵל	10
אָלָה	41
אֵלֶּה	5
אֵלָה	72
אֱלֹהִים	2
אֱלוֹהַּ	28
אַלּוֹן	81
אַלּוּף	27
אֱלִיל	55
אַלְמָנָה	29
אֶלֶף	(#101) 6, 160, 174
אֶלֶף	(#1749) 77, 160, 174
אֵם	11, 171
אִם	3
אָמָה	29
אַמָּה	10

אֱמוּנָה	31, 87	אֶפֶס	35, 174	אַשְׁרֵי	34, 88
אָמָל	67, 192, 233	אֵפֶר	54, 174	אַתְּ	25
אָמֵן	45, 87	אֶצְבַּע	44, 171	אֵת	(#5) 2, 160
אָמַן	20, 87, 192, 233	אֵצֶל	27, 189	אֵת	(#50) 4, 160, 189
אָמֵץ	36, 192, 233	אָרַב	36, 192, 233, 243	אַתָּה	55, 193, 240, 252
אָמַר	2, 87, 192, 233	אַרְבֶּה	51, 122	אַתָּה	5
אֵמֶר	32, 87, 174	אַרְבַּע	7, 122	אָתוֹן	41, 171
אִמְרָה	40, 87	אַרְבָּעָה	7	אַתֶּם	9
אֱמֶת	17, 87	אַרְבָּעִים	7	אֶתְנַן	77
אַמְתַּחַת	67	אָרַג	72, 172, 233, 243	בְּ	2, 189
אָן	35	אַרְגָּמָן	38	בְּאֵר	39, 171
אָנָּא	72	אָרוֹן	12, 168	בָּאַשׁ	60, 193, 243
אָנָה	35	אֶרֶז	24, 174	בָּגַד	31, 193
אֱנוֹשׁ	36	אֹרַח	28, 168, 174	בֶּגֶד	11, 174
אָנַח	72, 87, 192, 233, 258	אֲרִי	41	בִּגְלַל	81
אֲנָחָה	77, 87	אַרְיֵה	32	בַּד	(#782) 37, 160
אֲנַחְנוּ	17	אָרַךְ	41, 87, 193, 233, 243	בַּד	(#1136) 52, 160
אֲנִי	4	אֶרֶךְ	67, 87, 183	בָּדָד	77
אֳנִיָּה	43	אֹרֶךְ	20, 87, 174	בָּדַל	36, 193
אָנֹכִי	4	אַרְמוֹן	43	בֶּדֶק	81, 174
אָנַף	69, 87, 192, 233	אֶרֶץ	2, 171, 174	בָּהַל	38, 193, 243
אָסִיר	69, 87	אָרַר	26, 193, 233, 243, 270	בְּהֵמָה	13
אָסַף	12, 192, 233	אָרַשׂ	77, 193, 234	בֹּהֶן	64, 174
אָסַר	24, 87, 192, 233	אֵשׁ	7, 168	בַּהֶרֶת	75
אִסָּר	77, 87	אִשָּׁה	4	בּוֹא	2, 88, 193, 265
אַף	(#170) 10, 87, 160	אִשֶּׁה	26	בּוּז	(#1546) 69, 88, 160, 193, 265
אַף	(#309) 16, 160	אָשַׁם	41, 88, 193, 234	בּוּז	(#1755) 77, 88, 160
אֵפֹד	31	אָשָׁם	33, 88	בּוּס	75, 193, 265
אָפָה	50, 192, 240, 252	אַשְׁמָה	58, 88	בּוֹר	25
אֵפוֹא	67	אֲשֶׁר	2	בּוֹשׁ	17, 88, 193, 265
אָפִיק	60	אֹשֶׁר	81, 88, 193, 234	בַּז	50, 88
אֲפֵלָה	81	אֲשֵׁרָה	37	בָּזָה	36, 193, 252

Index of Hebrew Words

בָּזָה	81, 88
בָּזַז	35, 88, 193, 270
בָּחוּר	34
בָּחִיר	72, 88, 183
בָּחַן	46, 193, 243
בָּחַר	13, 88, 193, 243
בָּטַח	18, 88, 193, 258
בֶּטַח	36, 88, 174
בֶּטֶן	24, 171, 174
בִּי	75
בֵּין	7, 189
בִּין	13, 89, 193, 265
בִּינָה	38, 89
בִּירָה	60
בַּיִת	3
בָּכָה	18, 89, 193, 252
בְּכוֹר	17, 89
בִּכּוּרִים	62, 89
בְּכִי	45, 89
בְּכֹרָה	75, 89
בַּל	24
בָּלָה	64, 89, 194, 252
בַּלָּהָה	81
בְּלִי	28, 89
בְּלִיַּעַל	48, 183
בָּלַל	34, 194, 270
בָּלַע	36, 194, 258
בִּלְעֲדֵי	62, 189
בִּלְתִּי	19
בָּמָה	19
בְּמוֹ	81, 189
בֵּן	2
בָּנָה	7, 89, 194, 252
בַּעֲבוּר	31, 189
בַּעַד	19, 189
בָּעַל	65, 89, 194, 243
בַּעַל	14, 89, 174
בָּעַר	(#558) 27, 160, 194, 243
בָּעַר	(#1030) 48, 160, 194, 243
בָּעַת	65, 194, 243
בָּצוּר	49, 183
בָּצַע	65, 89, 194, 258
בֶּצַע	52, 89, 174
בָּקַע	31, 89, 194, 258
בִּקְעָה	58, 89
בָּקָר	13
בֹּקֶר	12, 174
בְּקֶרֶב	11, 179
בָּקַשׁ	11, 194
בַּר	69
בָּרָא	32, 194, 243, 262
בָּרָד	46
בְּרוֹשׁ	57
בַּרְזֶל	23
בָּרַח	26, 194, 243, 258
בָּרִיא	69, 183
בְּרִיחַ	37
בְּרִית	9
בֶּרֶךְ	49, 171, 174
בָּרַךְ	8, 90, 194, 243
בְּרֵכָה	62
בְּרָכָה	25, 90
בָּרָק	55
בָּרַר	65, 194, 243, 270
בֹּשֶׂם	45, 174
בָּשָׂר	51, 194
בָּשַׂר	10
בָּשַׁל	47, 194
בֹּשֶׁת	37, 88, 174
בַּת	(#82) 5, 160
בַּת	(#1616) 72, 160
בְּתוֹךְ	8, 189
בְּתוּלָה	31, 90
בְּתוּלִים	81, 90
גַּאֲוָה	58
גָּאוֹן	31
גָּאַל	(#372) 19, 90, 161, 194, 243
גָּאַל	(#1756) 78, 161, 194, 243
גְּאֻלָּה	69, 90
גַּב	75
גָּבַהּ	41, 90, 194
גֹּבַהּ	62, 90
גָּבֹהַּ	37, 90, 183
גְּבוּל	10
גִּבּוֹר	14, 90, 183
גְּבוּרָה	27, 90
גָּבִיעַ	69
גְּבִירָה	76, 90
גִּבְעָה	24
גָּבַר	50, 90, 194
גֶּבֶר	26, 90, 175
גָּג	44
גְּדוּד	44
גָּדוֹל	6, 90, 183
גְּדוּלָה	72, 90
גְּדִי	65
גָּדַל	18, 90, 195
גָּדֵל	72, 90, 175

גָּדַע	57, 195, 258	גַּנָּה	75	דֶּלֶת	21, 175
גָּדַר	81, 90, 195	גָּעַל	81, 195, 244	דָּם	8
גֶּדֶר	67, 90	גָּעַר	69, 91, 195, 244	דָּמָה	(#965) 45, 161, 196, 252
גּוֹי	5	גְּעָרָה	67, 91	דָּמָה	(#1690) 75, 161, 196, 252
גְּוִיָּה	72	גָּעַשׁ	81, 195, 244	דְּמוּת	50
גּוֹלָה	36, 91	גֶּפֶן	29, 168, 175	דָּמַם	58, 196, 270
גָּוַע	51, 195, 258	גֵּר	21, 91	דִּמְעָה	52
גּוּר	(#430) 22, 91, 161, 195, 265	גָּרָה	67, 195, 244, 252	דַּעַת	21, 100, 175
גּוּר	(#1839) 81, 161, 195, 265	גֵּרָה	78	דַּק	69, 92, 183
גּוֹרָל	23	גֹּרֶן	39, 171, 175	דָּקַק	75, 92, 196, 270
גָּזַז	67, 195, 270	גָּרַע	55, 195, 244, 258	דָּקַר	78, 196
גָּזִית	78	גָּרַשׁ	34, 195, 244	דָּרוֹם	62
גָּזַל	45, 195	גֶּשֶׁם	41, 175	דָּרַךְ	27, 92, 196, 244
גָּזַר	75, 195	דֹּב	75	דֶּרֶךְ	5, 92, 168, 175
גַּחֶלֶת	60	דְּבִיר	65	דָּרַשׁ	14, 196, 244
גַּיְא	26, 168	דָּבַק	29, 196	דֶּשֶׁא	69, 175
גִּיל	32, 195, 265	דָּבַר	3, 91	דָּשֵׁן	78, 92, 196
גַּל	(#1325) 60, 161	דָּבָר	3, 91, 196	דֶּשֶׁן	67, 92, 175
גַּל	(#1440) 65, 161	דֶּבֶר	33, 175	דָּת	54
גֻּלְגֹּלֶת	75	דְּבַשׁ	30	הַ ·	2
גָּלָה	13, 91, 195, 252	דָּג	58	הַ	5
גֻּלָּה	67	דָּגָה	67	הֶאָח	75
גִּלּוּלִים	32	דֶּגֶל	69, 175	הֶבֶל	24, 175
גָּלוּת	67, 91	דָּגָן	37	הָגָה	50, 196, 240, 252
גָּלַח	52, 195, 258	דּוֹד	27	הָדַף	78, 196, 234
גָּלַל	60, 91, 195, 270	דּוֹר	14	הָדַר	45
גַּם	4	דּוּשׁ	65, 196, 265	הוּא	3
גָּמוּל	58, 91	דַּי	38	הוֹד	51
גָּמַל	39, 91, 195	דִּין	(#1115) 51, 91, 161, 196, 265	הַוָּה	72
גָּמָל	30	דִּין	(#1279) 58, 91, 161	הוֹי	31
גַּן	37, 168	דָּכָא	60, 196, 262	הוֹן	49
גָּנַב	37, 91, 195	דַּל	32, 183	הִיא	6
גַּנָּב	62, 91				

הָיָה	2, 196, 240, 252	
הֵיכָל	22	
הִין	54	
הָלְאָה	65	
הָלַךְ	3, 196, 234	
הָלַל	(#282) 15, 92, 161, 196, 234, 270	
הָלַל	(#1501) 67, 161, 197, 234, 270	
הָלַם	75	
הֵם	6	
הֵמָּה	41, 92, 197, 240, 252	
הָמוֹן	22, 92	
הָמַם	72, 197, 234, 270	
הֵן	19	
הִנֵּה	3	
הִנָּה	(#570) 28, 161	
הִנָּה	(#982) 46, 161	
הָפַךְ	20, 92, 197, 234	
הַר	6	
הָרַג	14, 197, 234, 244	
הָרָה	(#728) 35, 92, 161, 197, 240, 244, 252	
הָרָה	(#1502) 67, 92, 161, 183	
הָרַס	35, 197, 234, 244	
וְ	2	
וָו	72	
זֹאת	5	
זָבַח	16, 92, 197, 258	
זֶבַח	14, 92, 175	
זֵד	72, 93, 183	
זָדוֹן	78, 93	
זֹה	78	
זֶה	3	
זָהָב	7	
זָהַר	54, 197, 244	
זוּ	67	
זוֹב	36, 93, 197, 265	
זוֹב	72, 93	
זוּלָה	65, 189	
זוֹנָה	41, 93	
זִיד	81, 93, 197, 265	
זַיִת	38	
זַךְ	78, 183	
זָכַר	10, 93, 197	
זֵכֶר	52, 93, 175	
זָכָר	22	
זִכָּרוֹן	51, 93	
זִמָּה	36	
זָמַם	72, 93, 197, 270	
זָמַר	34, 93, 197	
זָנָב	78	
זָנָה	27, 93, 197, 252	
זְנוּנִים	75, 93	
זָנַח	58, 197, 258	
זַעַם	75, 93, 197, 244	
זַעַם	54, 93, 175	
זָעַק	24, 93, 197, 244	
זְעָקָה	58, 93	
זָקֵן	(#241) 13, 94, 161, 183	
זָקֵן	(#1055) 49, 94, 161, 197	
זָקָן	58, 94, 168	
זָר	81	
זָר	25, 183	
זָרָה	39, 197, 244, 252	
זְרוֹעַ	21, 171	
זָרַח	60, 94, 197, 244, 258	
זָרַע	29, 94, 198, 244, 258	
זֶרַע	11, 94, 175	
זָרַק	41, 94, 198, 244	
חָבָא	42, 198, 234, 262	
חָבַל	(#1626) 72, 161, 198, 234	
חָבַל	(#1766) 78, 161, 198, 234	
חֶבֶל	32, 175	
חָבַק	72, 198, 234	
חָבֵר	67, 94	
חָבַר	50, 94, 198, 234	
חָבַשׁ	42, 198, 234	
חַג	27, 94	
חָגַג	69, 94, 198, 234, 270	
חָגַר	34, 198, 234	
חָדַל	29, 198, 234	
חֶדֶר	39, 175	
חָדָשׁ	81, 94, 198, 235	
חָדַשׁ	30, 94, 183	
חֹדֶשׁ	9, 94, 175	
חָוָה	13, 198, 240, 252	
חוֹחַ	78	
חוּל	81, 198, 235, 265	
חוֹל	54	
חוֹמָה	16	
חוּס	51, 198, 235, 265	

חוּץ	14	חָלָב	34	חֹמֶר	(#1370) 62, 162, 175
חוּשׁ	60, 198, 235, 265	חֵלֶב	21, 175	חֹמֶר	(#1629) 72, 162, 175
חוֹתָם	69, 98	חָלָה	23, 95, 199, 240, 253	חָמֵשׁ	6
חָזָה	29, 94, 198, 240, 252	חַלָּה	69	חֲמִשָּׁה	6
חֹזֶה	65, 94	חֲלוֹם	26, 96	חֲמִשִּׁים	6
חָזֶה	72	חַלּוֹן	43, 168	חֵן	25, 96
חָזוֹן	41, 94	חֳלִי	51, 95	חָנָה	15, 96, 199, 240, 253
חָזַק	9, 95, 198, 235	חָלִיל	55	חַנּוּן	72, 96, 184
חָזָק	29, 95, 183	חֲלִיפָה	75, 96	חֲנִית	32
חָטָא	10, 95, 198, 235, 262	חָלַל	20, 95, 184	חִנָּם	43
חֵטְא	42, 95	חָלָל	16, 95, 199, 235, 270	חָנַן	23, 96, 199, 235, 270
חַטָּא	58, 95, 183	חָלַם	46, 96, 199, 235	חָנַף	78, 97, 199, 235
חַטָּאת	9, 95	חָלַף	49, 96, 199, 235	חָנֵף	73, 97, 184
חִטָּה	45	חָלַץ	34, 199, 235	חֶסֶד	10, 175
חַי	10, 95, 183	חֲלָצַיִם	78	חָסָה	39, 97, 199, 240, 253
חִידָה	62	חָלַק	29, 96, 199, 235	חָסִיד	42, 184
חָיָה	9, 95, 198, 240, 252	חָלָק	81, 184	חָסֵר	(#1181) 54, 97, 162, 199, 235
חָיָה	(#390) 20, 95, 162	חֵלֶק	26, 96, 175	חָסֵר	(#1371) 62, 97, 162, 184
חָיָה	(#1768) 78, 95, 162	חֶלְקָה	52, 96	חָפָה	75, 199, 240, 253
חַיִּים	16, 95	חֹם	81, 96	חָפַז	81, 199, 235
חַיִל	10	חֶמְאָה	81	חָפֵץ	(#471) 24, 97, 162, 199, 236
חַיִל	32, 199, 235, 265	חָמַד	55, 96, 199, 235	חָפֵץ	(#1632) 73, 97, 162, 184,
חִיצוֹן	50, 183	חֶמְדָּה	65, 96	חֵפֶץ	39, 97, 175
חֵיק	39	חֵמָה	17, 96	חָפַר	(#1143) 52, 162, 199, 236
חֵךְ	60	חֲמוֹר	20	חָפַר	(#1372) 62, 162, 200, 236
חָכָה	69, 199, 240, 253	חָמוֹת	78	חָפַשׂ	52, 200, 236
חָכַם	47, 95, 199, 235	חֲמִישִׁי	34	חָפְשִׁי	62, 184
חָכָם	16, 95, 183	חֲמִישִׁית	34		
חָכְמָה	15, 95	חָמַל	37, 199, 235		
		חָמַם	52, 96, 199, 235, 270		
		חָמַס	28		
		חָמֵץ	78		

חֵץ	29	חָרָשׁ	40, 98	טוּר	49
חָצַב	65, 200, 236	חָרָשׁ	(#674) 32, 162, 200, 236, 245	טִיט	73
חָצָה	67, 97, 200, 240, 253	חָרָשׁ	(#1032) 48, 98, 162, 200, 236, 245	טַל	44
חֲצִי	17, 97			טָמֵא	(#262) 14, 99, 162, 201, 262
חָצִיר	62	חָשַׁד	47, 200, 236	טָמֵא	(#417) 21, 99, 162, 184
חֲצֹצְרָה	46	חָשַׂף	82, 200, 236	טֻמְאָה	40, 99
חָצֵר	13, 168	חָשַׁב	17, 98, 200, 236	טָמַן	44, 201
חֹק	17, 97	חָשָׂה	65, 200, 236, 240, 253	טָעַם	78, 99, 201, 245
חֻקָּה	19, 97			טַעַם	73, 99, 176
חָקַק	58, 97, 200, 236, 270	חָשַׁך	62, 98, 200, 236	טַף	37
		חֹשֶׁך	22, 98, 176	טֶרֶם	29
חָקַר	48, 97, 200	חֹשֶׁן	50, 176	טָרַף	50, 99, 201, 245
חֵקֶר	75, 97, 175	חָשַׁק	78, 200, 236	טֶרֶף	54, 99, 176
חֹר	73	חָתַם	48, 98, 200, 236	יָאַל	60, 201, 230, 245
חָרֵב	(#840) 40, 97, 162, 200, 236, 244	חָתַן	78, 98, 201, 236		
		חָתָן	57, 98	יְאֹר	26
חָרֵב	(#1850) 81, 97, 162, 184	חֹתֵן	55, 98	יְבוּל	73, 99
חֹרֶב	65, 97, 176	חָתַת	29, 98, 201, 237, 270	יָבַל	60, 99, 201, 230
חֶרֶב	7, 171, 176	טָבַח	78, 99, 201, 258	יָבֵשׁ	28, 100, 201, 230
חָרְבָּה	36	טַבָּח	43, 99	יַבָּשָׁה	70, 100
חָרַד	38, 200, 236, 244	טֶבַח	75, 99, 176	יָגוֹן	70
		טָבַל	65, 201	יְגִיעַ	65, 100
חָרָה	21, 98, 200, 240, 244, 253	טָבַע	82, 201, 258	יָגַע	49, 100, 201, 230, 258
		טַבַּעַת	31		
חָרוֹן	37, 98	טָהוֹר	20, 99, 184	יָד	3, 134
חַרְטֹם	78	טָהֵר	20, 99, 201, 245	יָדָה	19, 100, 201, 230, 253
חָרַם	31, 98, 200, 236, 244	טָהֳרָה	73, 99	יָדַע	4, 100, 201, 230, 258
חֵרֶם	46, 98, 176	טוֹב	(#92) 6, 99, 162, 184	יִדְּעֹנִי	79, 100
חָרַף	39, 98, 200, 236, 245	טוֹב	(#714) 34, 99, 162, 201, 265	יָהַב	42, 201, 230, 245
חֶרְפָּה	24, 98	טוּב	43, 99	יוֹבֵל	48
חָרַץ	82, 200, 236, 245	טוּחַ	78, 201, 265	יוֹם	2
חָרֵשׁ	57, 176	טוּל	69, 201, 265		

יוֹמָם	30	יַעַץ	22, 101, 202, 231, 245	יָרַשׁ	11, 102, 203, 231, 245
יוֹנָה	42	יַעַר	29, 176	יְרֻשָּׁה	74, 102
יָחַד	33, 100	יָפֶה	36, 101, 184	יֵשׁ	16
יַחְדָּו	20, 100	יֳפִי	58, 101	יָשַׁב	3, 102, 203, 231
יָחִיד	75, 184	יָצָא	3, 101, 202, 231, 262	יְשׁוּעָה	23, 102
יָחַל	36, 202, 230, 245	יָצַב	32, 202, 231	יְשִׁימוֹן	78
יָחַשׁ	57, 202, 230, 245	יָצַג	62, 202, 231	יָשֵׁן	65, 102, 203, 231
יָטַב	18, 202, 230	יִצְהָר	52	יָשַׁע	12, 102, 203, 231, 258
יַיִן	15	יָצַק	30, 202, 231	יֵשַׁע	40, 102, 176
יָכַח	28, 100, 202, 230, 258	יָצַר	27, 202, 231	יָשַׁר	48, 103, 203, 231
יָכֹל	12, 202, 230	יָצַת	48, 203, 231	יֹשֶׁר	70, 103, 176
יָלַד	6, 100, 202, 230	יֶקֶב	65, 176	יָשָׁר	18, 103, 184
יֶלֶד	21, 100, 176	יָקַץ	79, 203, 231	יָתֵד	51, 171
יָלִיד	73, 100, 184	יָקַר	79, 101, 203, 231	יָתוֹם	36
יָלַל	44, 202, 230, 270	יְקָר	62, 101	יָתַר	19, 103, 203, 231
יָם	7	יָקָר	40, 101, 184	יֶתֶר	20, 103, 176
יָמִין	15, 171	יָרֵא	(#150) 8, 102, 162, 203, 231, 245, 262	יִתְרוֹן	82, 103
יְמָנִי	42	יָרֵא	(#539) 27, 102, 162, 184	יֹתֶרֶת	79
יְמָנִית	42, 184	יִרְאָה	34, 102	כְּ	2, 189
יָנָה	58, 202, 230, 253	יָרַד	7, 203, 231, 245	כָּבֵד	(#353) 18, 103, 163, 203
יָנַק	42, 202, 230	יָרָה	(#675) 33, 102, 163, 203, 231, 245, 253	כָּבֵד	(#773) 37, 103, 163, 184
יָסַד	37, 101, 202, 230	יָרָה	(#1008) 47, 163, 203, 231, 245, 253	כָּבֵד	(#1563) 70, 163
יְסוֹד	57, 101	יָרֵחַ	48, 102	כָּבָה	51, 203, 253
יָסַף	12, 202, 230	יֶרַח	75, 102, 176	כָּבוֹד	12, 103
יָסַר	37, 101, 202, 230	יְרִיעָה	30	כַּבִּיר	82, 184
יָעַד	46, 101, 202, 231, 245	יָרֵךְ	42, 171	כָּבַס	31, 203
יָעַל	52, 202, 231, 245	יְרֵכָה	45	כֶּבֶשׂ	19, 176
יַעַן	20, 189			כָּבַשׁ	67, 203
				כַּד	60, 171
				כֹּה	5

כֹּהֵן	52, 103, 203, 245	
כֹּהֵן	5, 103	
כְּהֻנָּה	70, 103	
כּוֹכָב	39	
כּוּל	39, 203, 266	
כּוּן	11, 103, 204, 266	
כּוֹס	44, 171	
כָּזַב	65, 103, 204	
כָּזָב	44, 103	
כֹּחַ	17	
כָּחַד	43, 204, 245	
כָּחַשׁ	54, 204, 246	
כִּי	2	
כִּיוֹר	53	
כָּכָה	39	
כִּכָּר	25, 171	
כֹּל	2, 104	
כָּלָא	62, 104, 204, 262	
כֶּלֶא	82, 104, 176	
כֶּלֶב	43, 176	
כָּלָה	(#218) 12, 104, 163, 204, 253	
כָּלָה	(#1184) 54, 104, 163	
כַּלָּה	42	
כְּלִי	8	
כְּלָיוֹת	44	
כָּלִיל	67, 104, 184	
כָּלַם	39, 104, 204	
כְּלִמָּה	45, 104	
כֵּן	(#69) 5, 163	
כֵּן	(#1122) 51, 163	
כֵּן	(#1783) 79, 163	
כִּנּוֹר	36	
כָּנַס	79, 204	
כָּנַע	40, 204, 258	
כָּנָף	19, 171	
כִּסֵּא	16	
כָּסָה	15, 104, 204, 253	
כְּסִיל	25	
כֶּסֶף	7, 176	
כָּעַס	29, 104, 204, 246	
כַּעַס	55, 104, 176	
כַּף	12, 171	
כְּפִיר	44	
כָּפַר	19, 104, 204	
כֹּפֶר	78, 104, 176	
כַּפֹּרֶת	48, 104	
כַּפְתֹּר	60	
כַּר	75	
כָּרָה	70, 204, 246, 253	
כְּרוּב	21	
כֶּרֶם	20, 176	
כַּרְמֶל	67	
כָּרַע	40, 204, 246, 259	
כָּרַת	9, 204, 246	
כֶּשֶׂב	73, 176	
כָּשַׁל	26, 104, 204	
כָּתַב	11, 105, 204	
כְּתָב	62, 105	
כֻּתֹּנֶת	46	
כָּתֵף	25, 171	
כֹּתֶרֶת	51	
כָּתַת	62, 204, 270	
לְ	2, 168	
לֹא	2	
לָאָה	58, 204, 246, 253	
לְאֹם	44	
לֵב	4	
לֵבָב	4	
לְבַד	14	
לְבוֹנָה	55	
לְבוּשׁ	43, 105	
לָבִיא	75, 168	
לָבֵן	46, 184	
לְבֵנָה	75	
לָבַשׁ	19, 105, 205	
לַהַב	75, 105, 176	
לֶהָבָה	58, 105	
לָהַט	82, 205, 246	
לוּ	53	
לָוָה	(#1566) 70, 163, 205, 253	
לָוָה	(#1706) 76, 163, 205, 253	
לוּחַ	35	
לוּלֵי	70	
לוּן	62, 205, 266	
לְחִי	55, 171	
לֶחֶם	8, 176	
לָחַם	14, 105, 205, 246	
לָחַץ	58, 105, 205, 246	
לַחַץ	76, 105, 176	
לַיְלָה	11	
לִין	25, 205, 266	
לִיץ	47, 205, 266	
לָכַד	17, 205	

לִלְאֹת 73
לָמַד 21, 205
לָמָּה 13
לְמַעַן 10, 189
לָעַג 60, 205, 246
לְעֻמַּת 44, 189
לַפִּיד 70
לִפְנֵי 168
לָקַח 4, 205, 259
לָקַט 39, 205
לָשׁוֹן 18, 168
לִשְׁכָּה 32
מְאֹד 9
מֵאָה 5
מְאוּמָה 43
מָאוֹר 60, 86
מֹאזְנַיִם 68
מַאֲכָל 45, 87
מָאֵן 37, 205, 246
מָאַס 24, 205, 246
מָבוֹא 49, 88
מַבּוּל 73
מִבְחָר 76, 88
מִבְטָח 68, 88
מִבְצָר 39
מִגְדָּל 34, 90
מָגוֹר 79, 91
מְגִלָּה 55, 91
מָגֵן 28, 168
מַגֵּפָה 49, 108
מִגְרָשׁ 18
מַד 79
מִדְבָּר 10

מָדַד 30, 105, 205, 271
מִדָּה 29, 105
מָדוֹן 62, 91
מַדּוּעַ 24
מִדְיָן 82
מְדִינָה 30
מָה 5
מְהוּמָה 76
מָהַר 22, 105, 205, 246
מְהֵרָה 57, 105
מוּג 62, 205, 266
מוֹט 38, 105, 205, 266
מוֹטָה 76, 105
מוּל (#847) 40, 163, 189
מוּל (#925) 43, 163, 205, 266
מוֹלֶדֶת 54, 100
מוּם 56
מוּסָר 31, 101
מוֹעֵד 11, 101
מוֹפֵת 40
מוֹצָא 48, 101
מוֹקֵשׁ 48
מוּר 70, 205, 266
מוֹרָא 79, 102
מוּשׁ 56, 206, 266
מוֹשָׁב 34, 102
מוּת 4, 105, 206, 266
מָוֶת 15, 105
מִזְבֵּחַ 7, 92
מְזוּזָה 62
מְזִמָּה 59, 93

מִזְמוֹר 29, 93
מִזְרָח 24, 94
מִזְרָק 43, 94
מָחָה 42, 206, 246, 253
מְחִיר 68
מַחֲלֹקֶת 36, 96
מַחְמָד 73, 96
מַחֲנֶה 11, 96, 168
מַחְסֶה 57, 97
מַחְסוֹר 73, 97
מָחַץ 70, 206, 246
מַחֲצִית 65, 97
מָחָר 30, 106
מָחֳרָת 43, 106
מַחֲשָׁבָה 29, 98
מַחְתָּה 54
מְחִתָּה 79, 98
מַטֶּה 59
מַטֶּה 10
מִטָּה 46
מָטַר 62, 106, 206
מָטָר 39, 106
מַטָּרָה 65
מִי 7
מַיִם 5
מִין 44
מִישׁוֹר 53, 103
מֵישָׁרִים 59, 103
מַכְאוֹב 65
מַכָּה 32, 109
מָכוֹן 62, 103
מְכוֹנָה 50, 103
מִכְסֶה 66, 104

מָכַר	22, 106, 206	
מִכְשׁוֹל	70, 104	
מָלֵא	(#180) 10, 106, 163, 206, 262	
מָלֵא	(#554) 27, 106, 163	
מָלֵא	39, 106	
מַלְאָךְ	12	
מְלָאכָה	14	
מִלָּה	39	
מִלּוּאִים	68, 106	
מְלוּכָה	51, 106	
מֶלַח	53, 177	
מִלְחָמָה	8, 105	
מָלַט	20, 206	
מָלַךְ	8, 106, 206	
מֶלֶךְ	2, 106, 177	
מַלְכָּה	41, 106	
מַלְכוּת	21, 106	
מִמְכָּר	82, 106	
מַמְלָכָה	18, 106	
מֶמְשָׁלָה	62, 107	
מִן	2, 132	
מָן	73	
מָנָה	(#1010) 47, 106, 163, 206, 253	
מָנָה	(#1711) 76, 106, 163	
מְנוּחָה	56, 108	
מְנוֹרָה	36	
מִנְחָה	12	
מָנַע	46, 206, 259	
מַס	53	
מִסְגֶּרֶת	60, 111	
מָסָךְ	50	
מַסֵּכָה	49, 109	
מְסִלָּה	48	
מָסַס	56, 206, 271	
מַסַּע	76, 109	
מִסְפֵּד	66, 111	
מִסְפָּר	16, 111	
מִסְתָּר	82, 111	
מַעְגָּל	73, 112	
מֵעָה	43	
מָעוֹז	39	
מָעוֹן	62	
מָעַט	54, 106, 206, 246	
מְעַט	20, 106, 184	
מְעִיל	47	
מַעְיָן	53	
מָעַל	40, 107, 206, 246	
מַעַל	(#292) 16, 113, 163, 189	
מַעַל	(#992) 46, 107, 163, 177	
מַעֲלָה	31, 113	
מַעֲלֶה	54	
מַעֲלָל	36, 113	
מַעֲרָב	70, 114	
מְעָרָה	37	
מַעֲרָכָה	59, 114	
מַעֲרֶכֶת	87, 114	
מַעֲשֶׂה	10, 114	
מַעֲשֵׂר	43	
מָצָא	7, 206, 262	
מַצָּב	82, 110	
מַצֵּבָה	42, 110	
מְצָד	76, 171	
מַצָּה	30	
מְצוּדָה	60	
מִצְוָה	13, 117	
מָצוֹר	57, 118	
מֵצַח	73, 177	
מְצִלְתַּיִם	73, 168	
מִצְנֶפֶת	76	
מִקְדָּשׁ	23, 119	
מָקוֹם	7, 119	
מָקוֹר	61	
מַקֵּל	61, 168	
מִקְלָט	57	
מִקְנֶה	23, 120	
מִקְנָה	68, 120	
מִקְצוֹעַ	76	
מָקַק	82, 206, 271	
מִקְרָא	53, 120	
מִקְרֶה	82, 121	
מֹר	76	
מַר	39, 107, 184	
מַרְאָה	76, 121	
מַרְאֶה	19, 121	
מְרַאֲשׁוֹת	73, 121	
מָרַד	50, 206, 246	
מָרָה	34, 107, 206, 246, 253	
מָרוֹם	30, 123	
מֶרְחָק	61, 123	
מָרַט	70, 206, 246	
מְרִי	53, 107	
מֶרְכָּבָה	34, 124	
מִרְמָה	38	
מִרְעֶה	73, 124	
מַרְעִית	82, 124	
מַרְפֵּא	73, 125	
מָרַר	66, 107, 206, 246, 271	

מַשָּׂא (#719) 35, 110, 164	מָתְנַיִם 33	נָגַר 82, 207, 225
מַשָּׂא (#1254) 57, 110, 164	נָא 7	נָגַשׂ 53, 207, 225
מַשְׂאֵת 68, 110	נָאוֶה 82, 185	נָגַשׁ 17, 207, 225
מִשְׂגָּב 63, 125	נְאֻם 8	נָדַב 63, 108, 208, 225
מָשׂוֹשׂ 66, 125	נָאַף 44, 207, 225, 247	נְדָבָה 49, 108
מַשְׂכִּיל 70, 126	נָאַץ 52, 207, 225, 247	נָדַד 50, 189, 218, 268
מְשׂוּבָה 73, 127	נָבָא 18, 107, 207, 215, 225, 262	נָדָה 46
מָשַׁח 25, 107, 207, 259	נָבַט 25, 207, 225	נָדַח 31, 208, 225, 259
מִשְׁחָה 56, 107	נָבִיא 9, 107	נָדִיב 49, 108, 185
מַשְׁחִית 82, 127	נָבֵל 57, 107, 207, 225	נָדַר 44, 108, 208, 225
מָשִׁיחַ 39, 107, 185	נֵבֶל (#1012) 47, 164, 177	נֶדֶר 28, 108, 177
מָשָׁךְ 40, 207	נֵבֶל (#1869) 82, 164, 177	נָהַג 45, 208, 226, 247
מִשְׁכָּב 33, 128	נָבָל 61, 185	נָהַל 82, 208, 226, 247
מִשְׁכָּן 16, 128	נְבָלָה 73	נָהַר 18
מָשַׁל (#438) 22, 107, 164, 207	נְבֵלָה 32, 107	נוּד 50, 208, 266
מָשַׁל (#1389) 63, 107, 164, 207	נָבַע 79, 207, 225, 259	נָוֶה 43
מָשָׁל 37, 107, 274	נֶגֶב 46	נָוֶה 68
מִשְׁמָר 54, 129	נָגַד 8, 207, 225	נוּחַ 16, 108, 208, 266
מִשְׁמֶרֶת 23, 129	נֶגֶד 15, 189	נוּס 14, 208, 266
מִשְׁנֶה 41	נֹגַהּ 59, 177	נוּעַ 36, 208, 266
מִשְׁעֶנֶת 79, 129	נָגַח 79, 207, 225, 259	נוּף 42, 108, 208, 266
מִשְׁפָּחָה 9	נָגִיד 35	נָזָה 52, 208, 226, 254
מִשְׁפָּט 7, 129	נְגִינָה 70, 108	נָזִיר 66, 109
מַשְׁקֶה 59, 130	נָגַן 68, 108, 207, 225	נָזַל 66, 208, 226
מִשְׁקָל 31, 130	נָגַע 15, 108, 207, 225, 259	נֶזֶם 63, 177
מָשָׁשׁ 82, 207, 271	נֶגַע 23, 108, 177	נָזַר 82, 109, 208, 226
מִשְׁתֶּה 33, 130	נָגַף 31, 108, 207, 225	נֵזֶר 50, 109, 177
מָתוֹק 76, 185		
מָתַי 35		
מְתִים 54		
מַתָּנָה 63, 110		

נָחָה	38, 208, 226, 247, 254	נַעַר	10, 177	נָשַׁךְ	79, 210, 227
נְחוּשָׁה	82	נָעַר	79, 209, 226, 247	נְשָׁמָה	52
נָחַל	28, 109, 208, 226, 247	נַעֲרָה	23	נֶשֶׁף	76, 177
נַחַל	16, 177	נָפַח	76, 209, 227, 259	נָשַׁק	43, 210, 227
נַחֲלָה	11, 109	נָפַל	7, 209, 227	נֶשֶׁר	49, 177
נָחַם	19, 208, 226, 247	נָפַץ	59, 209, 227	נֶתַח	73, 177
נָחַשׁ	79, 208, 226, 247	נֶפֶשׁ	5, 171, 177	נְתִיבָה	56
נָחָשׁ	44	נָצַב	24, 110, 209, 227	נָתִין	63
נְחֹשֶׁת	16	נָצַח	26, 209, 227, 259	נָתַךְ	56, 210, 227
נָטָה	11, 208, 226, 254	נֵצַח	38, 177	נָתַן	3, 110, 210, 227
נָטַע	28, 209, 226, 259	נְצִיב	76, 110	נָתַץ	36, 210, 228
נָטַף	61, 209, 226	נָצַל	12, 209, 227	נָתַק	48, 110, 210, 228
נָטַשׁ	38, 209, 226	נָצַר	27, 209, 227	נֶתֶק	70, 110, 177
נִיחוֹחַ	35	נָקַב	59, 209, 227	נָתַשׁ	56, 210, 228
נָכָה	6, 109, 209, 226, 254	נְקֵבָה	54	סָבַב	14, 111, 210, 271
נֹכַח	50, 190	נָקָה	35, 110, 209, 227, 254	סָבִיב	8, 111, 190
נָכַר	31, 109, 209, 226	נָקִי	35, 110, 185	סָגָן	63
נֵכָר	40, 109	נָקַם	41, 110, 210, 227	סָגַר	21, 111, 210
נָכְרִי	33, 109, 185	נָקָם	63, 110	סוּג	52, 210, 266
נֵס	56	נְקָמָה	48, 110	סוֹד	56
נָסָה	40, 209, 226, 254	נָקַף	63, 210, 227	סוּךְ	83, 210, 266
נָסַךְ	50, 109, 209, 226	נֵר	35	סוּס	16
נֶסֶךְ	28, 109, 177	נָשָׂא	5, 110, 210, 227, 262	סוּף	47
נָסַע	15, 109, 209, 226, 259	נָשַׂג	31, 210, 227	סוּפָה	68
נְעוּרִים	33	נָשִׂיא	17, 110	סוּר	9, 210, 266
נָעִים	73, 185	נָשָׁא	70, 210, 227, 262	סוּת	61, 210, 266
נַעַל	54, 171, 177	נָשָׁה	61, 210, 227, 254	סָחַר	56, 211, 247
		נָשַׁךְ	76, 177	סִיר	46, 168
				סִכָּה	44
				סָכַךְ	66, 211, 271
				סָכַן	73, 211
				סַל	68
				סֶלָה	24

סָלַח	33, 211, 259	עֲגָלָה	76, 112	עָזַר	24, 112, 212, 237
סָלַל	76, 111, 211, 271	עַד	25, 112	עֵזֶר	63, 112, 178
סֹלְלָה	79, 111	עַד	(#33) 3, 164, 190	עֶזְרָה	49, 112
סֶלַע	28, 177	עַד	(#678) 33, 164	עָטָה	74, 212, 240, 254
סֹלֶת	30, 177	עֵדָה	14, 101	עָטַף	79, 212, 237
סָם	66	עֵדוּת	27, 112	עֲטָרָה	53
סָמַךְ	32, 211	עֲדִי	70	עַיִן	4, 168
סָעַד	76, 211, 247	עֵדֶר	39, 178	עָיֵף	63, 185
סְעָרָה	61	עוֹד	6	עִיר	3, 172
סַף	50	עוּד	38, 112, 211, 237, 267	עַיִר	83, 114, 185
סָפַד	45, 111, 211	עָוָה	63, 112, 211, 240, 254	עָכַר	70, 212, 237
סָפָה	59, 211, 254	עָוֶל	56, 178	עַל	38
סַפִּיר	79	עַוְלָה	42	עַל	5, 141
סָפַר	19, 111, 211	עוֹלֵל	79	עָלָה	4, 113, 212, 241, 254
סֵפֶר	13, 111, 177	עוֹלָם	7	עָלֶה	59
סֹפֵר	30, 111	עָוֹן	11, 112	עֹלָה	9, 113
סָקַל	54, 211	עוֹף	25, 112	עָלַז	63, 212, 237
סָרִיס	34	עוּף	48, 112, 211, 237, 267	עֲלִיָּה	57, 113
סֶרֶן	56, 177	עוֹר	20	עֶלְיוֹן	30, 119, 185
סָרַר	63, 211, 247, 271	עֵוֵר	49, 185	עֲלִילָה	52, 113
		עוּר	22, 211, 237, 267	עָלַל	59, 113, 212, 237, 271
סָתַם	74, 211	עֲוַת	76, 212, 237	עָלַם	47, 212, 237
סָתַר	22, 111, 211	עַז	53, 112, 185	עַם	3
סֵתֶר	44, 111, 178	עֵז	26, 152	עִם	4, 133
עָב	44	עֹז	(#463) 23, 112, 164	עָמַד	6, 113, 212, 237
עָבַד	9, 111, 211, 237	עֹז	(#1399) 63, 112, 164	עָמָד	34, 190
עֶבֶד	4, 111, 178	עָזַב	12, 212, 237	עַמּוּד	19, 113
עֲבוֹדָה	15, 111	עָזַז	79, 112, 212, 237, 271	עָמִית	76
עָבַר	6, 112, 211, 234			עָמַל	76, 113, 212, 237
עֵבֶר	21, 112, 178			עָמָל	30, 113
עֶבְרָה	42			עָמֹק	63, 113, 185
עֲבֹת	59, 168				
עֵגֶל	41, 112, 178				
עֶגְלָה	50, 112				

Index of Hebrew Words

עֵמֶק 25, 113, 178	עֲרָבָה 28	עָשַׁר 63, 115, 213, 238
עֵנָב 59	עָרָה 68, 114, 213, 241, 247, 254	עֹשֶׁר 39, 115, 178
עֶנֶג 83, 212, 237	עֶרְוָה 30, 114	עַשְׁתֵּי 59
עָנָה (#152) 9, 164, 212, 241, 254	עָרוֹם 80, 114, 185	עֵת 9, 168
עָנָה (#449) 23, 113, 164, 212, 241, 254	עָרוֹם 66, 185	עַתָּה 7
עָנָה (#1467) 66, 164, 212, 241, 254	עָרִיץ 57, 114, 185	עַתּוּד 46
עָנָו 50, 113, 185	עָרַךְ 23, 114, 213, 238, 247	עָתַר 57, 213, 238
עָנִי 22, 113, 185	עֵרֶךְ 42, 114, 178	פֵּאָה 22
עֳנִי 40, 113	עָרֵל 41, 185	פָּאַר 74, 115, 213, 247
עָנָן 79, 212, 237, 271	עָרְלָה 66	פָּגַע 33, 213, 259
עָנָן 21	עֲרֵמָה 80	פֶּגֶר 54, 178
עַפְעַפַּיִם 83	עֹרֶף 42, 178	פָּגַשׁ 70, 213
עָפָר 19	עֲרָפֶל 68	פָּדָה 28, 213, 254
עֵץ 8	עָרַץ 68, 114, 213, 238, 247	פֹּה 22
עֶצֶב 63	עֶרֶשׂ 83, 172, 178	פֶּה 6
עָצַב 68, 212, 237	עֵשֶׂב 43, 178	פּוּחַ 83, 213, 267
עֵצָה 21, 101	עָשָׂה 2, 114, 213, 241, 254	פּוּץ 26, 213, 267
עָצוּם 44, 113, 185	עָשׂוֹר 66, 114	פָּזַר 83, 213
עָצֵל 70, 185	עֲשִׂירִי 46	פַּח 50
עֶצֶם 63, 113, 212, 238	עָשַׂר 83, 114, 213, 238	פַּחַד 51, 115, 213, 247
עֶצֶם 17, 172, 178	עֶשֶׂר 8, 114	פַּחַד 31, 115, 178
עָצַר 33, 213, 238	עֶשֶׂר 6, 114	פֶּחָה 47
עֲצָרָה 80	עֶשְׂרֵה 8	פַּחַת 83, 178
עָקֵב 70	עֲשָׂרָה 6	פֶּטֶר 80, 178
עָקֵב 68, 178	עִשָּׂרוֹן 43	פִּילֶגֶשׁ 40, 172
עָקַר 76, 185	עֶשְׂרִים 6	פָּלָא 25, 115, 213, 262
עָקַשׁ 83, 185	עָשִׁיר 53, 115, 185	פֶּלֶא 74, 115, 178
עָרַב 63, 213, 238, 247	עָשֵׁן 50	פֶּלֶג 83, 178
עָרַב 83	עֹשֶׁק 68, 114, 178	פָּלַט 48, 115, 213
עֶרֶב 17, 114, 178	עָשַׁק 39, 114, 213, 238	פָּלִיט 59, 115
		פְּלֵיטָה 47, 115

פָּלַל 22, 115, 213, 271

פֶּן 16

פָּנָה 16, 115, 214, 254

פִּנָּה 45

פָּנִים 3, 115, 168

פְּנִימָה 70, 115

פְּנִימִי 44, 115, 185

פֶּסַח 31, 178

פָּסַח 71, 185

פָּסִיל 53, 115

פֶּסֶל 44, 115, 178

פָּעַל 28, 116, 214, 248

פֹּעַל 40, 116, 178

פְּעֻלָּה 71, 116

פַּעַם 18, 172, 178

פָּצָה 68, 214, 254

פָּקַד 9, 116, 195, 214

פְּקֻדָּה 44, 116

פִּקּוּדִים 52, 116

פָּקַח 56, 214

פָּקִיד 74, 116

פַּר 16

פֶּרֶא 83, 179

פָּרַד 49, 214, 248

פֶּרֶד 71, 179

פָּרָה (#998) 46, 116, 164, 214, 248, 254

פָּרָה (#1068) 49, 164

פֶּרַח 63, 116, 179

פָּרַח 42, 116, 214, 248, 259

פְּרִי 18, 116

פָּרֹכֶת 51

פָּרַס 71, 116, 214, 248

פַּרְסָה 56, 116

פָּרַע 66, 214, 248, 259

פָּרַץ 33, 116, 214, 248

פֶּרֶץ 59, 116, 179

פָּרַק 83, 214, 248

פָּרַר 33, 214, 248, 271

פָּרַשׂ 25, 214, 248

פָּרָשׁ 29

פָּשָׂה 54, 214, 254

פָּשַׁט 35, 214

פָּשַׁע 37, 116, 214, 259

פֶּשַׁע 21, 116, 179

פֵּשֶׁת 66, 179

פַּת 71

פִּתְאֹם 51

פָּתָה 48, 116, 255

פָּתוּחַ 80

פֶּתַח 15, 117, 179

פָּתַח 16, 117, 214, 259

פֶּתִי 63, 116

פָּתִיל 80

צֹאן 10, 168

צֶאֱצָאִים 80, 101

צָבָא (#107) 6, 117, 164, 275

צָבָא (#1589) 71, 117, 164, 214, 262

צְבִי (#1347) 61, 164

צְבִי (#1730) 76, 164

צַד 43

צַדִּיק 12, 117, 186

צָדַק 37, 117, 215

צֶדֶק 17, 117, 179

צְדָקָה 14, 117

צָהֳרַיִם 53

צַוָּאר 37

צוּד 64, 117, 215, 267

צִוָּה 6, 117, 215, 255

צוּם 56, 117, 215, 267

צוֹם 49, 117

צוּק 76, 215, 267

צוּר (#485) 24, 164

צוּר (#956) 45, 164, 215, 267

צָחַק 74, 215, 248

צַיִד 71, 117

צֵידָה 83, 117

צִיָּה 66

צִיץ 71

צֵל 30

צָלַח 26, 215, 260

צֶלֶם 68, 179

צַלְמָוֶת 61

צֵלָע 38, 172

צַמָּא 64, 117

צָמֵא 83, 117, 215, 262

צֶמֶד 68, 179

צָמַח 43, 117, 215, 260

צֶמַח 77, 117, 179

צֶמֶר 66, 179

צָמַת 68, 215

Index of Hebrew Words

צָנָה	57	קָדַם	49, 118, 216	קֶמַח	71, 179
צָעַד	71, 179	קֶדֶם	49	קֵן	74
צָעִיר	53, 186	קֶדֶם	29, 118, 179	קָנָא	42, 120, 216, 262
צָעַק	29, 215, 248	קַדְמָה	49, 118	קִנְאָה	35, 120
צְעָקָה	56	קַדְמֹנִי	83, 118, 186	קָנָה	22, 120, 216, 255, 259
צָפָה	(#680) 33, 165, 215, 255	קָדְקֹד	80	קָנֶה	27
צָפָה	(#834) 40, 165, 215, 255	קָדַר	64, 216	קִנְיָן	83, 120
צָפוֹן	15, 142	קָדַש	14, 119, 216	קָסַם	55, 120, 216
צִפּוֹר	38, 169	קֹדֶש	7, 119, 179	קֶסֶם	80, 120, 179
צָפַן	42, 215	קָדַש	80, 119	קְעָרָה	64
צְפַרְדֵּעַ	74, 172	קָהָל	38, 119, 216, 248	קֵץ	26, 120
צַר	(#490) 24, 118, 165	קָהָל	17, 119	קָצָה	41
צַר	(#1047) 48, 118, 165, 186	קַו	74	קָצֶה	21, 120
צָרָה	25, 118	קָוָה	33, 119, 216, 255	קָצִין	77
צָרַע	57, 118, 215, 248, 260	קוֹל	6	קָצִיר	32, 120
צָרַעַת	41, 118	קוּם	6, 119, 216, 267	קָצַף	42, 120, 216
צָרַף	42, 215, 248	קוֹמָה	34, 119	קֶצֶף	47, 120, 179
צָרַר	(#681) 33, 118, 165, 215, 248, 271	קוֹץ	80	קָצַץ	71, 120, 216, 272
צָרַר	(#1070) 49, 118, 165, 215, 248, 271	קָטֹן	24, 186	קָצַר	(#855) 40, 120, 165, 216
קָבַב	71, 215, 271	קָטָן	48, 186	קָצַר	(#1598) 71, 165, 216
קְבוּרָה	71, 118	קָטַר	18, 119, 216	קָרָא	(#70) 5, 120, 165, 217, 248, 262
קָבַל	71, 215	קְטֹרֶת	28, 119	קָרָא	(#301) 16, 165, 217, 249, 263
קָבַץ	17, 216	קִינָה	61	קָרַב	9, 121, 217, 249
קָבַר	16, 118, 216	קַיִץ	57	קֶרֶב	11, 121, 179
קֶבֶר	25, 118, 179	קַיִץ	54, 216, 267	קָרֵב	77, 121, 186
קָדַד	68, 216, 271	קִיר	24	קָרְבָּן	22, 121
קָדוֹש	18, 119, 186	קַל	79, 119, 186	קָרָה	55, 121, 217, 249, 255
קָדִים	25, 118	קָלוֹן	64	קָרוֹב	23, 121, 186
		קָלַל	22, 119, 216, 271		
		קְלָלָה	46, 119		
		קָלַע	66, 179		
		קָמָה	83, 119		

קָרְחָה	70
קִרְיָה	46
קֶרֶן	23, 172, 179
קֶרֶס	83, 179
קָרַע	27, 217, 249, 260
קֶרֶשׁ	31, 179
קַשׁ	66
קָשַׁב	34, 217
קָשָׁה	47, 121, 217, 255
קָשֶׁה	41, 121, 186
קָשַׁר	35, 121, 217
קֶשֶׁר	66, 121, 179
קֶשֶׁת	23, 179
רָאָה	3, 121, 217, 249, 255
רֹאֶה	80, 121
רֹאשׁ	(#80) 5, 121, 165
רֹאשׁ	(#1735) 77, 165
רִאשׁוֹן	13, 121, 186
רֵאשִׁית	31, 121
רֹב	15, 122
רַב	(#119) 7, 122, 165, 186
רַב	(#975) 45, 122, 165
רָבַב	53, 122, 217, 272
רְבָבָה	61, 122
רָבָה	11, 122, 217, 255
רִבּוֹא	80, 122, 172
רְבִיעִי	29, 122
רָבַע	77, 122, 217, 260
רָבַץ	45, 217
רָגַז	37, 217
רָגַל	49, 122, 217
רֶגֶל	10, 122, 172, 179
רַגְלִי	77, 122, 186
רֶגֶם	66, 217
רָגַע	74, 122, 217, 260
רֶגַע	55, 122, 180
רָדָה	55, 217, 255
רָדַף	15, 217
רָוָה	71, 217, 255
רָוַח	71, 122, 218, 260
רוּחַ	7, 122, 169
רוּם	12, 123, 218, 267
רוּעַ	35, 123, 218, 267
רוּץ	19, 218, 267
רוּשׁ	52, 218, 267
רָחַב	49, 123, 218, 249
רֹחַב	20, 123
רָחָב	57, 123, 186
רְחוֹב	35, 123, 172
רָחוּם	74, 123, 186
רָחוֹק	23, 123, 186
רָחַם	33, 123, 218, 249
רֶחֶם	49, 123, 180
רַחֲמִים	38, 123
רָחַץ	24, 218, 249
רָחַק	28, 123, 218, 249
רִיב	(#492) 24, 123, 165, 218, 267
רִיב	(#547) 27, 123, 165
רֵיחַ	28, 122
רִיק	(#1308) 63, 130
רִיק	(#1739) 82, 130, 218, 267
רֵיק	71, 124, 186
רֵיקָם	66, 124
רַךְ	66, 186
רָכַב	23, 124, 218
רֶכֶב	17, 124, 180
רְכוּשׁ	47
רָכַל	64, 218
רִמּוֹן	43
רֹמַח	68, 180
רְמִיָּה	68
רָמַס	59, 218
רָמַשׂ	64, 124, 218
רֶמֶשׂ	64, 124, 180
רִנָּה	43, 124
רָנַן	30, 124, 218, 272
רַע	9, 124, 186
רָע	9
רֹעַ	59, 124
רֵעַ	13
רָעֵב	(#1263) 57, 124, 165, 186
רָעֵב	(#1670) 74, 124, 165, 218, 249
רָעֵב	20, 124
רָעָה	(#137) 8, 124, 166
רָעָה	(#255) 14, 124, 166, 218, 249, 255

שָׁאַב 59, 219, 249
שָׁאַג 56, 219, 249
שְׁאוֹל 26, 169
שָׁאוֹן 64
שָׁאַל 13, 126, 219, 249
שְׁאֵלָה 74, 126
שַׁאֲנָן 83, 186
שָׁאַף 71, 220, 249
שָׁאַר 17, 126, 220, 207, 249
שְׁאָר 50, 126
שְׁאֵר 66
שְׁאֵרִית 26, 126
שָׁבָה 33, 127, 220, 255
שָׁבוּעַ 58
שְׁבוּעָה 45, 127
שָׁבוּת 46, 127
שֵׁבֶט 13, 180
שְׁבִי 32, 127
שְׁבִיעִי 20
שְׁבִית 71, 127
שִׁבֹּלֶת 66
שָׁבַע 13, 127, 220, 260
שֶׁבַע 6
שִׁבְעִים 6
שָׁבַר (#280) 15, 127, 166, 220
שָׁבַר (#1238) 56, 166, 220
שֶׁבֶר 35, 127, 180
שָׁבַת 25, 127, 220
שַׁבָּת 19, 127, 169
שַׁבָּתוֹן 80, 127

שָׂחַק 40, 125, 219, 249
שָׂטָן 50
שֵׂיבָה 59
שִׂיחַ (#1265) 57, 126, 166, 219, 267
שִׂיחַ (#1603) 71, 126, 166
שִׂים 5, 219, 267
שָׂכִיר 61, 126, 186
שֶׂכֶל 66, 126, 180
שָׂכַל 28, 126, 219
שָׂכַר 57, 126, 219
שָׂכָר 47, 126
שַׂלְמָה 66
שְׂמֹאל 30
שָׂמַח 15, 126, 219, 260
שָׂמֵחַ 56, 126, 186
שִׂמְחָה 21, 126
שִׂמְלָה 45
שָׂנֵא 15, 126, 219, 263
שִׂנְאָה 64, 126
שָׂעִיר 30
שֵׂעָר 47
שְׂעֹרָה 42
שָׂפָה 13
שַׂק 32
שַׂר 7
שָׂרִיד 46
שָׂרַף 18, 126, 219, 249
שְׂרֵפָה 74, 126
שָׂשׂוֹן 55, 125
שֶׁ 15

רַעְיָה 83
רַעַם 80, 218, 249
רַעֲנָן 59, 186
רָעַע 20, 124, 218, 249, 260, 272
רַעַשׁ 64, 125, 180
רָעַשׁ 46, 125, 219, 249
רָפָא 25, 125, 219, 263
רָפָה 34, 219, 255
רָצָה 32, 125, 219, 255
רָצוֹן 29, 125
רָצַח 33, 219, 260
רָצַץ 59, 219, 272
רַק 19
רָקִיעַ 64
רִקְמָה 77
רָקַע 80, 219, 260
רָשַׁע 41, 125, 219, 260
רֶשַׁע 45, 125, 180
רָשָׁע 10, 125, 186
רִשְׁעָה 68, 125
רֶשֶׁת 55, 180
שְׂבָכָה 64
שָׂבַע 20, 125, 219, 260
שָׂבֵעַ 83, 125, 186
שָׂגַב 57, 125, 219
שָׂדֶה 8
שֶׂה 33
שׂוּשׂ 48, 125, 219, 267
שְׂחוֹק 71, 125

שְׁגָגָה 60

שָׁגָה 56, 220, 255

שַׁד 56

שֹׁד 51, 127

שָׁדַד 28, 127, 220, 272

שַׁדַּי 32

שֹׁהַם 80, 180

שָׁוְא 30

שׁוֹאָה 77

שׁוּב 3, 127, 220, 267

שָׁוָה 67, 220, 255

שׁוֹט 74, 220, 268

שׁוֹטֵר 51

שׁוּל 80

שָׁוַע 56, 127, 220, 260

שַׁוְעָה 80, 127

שׁוֹעֵר 40

שׁוֹפָר 24

שׁוֹק 60, 172

שׁוֹר 23

שׁוּר 68, 220, 268

שׁוּשַׁן 64

שָׁזַר 56, 220

שֹׁחַד 53, 180

שָׁחַח 61, 220, 250, 260, 272

שָׁחַט 22, 220, 250

שְׁחִין 74

שָׂחַק 57, 180

שָׁחַר 77, 220, 250

שַׁחַר 53, 180

שָׁחַת 15, 127, 220, 250

שַׁחַת 53, 180

שָׂטָה 47

שָׁטַף 45, 220

שִׁיר (#418) 21, 128, 166, 221, 268

שִׁיר (#455) 23, 128, 166

שִׁירָה 74, 128

שִׁית 22, 221, 268

שָׁכַב 12, 128, 221

שִׁכּוֹר 74, 128, 187

שָׁכַח 20, 221, 260

שָׂכַל 52, 221

שָׁכַם 26, 221

שְׁכֶם 55

שָׁכַן 17, 128, 221

שָׁכֵן 60, 128

שָׁכַר 61, 128, 221

שֵׁכָר 53, 128

שֶׁלֶג 58, 180

שָׁלוֹם 10, 128

שָׁלַח 4, 221, 260

שֻׁלְחָן 24

שָׁלִישׁ 64

שְׁלִישִׁי 19

שְׁלִישִׁיָּה 19

שָׁלַךְ 17, 221

שָׁלָל 24, 128

שָׁלַל 71, 128, 221, 272

שָׁלֵם (#349) 18, 128, 166, 221

שָׁלֵם (#1024) 47, 128, 166, 187

שֶׁלֶם 22, 128, 180

שָׁלַף 51, 221

שָׁלֹשׁ 5

שִׁלְשׁוֹם 51

שְׁלֹשִׁים 5

שָׁם 4

שֵׁם 4

שָׁמַד 21, 221

שַׁמָּה 38, 128

שְׁמוּעָה 48, 129

שָׁמַט 83, 221

שָׁמַיִם 7

שְׁמִינִי 45

שָׁמֵם 21, 128, 221, 272

שְׁמָמָה 29, 128

שָׁמֵן 84, 187

שֶׁמֶן 12, 180

שְׁמֹנֶה 15

שְׁמֹנִים 15

שָׁמַע 3, 129, 221, 260

שֵׁמַע 64, 129, 180

שָׁמַר 7, 129, 221

שֶׁמֶשׁ 16, 169, 180

שֵׁן 29, 169

שָׁנָה (#51) 4, 129, 166

שָׁנָה (#1534) 69, 129, 166, 221, 255

שֵׁנָה 53, 102

שָׁנִי 36

שֵׁנִי 15

שְׁנַיִם 4

שָׂסָה 80, 222, 255

שָׁעָה 74, 222, 250, 256

שָׁעַן 55, 129, 222, 250

שַׂעַר 8, 180

שִׁפְחָה 27
שָׁפַט 12, 129, 222
שֶׁפֶט 67, 129, 180
שְׁפִי 84
שָׁפַךְ 18, 222
שָׁפֵל 45, 129, 222
שָׁפָל 64, 129, 187
שְׁפֵלָה 58, 129
שָׁקַד 77, 222
שָׁקָה 27, 129, 222, 256
שִׁקּוּץ 47
שָׁקַט 36, 222
שָׁקַל 53, 130, 222
שֶׁקֶל 21, 120, 180
שָׁקַף 77, 222
שֶׁקֶץ 80, 180
שֶׁקֶר 18, 180
שָׁרַץ 71, 130, 222, 250
שֶׁרֶץ 69, 130, 181
שָׁרַק 82, 222, 250
שְׁרִרוּת 84
שֹׁרֶשׁ 43, 181
שָׁרַת 20, 222, 250
שֵׁשׁ (#173) 10, 166
שֵׁשׁ (#800) 38, 166
שִׁשִּׁי 47
שִׁשִּׁים 10
שָׁתָה 11, 130, 222, 256
שָׁתַל 84, 222
תָּא 64
תַּאֲוָה 50, 86
תְּאֵנָה 38

תֹּאַר 69, 181
תֵּבָה 47
תְּבוּאָה 35, 88
תְּבוּנָה 36, 89
תֵּבֵל 41, 172
תֶּבֶן 64, 181
תַּבְנִית 58, 89
תֹּהוּ 58
תְּהוֹם 41, 169
תְּהִלָּה 28, 92
תַּהְפּוּכָה 84, 92
תּוֹדָה 44, 100
תָּוֶךְ 8
תּוֹכַחַת 52, 100
תּוֹלְדוֹת 38, 100
תּוֹלַעַת 38
תּוֹעֵבָה 18, 130
תּוֹצָאוֹת 51, 101
תּוּר 52, 222, 268
תּוֹר 72, 172
תּוֹרָה 11, 102
תּוֹשָׁב 72, 102
תּוּשִׁיָּה 77
תַּזְנוּת 55, 93
תְּחִלָּה 53
תְּחִנָּה 51, 96
תַּחֲנוּן 61, 96
תַּחַשׁ 72, 181
תַּחַת 6, 130, 190
תַּחְתּוֹן 74, 130, 187
תַּחְתִּית 60, 130, 187
תִּיכוֹן 80, 187
תֵּימָן 52, 172
תִּירוֹשׁ 39

תְּכֵלֶת 32
תָּכַן 61, 222
תָּלָה 46, 222, 256
תָּם 69, 130, 187
תֹּם 53, 130
תְּמוֹל 53
תְּמוּנָה 84
תָּמִיד 19
תָּמִים 21, 130, 187
תָּמַךְ 57, 222
תָּמַם 26, 130, 222, 272
תִּמֹרָה 58
תַּן 69, 169
תְּנוּפָה 46, 108
תַּנּוּר 69, 169
תַּנִּין 69
תָּעַב 55, 130, 222, 250
תָּעָה 31, 223, 250, 256
תַּעַר 74, 181
תֹּף 64
תִּפְאֶרֶת 32, 115
תְּפִלָּה 23, 115
תָּפַשׂ 26, 223
תִּקְוָה 44, 119
תָּקַע 25, 223, 260
תְּרוּמָה 23, 123
תְּרוּעָה 52, 123
תְּרָפִים 69
תְּשׁוּעָה 42, 102
תְּשִׁיעִי 61
תֵּשַׁע 23
תִּשְׁעִים 23

Index of Aramaic Words

The following index contains an alphabetical listing of the Aramaic words found throughout this volume. This index does not include inflected forms listed within entries.

אַב 136	אמן 143	אֲרַע 133
אבד 137	אמר 132	אֲרַק 150
אֶבֶן 137	אִמַּר 143	אַרְתַּחְשַׁשְׁתָּא 138
אִגְּרָה 143	אֵנֶב 143	אֵשׁ 143
אֱדַיִן 132	אֲנָה 134	אֶשָּׁא 150
אֲדָר 149	אִנּוּן 143	אָשַׁף 139
אַדַּר 149	אִנִּין 150	אֶשַּׁרְן 146
אֲדַרְגָּזַר 145	אֲנַחְנָא 141	אֶשְׁתַּדּוּר 146
אֲדַרְזְדָא 149	אנס 150	אָת 143
אֶדְרָע 149	אֲנַף 146	אתה 134
אַזְדָּא 145	אֱנָשׁ 133	אַתּוּן 136
אזה 143	אַנְתְּ 134	אֲתַר 140
אזל 138	אַנְתָּה 150	בְּ 132
אָח 145	אַנְתּוּן 150	בְּאִישׁ 150
אֲחִידָה 149	אֵסוּר 143	באש 150
אַחְמְתָא 149	אָסְנַפַּר 150	בְּאתַר 143
אַחַר 143	אָסְפַּרְנָא 138	בָּבֶל 133
אָחֳרִי 149	אֱסָר 138	בָּבֶל 150
אָחֳרֵין 149	אָע 140	בדר 150
אָחֳרָן 136	אַף 141	בְּהִילוּ 150
אֲחַשְׁדַּרְפַּן 136	אַפֶּרְסִי 150	בהל 137
אִילָן 139	אֲפַרְסְכָי 146	בטל 139
אֵימְתָן 149	אֲפַרְסַתְכָי 150	בֵּין 143
אִיתַי 134	אפתם 150	בִּינָה 150
אכל 138	אֶצְבַּע 143	בִּירָה 150
אַל 141	אַרְבַּע 137	בית 150
אֵל 150	אַרְגְּוָן 143	בַּיִת 132
אֱלָהּ 132	אֲרוּ 140	בָּל 150
אֱלָהִין 132	אֲרַח 146	בֵּלְאשַׁצַּר 137
אֵלֶּה 145	אַרְיֵה 136	בלא 150
אֵלּוּ 140	אַרְיוֹךְ 140	בְּלוֹ 143
אִלֵּין 140	אֲרִיךְ 150	בֵּלְשַׁאצַּר 138
אִלֵּךְ 134	אַרְכֻּבָּא 150	בנה 133
אֲלַף 140	אַרְכָה 146	בִּנְיָן 150
אַמָּה 141	אַרְכְּוָי 146	בנס 150
אֱמָה 137	אַרְעִי 150	בְּעָא 135

בְּעוּ	146	דָּא	139	דְּתָא	146
בְּעֵל	143	דֹּב	151	דְּתָבַר	146
בִּקְעָה	150	דבח	151	הֵ	138
בקר	140	דְּבַח	151	הָא	151
בַּר	134, 137	דבק	151	הֵא	151
בְּרַך	141	דִּבְרָה	146	הַדָּבַר	141
ברך	150	דִּי	132	הַדָּם	146
בְּרַך	150	דְּהַב	133	הדר	143
בְּרַם	140	דקק	136	הֲדַר	144
בְּשַׂר	143	דור	135	הוּא	134
בַּת	146	דּוּרָא	151	הוה	132
בָּאתַר	143	דּוש	151	הִיא	138
גֹב	136	דַּחֲוָה	151	הֵיכַל	135
גְּבוּרָה	146	דחל	139	הלך	144
גְּבַר	133	דִּי	139	הֲלָך	144
גְּבַּר	151	דִּין	146	הֵמוֹ	135
גְּדָבַר	146	דִּין	140	הִמּוֹן	135
גדד	146	דַּיָּן	151	הֲמְנִיךְ	139
גּוֹא	135	דִּינֵא	151	הֵן	134
גֵּוָה	151	דֵּך	139	הַנְזָקָה	151
גוח	151	דָּך	138	הַרְהֹר	151
גִּזְבַּר	151	דִּכֵּן	143	הִתְנַדָּבוּ	151
גזר	139	דְּכַר	143	וְ	132
גְּזֵרָה	146	דִּכְרוֹן	151	זבן	151
גִּיר	151	דָּכְרָן	146	זְהִיר	151
גַּלְגַּל	151	דלק	151	זוד	151
גלה	136	דמה	146	זון	152
גָּלוּ	141	דְּנָה	132	זוע	141
גְּלָל	146	דָּנִיֵּאל	132	זִיו	139
גמר	151	דקק	136	זָכוּ	152
גְּנַז	143	דָּר	141	זְכַרְיָה	146
גַּף	143	דָּרְיָוֶשׁ	134	זמן	146
גְּרַם	151	דְּרַע	151	זְמָן	136
גְּשֵׁם	139	דָּת	134	זְמָר	141

טַרְפְּלָי	153	חֵמָא	147	זְמַר	152
יבל	144	חֲמַר	139	זַן	141
יַבֶּשֶׁת	153	חִנְטָה	147	זְעֵיר	152
יַד	134	חֲנֻכָּה	142	זעק	152
ידה	147	חנן	147	זקף	152
ידע	132	חֲנַנְיָה	152	זְרֻבָּבֶל	152
יהב	133	חַסִּיר	152	זְרַע	152
יְהוּד	138	חסן	147	חֲבוּלָה	152
יְהוּדִי	136	חֶסֶן	147	חבל	139
יוֹם	134	חֲסַף	136	חֲבָל	144
יוֹצָדָק	153	חצף	147	חֲבַר	144
יטב	153	חרב	152	חַבְרָה	152
יכל	134	חַרְטֹם	140	חַגַּי	146
יָם	147	חרך	152	חַד	134
יסף	153	חֲרַץ	152	חֲדֵה	152
יעט	144	חשב	152	חֶדְוָה	152
יצב	153	חֲשׁוֹךְ	152	חֲדַת	152
יַצִּיב	140	חשח	152	חוה	134
יקד	137	חַשְׁחָה	152	חוט	152
יְקֵדָה	153	חַשְׁחוּ	152	חִוָּר	152
יַקִּיר	147	חשל	152	חזה	133
יְקָר	138	חתם	152	חֱזוּ	135
יְרוּשְׁלֶם	133	טאב	152	חֱזוֹת	146
יְרַח	147	טָב	147	חטא	146
יַרְכָה	153	טַבָּח	152	חֲטִי	147
יִשְׂרָאֵל	137	טוּר	147	חַי	138
יֵשׁוּעַ	153	טְוָת	153	חיה	139
יָת	153	טִין	147	חֵיוָה	133
יתב	140	טַל	140	חַיִל	138
יַתִּיר	137	טלל	153	חַכִּים	134
כְּ	132	טעם	144	חָכְמָה	137
כִּדְבָה	153	טְעֵם	133	חֵלֶם	133
כָּה	153	טְפַר	147	חלף	141
כהל	142	טרד	142	חֲלָק	144

כָּהֵן	137	לְחֶם	153	מִן	132		
כַּוָּה	153	לְחֵנָה	144	מְנֵא	144		
כּוֹרֶשׁ	137	לֵילֵי	140	מִנְדָּה מִדָּה	147		
כִּכַּר	153	לִשָּׁן	138	מַנְדַּע	142		
כֹּל	132	מְאָה	137	מנה	140		
כלל	137	מֹאזְנֵא	153	מִנְחָה	147		
כֵּן	137	מֵאמַר	147	מִנְיָן	154		
כְּנֵמָא	140	מָאן	138	מַעֲבָד	154		
כנשׁ	144	מְגִלָּה	153	מְעֵה	154		
כְּנָת	138	מגר	153	מֵעָל	154		
כְּסַף	135	מַדְבַּח	153	מָרֵא	139		
כְּעַן	135	מִדָּה	147	מְרַד	154		
כְּעֶנֶת	142	מְדוֹר	142	מָרָד	147		
כפת	142	מָדַי	138	מרט	154		
כֹּר	153	מְדִינָה	136	מֹשֶׁה	154		
כָּרְבְּלָה	153	מָה	134	מְשַׁח	147		
כרה	153	מוֹת	154	מִשְׁכַּב	139		
כָּרוֹז	153	מָזוֹן	147	מִשְׁכַּן	154		
כרז	153	מחא	142	מַשְׁרוֹקִי	142		
כָּרְסֵא	144	מַחְלְקָה	154	מִשְׁתֵּא	154		
כַּשְׂדָּי	135	מטא	137	מַתְּנָה	144		
כתב	137	מִישָׁאֵל	154	נבא	154		
כְּתָב	135	מֵישַׁךְ	134	נְבוּאָה	154		
כְּתַל	147	מלא	147	נְבוּכַדְנֶצַּר	133		
לְ	132	מַלְאַךְ	147	נִבְזְבָּה	147		
לָא	132	מִלָּה	133	נְבִיא	137		
לֵב	153	מלח	154	נֶבְרְשָׁה	154		
לְבַב	138	מְלַח	154	נגד	154		
לְבוּשׁ	147	מֶלֶךְ	132	נֶגֶד	154		
לבשׁ	144	מְלַךְ	154	נֹגַהּ	154		
לָהֵן	144	מַלְכָּה	147	נדב	144		
לָהֵן	138	מַלְכוּ	132	נִדְבָּךְ	148		
לֵוָי	142	מלל	140	נדד	154		
לְוָת	153	מַן	136	נִדְנֶה	154		

נְהוֹר	154	סבר	155	עִיר	144
נְהִיר	154	סגד	135	עַל	132
נַהִירוּ	148	סְגֵן	140	עֵלָּא	155
נְהַר	134	סגר	155	עֵלָּה	144
נוד	154	סוּמְפֹּנְיָה	142	עֲלָוָה	155
גְּוָלוּ	144	סוף	148	עֵלִּי	133
נוּר	134	סוֹף	140	עֶלִּי	155
נזק	144	סלק	137	עֶלְיוֹן	142
נְחָשׁ	136	סעד	155	עלל	134
נחת	139	סְפַר	140	עָלַם	133
נטל	148	סָפַר	139	עָלְמִי	155
נטר	154	סָרְבָּל	148	עֲלַע	155
נְכַס	148	סְרַךְ	140	עַם	134
נְמַר	154	סתר	155	עִם	133
נסח	154	סתר	155	עַמִּיק	155
נְסַךְ	154	עבד	133	עֲמַר	155
נְסַךְ	155	עֲבֵד	137	ענה	133
נפל	135	עֲבֵד נְגוֹ	134	עֲנָה	156
נפק	135	עֲבִידָה	139	עֲנָן	156
נִפְקָה	148	עֲבַר	135	עֲנַף	142
נִצְבָּה	155	עַד	132	עֲנַשׁ	156
נצח	155	עדה	136	עֱפִי	145
נצל	144	עִדּוֹא	148	עֲצִיב	156
נְקֵא	155	עִדָּן	135	עקר	148
נקש	155	עוד	155	עִקַּר	145
נשׂא	144	עֲוָיָה	155	עַר	148
נְשִׁין	155	עוֹף	148	ערב	142
נִשְׁמָה	155	עוּר	155	עֲרָד	156
נְשַׁר	148	עֵז	155	עַרְוָה	156
נִשְׁתְּוָן	144	עִזְקָה	148	עֲשַׂב	140
נְתִין	155	עֶזְרָא	144	עֲשַׂר	139
נְתַן	138	עֲזַרְיָה	155	עֶשְׂרִין	156
נתר	155	עֲטָה	155	עשת	156
סבל	155	עַיִן	140	עֲתִיד	156

רְבִיעִי	136	צְלֵם	134	עַתִּיק	145
רַבְרְבָן	136	צְפִיר	156	פֶּחָה	136
רגז	156	צְפַּר	142	פְּחַר	156
רְגַז	156	קבל	145	פַּטִּישׁ	148
רְגַל	137	קֳבֵל	133	פלג	156
רגשׁ	145	קַדִּישׁ	135	פְּלַג	156
רֵו	149	קֳדָם	132	פְּלֻגָּה	156
רוּחַ	136	קַדְמָה	148	פלח	136
רום	142	קַדְמָי	145	פָּלְחָן	156
רום	141	קום	132	פֻּם	139
רָז	136	קטל	138	פַּס	148
רְחוּם	142	קְטַר	145	פְּסַנְטֵרִין	142
רַחִיק	157	קַיְט	156	פַּרְזֶל	133
רַחֲמִין	157	קָיָם	148	פרס	156
רחץ	157	קִיתָרוֹס	142	פְּרֵס	148
רֵיחַ	157	קִיתָרוֹס	142	פָּרָס	139
רמה	135	קָל	138	פַּרְסִי	148
רְעוּ	149	קנה	156	פרק	156
רַעְיוֹן	139	קצף	156	פרשׁ	156
רַעֲנַן	157	קְצַף	156	פַּרְשֶׁגֶן	145
רעע	149	קצץ	156	פשׁר	148
רפס	149	קְצָת	145	פְּשַׁר	132
רשׁם	138	קרא	136	פִּתְגָם	139
שָׂב	141	קרב	136	פתח	148
שַׂבְּכָא	142	קְרָב	156	פְּתָי	148
שׂגא	145	קִרְיָה	136	צבה	136
שַׂגִּיא	135	קֶרֶן	135	צְבוּ	156
שָׂהֲדוּתָה	157	קְרַץ	148	צבע	141
שְׂטַר	157	קְשֹׁט	149	צַד	148
שׂים	133	רֵאשׁ	135	צְדָא	156
שׂכל	157	רַב	133	צִדְקָה	156
שָׂכְלְתָנוּ	145	רבה	139	צַוַּאר	145
שׂנא	149	רְבוֹ	145	צלה	148
שְׂעַר	145	רְבוּ	141	צלח	142

שָׁאַל	139	שְׁלַם	145	שְׁתַר בּוֹזְנַי	143
שְׁאֵלָה	157	שְׁלָם	142	תְּבַר	157
שְׁאַלְתִּיאֵל	157	שֵׁם	135	תְּדִיר	149
שְׁאָר	135	שְׁמַד	157	תּוּב	137
שְׁבַח	141	שְׁמַיִן	132	תְּוָה	157
שְׁבַט	157	שְׁמַם	157	תּוֹר	138
שְׁבִיב	149	שְׁמַע	137	תְּחוֹת	141
שְׁבַע	140	שָׁמְרַיִן	149	תְּלַג	158
שְׁבַק	141	שַׁמָּשׁ	157	תְּלִיתָי	149
שְׁבַשׁ	157	שֶׁמֶשׁ	157	תְּלָת	136
שֵׁגַל	145	שִׁמְשַׁי	142	תַּלְתָּא	145
שְׁדַר	157	שֵׁן	141	תְּלָתִין	149
שַׁדְרַךְ	135	שְׁנָה	133	תְּמַהּ	145
שָׁוָה	145	שְׁנָה	138	תִּמַּהּ	143
שׁוּר	142	שְׁנָה	157	תִּנְיָן	158
שׁוּשַׁנְכָי	157	שָׁעָה	141	תִּנְיָנוּת	158
שְׁחַת	145	שְׁפַט	157	תִּפְתָּי	149
שֵׁיזִב	137	שַׁפִּיר	149	תַּקִּיף	141
שֵׁיצִיא	157	שְׁפַל	143	תְּקַל	158
שְׁכַח	134	שְׁפַל	157	תְּקֵל	149
שְׁכַן	149	שְׁפַר	145	תְּקַן	158
שְׁלֵה	157	שַׁפַּרְפָּר	157	תְּקַף	141
שְׁלוּ	141	שָׁק	157	תְּקֹף	158
שָׁלֵוָה	157	שָׁרָה	140	תָּקְף	158
שְׁלַח	135	שָׁרָשׁ	145	תְּרֵין	143
שְׁלַט	138	שֵׁשְׁבַּצַּר	149	תְּרַע	149
שָׁלְטָן	149	שֵׁת	149	תָּרָע	158
שִׁלְטֹן	135	שְׁתָה	141	תַּתְּנַי	143
שַׁלִּיט	136	שִׁתִּין	143		

Biblical Hebrew Vocabulary in Context

Miles V. Van Pelt and Gary D. Pratico

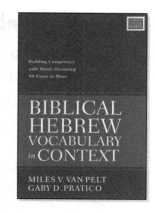

Biblical Hebrew Vocabulary in Context by Miles V. Van Pelt and Gary D. Pratico is a biblical Hebrew language resource designed to reinforce a student's basic vocabulary by reading words that occur fifty times or more in the context of the Hebrew Bible. All 642 of these Hebrew words have been collated into 195 key biblical verses and/or verse fragments to help students practice and retain their Hebrew vocabulary. In lieu of rote memorization, *Biblical Hebrew Vocabulary in Context* reinforces essential vocabulary by reading words in the context of the Hebrew Bible. The book includes two primary sections. The first section provides room for students to write their own glosses of the biblical verse and to parse as they feel necessary. An English translation is also provided and any term that appears less than fifty times is glossed. Proper names are identified with gray text. The second section of the book provides the same biblical verses from the first section but with minimal room to write glosses and parse and without an English translation for aid. The end of the book includes a Hebrew-English lexicon of all the words occurring fifty times or more in the Hebrew Bible.

Available in stores and online!

Basics of Hebrew Discourse

A Guide to Working with Hebrew Prose and Poetry

Matthew H. Patton, Frederic Clarke Putnam, and Miles V. Van Pelt

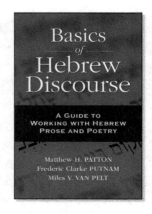

Basics of Hebrew Discourse: A Guide to Working with Hebrew Prose and Poetry by Matthew H. Patton, Frederic Clarke Putnam, and Miles V. Van Pelt is a syntax resource for intermediate Hebrew students. This Basics book introduces students to the principles and exegetical benefits of discourse analysis (text linguistics) when applied to biblical Hebrew prose and poetry. Where standard Hebrew reference grammars have traditionally worked to describe the relationship between words and phrases within discrete clauses (micro syntax), discourse analysis works to describe those relationships that exist between clauses and texts (macro syntax).

This resource fills a needed gap for intermediate Hebrew students and gives them the tools to work with Hebrew syntax on the macro level. Professors and pastors working with Hebrew will also find this one-of-a-kind resource highly valuable.

Available in stores and online!

CPSIA information can be obtained
at www.ICGtesting.com
Printed in the USA
LVHW021639090821
694563LV00001B/1

9 780310 532828